ROUTLEDGE LIBRARY EDITIONS:
17TH CENTURY PHILOSOPHY

Volume 5

RHETORIC AND PHILOSOPHY IN HOBBES' LEVIATHAN

RHETORIC AND PHILOSOPHY IN HOBBES' LEVIATHAN

RAIA PROKHOVNIK

Routledge
Taylor & Francis Group

LONDON AND NEW YORK

First published in 1991 by Garland

This edition first published in 2020
by Routledge
2 Park Square, Milton Park, Abingdon, Oxon OX14 4RN

and by Routledge
52 Vanderbilt Avenue, New York, NY 10017

*Routledge is an imprint of the Taylor & Francis Group, an informa
business*

British Library Cataloguing in Publication Data
A catalogue record for this book is available from the British Library

ISBN: 978-0-367-27875-5 (Set)
ISBN: 978-0-429-29844-8 (Set) (ebk)
ISBN: 978-0-367-33103-0 (Volume 5) (hbk)
ISBN: 978-0-367-33105-4 (Volume 5) (pbk)
ISBN: 978-0-429-31799-6 (Volume 5) (ebk)

Publisher's Note
The publisher has gone to great lengths to ensure the quality of this
reprint but points out that some imperfections in the original copies
may be apparent.

Disclaimer
The publisher has made every effort to trace copyright holders and
would welcome correspondence from those they have been unable to
trace.

RHETORIC AND PHILOSOPHY IN HOBBES' *LEVIATHAN*

Raia Prokhovnik

GARLAND PUBLISHING, INC.
New York —————— London
1991

Library of Congress Cataloging-in-Publication Data

Prokhovnik, Raia.
Rhetoric and philosophy in Hobbes' Leviathan/ Raia Prokhovnik.
p. cm.—(Political theory and political philosophy)
Revision of the author's thesis (Ph.D.—London School of Economics and
Political Science, 1981).
Includes bibliographical references.
ISBN 0-8153-0142-1 (alk. paper)
1. Hobbes, Thomas, 1588–1679. Leviathan. 2. Hobbes, Thomas, 1588–
1679—Literary art. I. Title. II. Series.
JC153.H659P76   1991
320.1'092—dc20   91-10709

Printed on acid-free, 250-year-life paper.
MANUFACTURED IN THE UNITED STATES OF AMERICA

For Gary, Eleanor and Conal
and to the memory of Kay

TABLE OF CONTENTS

LIST OF ILLUSTRATIONS

PREFACE

Since this thesis was written, many aspects of Hobbes' thinking have been explored in books and articles. The area of studies on rhetoric has also flourished, particularly amongst American writers. These developments, where they have a bearing on the subject of this dissertation, have been incorporated into the text and the updated bibliography. However nothing published in the last ten years has touched directly upon the issues discussed in this thesis. The best general work on Hobbes in that time is Richard Tuck, *Hobbes* (Oxford University Press, 1989), while Michael Oakeshott's *Introduction* to his edition of *Leviathan* (Blackwell, Oxford, 1946) remains the freshest and most stimulating general treatment of Hobbes' thinking. The work of Quentin Skinner and his associates, on the historical context of ideas, has grown over the past ten years and is to be welcomed. It may perhaps help to break down the propensity to tuck bits of Hobbes' thinking into different boxes, as though they were separate.

I would like to thank Dr. Robert Orr for the generous encouragement he gave me, and for all the valuable criticism he gave my thesis, and the London School of Economics for the Graduate Studentship which enabled me to continue the research for this thesis. I would also like to thank Dr. Conal Condren for his many fine critical insights, my father for the 'manifold facets' of his confidence in me, and Gary Browning for many congenial hours spent discussing political philosophy, and for a shared world.

CHAPTER 1
The Notion of Rhetoric

Since the early Sophists taught and practised rhetoric, the term has accumulated a whole variety of meanings, significances and connotations. In the same way that many other words in our vocabulary, such as 'democracy', 'science', 'philosophy' and 'nature', have histories whose courses can be charted, of changes of meaning and use, so the term 'rhetoric' has been used, throughout the history of western thought, to refer to different conceptions and understandings. For the Sophists, rhetoric was both an art and a science; for Plato the rhetorical methods of the poets were opposed to philosophy; for Aristotle 'good' rhetoric was distinguished from 'bad' rhetoric; for the sixteenth century handbook writers, rhetoric provided the means for discourse to both teach and entertain; while for Hobbes rhetoric is a morally neutral technique but some uses of language are reprehensible. And in the modern resurgence of interest in the subject, claims are made for the philosophical character of the postulates of rhetoric. To elucidate the frame of reference within which the term is to be understood, and so identify the meaning one wishes to employ, is the first task of someone who now wishes to use the term 'rhetoric' to approach a piece of writing.

In contemporary currency, the term 'rhetoric' has a strong pejorative connotation, signifying elegant but empty speech designed, not only to impress and persuade but also to deceive an audience into subscribing to and acting upon a conviction which sober common sense would condemn. The term carries with it the suspicion of being a disguise and smokescreen for a fundamentally unacceptable purpose, the suspicion that a speaker or writer who 'uses rhetoric' is one who seeks to hide a motive with which we really would not agree, behind a dazzlingly compelling facade.

The discredit that surrounds the term in contemporary usage is reflected in the predominance of pejorative definitions offered by the Shorter Oxford dictionary. 'Rhetoric' is defined as, firstly, the art of, or a treatise on "using language so as to persuade or influence others; the body of rules to be observed by a speaker or writer in order that he may express himself with eloquence"; secondly, as "elegance or eloquence of language; eloquent speech or writing. Speech or writing in terms calculated to persuade; hence, language characterised by artificial or ostentatious expression"; and thirdly, as "skill in or faculty of using eloquent and persuasive language". It goes on to define 'rhetorical' as "eloquent, eloquently expressed"; "expressed in terms calculated to persuade; hence, of the nature of mere rhetoric (as opposed to sober statement or argument)"; "of, belonging to, concerned with, or comprised in, the art of rhetoric"; and "of persons: given to the use of rhetoric".

But as well as reflecting the discredit into which the term has fallen in contemporary usage, these definitions also indicate two significant features of rhetoric. They indicate, in the first place, that rhetoric is concerned with discourse, with the uses of language through its grammar, syntax and other structural components, and through semantics and dialectic. At its narrowest, rhetoric refers to speech in which language is used solely for its persuasive effect upon an audience, regardless of whether or not its reasoning is sound, and in which language is solely designed to persuade an audience to undertake a certain course of action. At its widest, rhetoric may take as its province the manner in which all spoken and written discourse expresses and conveys meaning, to some form of audience, in conversation, oratory, practical life, dialogue, lecturing, poetry, drama, novels, debates, and in written works across the whole range of intellectual inquiry. And secondly, the definitions indicate the plurality of levels on which the term may operate. 'Rhetoric' may refer to the techniques involved in discourse about practical activities, to the affective character of language at several levels of abstraction, and to the theoretical basis of the practice, in the study of the set of techniques and language used and the postulates they exhibit. Thus rhetoric may be, according to the level at which it is examined, a practice, an art, a set of rules, a medium of persuasion, an intellectual discipline, and the study of the medium of linguistic expression itself. And a piece of writing or speech may be studied to assess its character in terms of any of these levels, in relation to the audience for which it was designed or to which it was directed.

The following discussion will concentrate on two meanings of 'rhetoric'. Firstly there is rhetoric as the art of persuasion in the practical world, and secondly as the comprehensive expression of thinking in the language a writer or speaker uses. In the second meaning of rhetoric, attention is focussed upon the way language is used to organise and express thinking and is not simply a static mirror reflection of thinking. The purpose of concentrating on these meanings and of distinguishing between them, is to present in clear contrast two of the principal ways by which the rhetoric of Hobbes' *Leviathan* could be studied. The first view might lead to a study of Hobbes' work as a piece of polemical writing, designed as a contribution to political debate in the 1640s and 1650s and intended to influence the course of events.[1] The first view might also be put forward to preface an argument that *Leviathan* is a work of philosophy, and as such is a work in which 'rhetoric' has no role to play at all. The second view, which is put forward in this thesis, leads to a study of *Leviathan* in which the philosophical character of the work is examined through Hobbes' use of language, comprehensively understood. The line of reasoning involved argues, firstly, that any piece of thinking may be studied in terms of the manner in which a writer or speaker uses language to express and organise his thought and, secondly, that more specifically, a piece of philosophical thinking may be studied in this way.

Although the two meanings of rhetoric to be considered in this chapter are not necessarily mutually exclusive nor directly opposed, since they may be seen to focus upon different kinds of discourse or even upon different levels of the same piece of discourse, two of the approaches they lead to can be taken to imply directly conflicting relationships between thinking, language and meaning in philosophy. Thus it is important to examine and distinguish these two approaches before proceeding with the study of the rhetoric of *Leviathan* in the following chapters.

There are two lines of argument about the relationship between rhetoric and philosophy that can be developed from the notion of rhetoric as the art of persuasion in the practical world, and I want, first of all, to outline the view that makes the sharper division between this notion of rhetoric and philosophy.

What is under consideration when discussing the general character of rhetoric as the art of persuasion in the practical world (and this is common ground to both lines of argument about the relationship between rhetoric and philosophy), is the mode of discourse appropriate in a world made up of contingent circumstances, where complete knowledge is inaccessible, where there is uncertainty about the future course of events, and where abstract principles have a limited viability - where "one speaks to win, not to impress with irrelevant learning".[2] The practical world is made up of human actions based on choices between uncertainties, and rhetoric is the infinitely adaptable mode of discourse adopted in this world. The practical world characteristically consists of actions undertaken on the basis of relatively unreflective choices between alternative concrete courses of action, and thus thinking and speaking and writing is in terms of the relative desirabilities of the alternatives presented by the convergence of situation and human will. To see the practical world, not in terms of making choices and acting upon them, but as an opportunity for reflection upon the nature and character of the choices and upon their presuppositions, is to leave the practical world behind and enter the realm of philosophy.[3]

The role of the rhetorician in this scheme is to reduce the complexity of the specific situation to the presentation of a simple alternative, and his argument, designed to appeal to a particular audience, is framed in terms and contains the degree of precision required in order to make that appeal effective, and not much further. To pass beyond what is immediately relevant to the situation at hand is to argue ineffectively, and part of the rhetorical skill is to be attuned to what constitutes relevance in the particular situation. Thus although the Sophists were attacked in some quarters for their relativistic outlook, it is a feature of the world of practical activity, when viewed from the outside, that the prime criterion of argument is the relativistic one in which relevance and effectiveness figure jointly, that what count as relevant considerations to be brought to bear differ according to circumstance, and that no particular decision can be dictated by an abstract, general principle.

Another aspect of the contingent character of the practical world in which rhetoric operates is that rhetoric cannot choose in advance the situations to be resolved. These situations are delivered to it in no discernible order or pattern, and the necessity of *making* a choice overrides the requirement of having a complete and accurate knowledge before a conclusion can be formed and a decision reached. In this way also, the province of rhetoric can be distinguished from (but not as yet opposed to) that of disciplines like science and philosophy, which do not carry with them the urgency of decision.

Two activities in which rhetorical discourse in this sense is most formally developed, are law in the context of the courtroom and politics, and it is no coincidence that these two activities help to define the civil life of a society. For what rhetoric is in the sphere of public life governed by the conventions of civil conduct, is discourse within and about the shared public idiom - a set of considerations drawn from other activities, a collection of references to acknowledged and aspiring authorities, and a cluster of shared general moral assumptions and commonplaces. Rhetorical discourse uses these resources in particular cases in whatever mixture will present an argument in favour of one course of action and against its alternatives; an argument which is simple, intelligible and appealing to the audience with whom, in some sense, the choice rests. Law and politics are activities which are primarily propelled by action undertaken on the basis of choices made in a linguistic context or forum, between alternative rhetorically framed arguments.

Rhetoric in this sense is, furthermore, characterised by its concern with questions of value and significance. Its role is always to evaluate the desirability of alternatives, to advocate and to persuade. And it is at this point that the two lines of argument about the relation between this meaning of rhetoric and philosophy begin to diverge. According to the argument which draws the sharper division, the practical and theoretical worlds presuppose relationships between facts and values which are quite distinct and significantly opposed. In the theoretical world, the argument runs, facts have value according to the internal connections established within the subject, and external considerations of desirability, relevance and audience accommodation, have no effect on the value of facts; in the practical world an external criterion of desirability imposes value on facts as they appear in contexts of circumstance.

This line of argument continues by placing rhetorical reasoning in strict opposition to the logical reasoning seen to characterise speech and writing in the theoretical world. Rhetorical argument, it holds, presupposes a form of reasoning which is distinct from logical reasoning, for the validity of its conclusions depends upon their success or failure in persuading an audience to choose a certain course of action, whereas the validity of conclusions in logical reasoning depends entirely upon the internal consistency of the steps that led to the conclusion, and not upon the approval of the audience or the acceptableness of the conclusion reached. While logical reasoning takes place within a set of postulates whose validity is not questioned, in rhetorical reasoning both the postulates and specific considerations marshalled by the rhetorician may be called into doubt at any time, and their value dismissed upon a mere statement of dissent by the audience. In the shifting sands of rhetorical 'truth' many arguments may be necessary in order to persuade, whereas in the theoretical world one argument is sufficient to demonstrate the truth of a given proposition. And whereas a logical proof is either true or false, a rhetorical proof results only in a degree of assent and its value is measured in degrees of assent.

It follows, according to this line of argument, that rhetorical reasoning operates on the basis of identifications whereas logical reasoning involves definitions. Identification and definition may be seen as two ways of associating or connecting ideas, thoughts or concepts, of giving meaning to one thing by linking it to another whose meaning is familiar and accepted. Definition is the appropriate form of linking when we want to know something, in exact terms, about the thing itself - indeed, not merely something about the thing, but that which explains its nature. The focus of attention in definition is the thing itself; but with identification the focus of attention is on the marks of identity which relate this thing with other things, and we want to know only enough about each of the other things to make the relationships between them and the thing identified intelligible. Furthermore, an identification is a looser and more tentative kind of connection and does not require the exactness of a definition. In rhetorical reasoning then, the argument proceeds by considering whether this can be identified in terms of its relations with that. The identifications of rhetoric are "fruitful connections between disparate insights",[4] where fruitful means persuasive. Rhetoric is concerned to show an identification, or to upset one by establishing another. And although a rhetorical argument is sometimes made along the lines that the thing under consideration will become clear once it has been defined, in the realm of human affairs, which is a world of contingent circumstances, such a definition can be no more than a classification, which by itself adds little to our understanding of the part it plays in a particular set of circumstances. Such a definition is, under these conditions, actually an identification, a proposition which must be supported by an argument referring to the contingent situation before it has been established as connected to it.

Furthermore, definition takes place between things at the same level of abstraction, whereas identifications may be made by relating things of different orders. For instance, in rhetorical reasoning, perhaps the most common form of identification is between principles and practice, and rhetoric here is the art of connecting the two. In fact, an 'application of principle' requires the mediation of an identification to, so to speak, absorb the principle into the real world of contingent circumstances.

Identification is also strictly distinguished from definition by its overall unsystematic character. The manner in which argument by identification proceeds by setting out the marks of identity of a this in terms of those particulars, seen as or appealed to or invoked as relevant, in unsystematic fashion, is typical of rhetorical reasoning. And this kind of argument may be contrasted to an argument which proceeds by systematically defining something in terms of its characteristics, which is typical of philosophy. And whereas philosophy has traditionally regarded identification as a somewhat second-rate manner of reasoning, because its connections are altogether looser, the value of rhetoric lies precisely in its lack of system; this form of reasoning allows the rhetorician to adapt his argument according to the pressures of contingent particulars and audience, whereas the reasoning of philosophy constantly seeks to transcend the particularity of the contingent and the mutable.

The contrast with philosophy can be extended by considering the rhetorical notions of truth and reality. Beginning from the rhetorical focus upon experience rather than ideas, which leads to a view of ideas as valuable in so far as they are useful, relevant and effective rather than subjects for reflection, and to the organising principle of whatever is appropriate in the particular case, rhetoric presupposes a conception of truth as that which is opposed to a lie or untruth, rather than as that which is opposed to objective error as in mathematics or logic. The contingent nature of the reality with which the rhetorician deals is joined with the contingent nature of language, in the rhetorical perception of discourse as both expressing and ordering insights into reality, so that both reality and discourse are permeated with moral value. Thus, for example, according to the rhetorical notions of truth and reality, terms like 'justice', 'obligation' and 'right', as part of the vocabulary of politics and law, take their meaning from being identified with particular contingent actions, and are used for their persuasive moral force. An examination of the conditions of these terms as concepts, on the other hand, would only result for the rhetorician in distancing them from particular contingent situations, and so limit their flexibility, effectiveness, relevance and usefulness.

Finally it follows, according to this line of argument, that rhetoric and philosophy are strictly distinguished not only in the meanings which words like 'justice', 'obligation' and 'right' have and in the use to which they are put, but on the question of language more generally. Rhetoric uses language for its persuasive force, and the kind of language which contains the greatest emotive force is appropriate to rhetorical argument. In particular, figurative language is doubly effective, firstly because of the powerful images it conjures up, which if skilfully handled are extremely persuasive, and secondly because the absence of reasoned argument is disguised. Philosophy, on the other hand, ought only to use neutral language, since it is concerned with internal coherence and logical truth and falsity and not affectiveness. Consequently, figurative language is inappropriate in philosophy and ought to be abjured in philosophy for the same reasons that make it appropriate in rhetoric.

Within these notions of truth and reality, then, rhetoric is capable of presenting phenomena in a manner which is denied to philosophy by virtue of its framework of metaphysical assumptions. However, beyond these limits, the rhetorical assumptions lose their intelligibility. From within the province of rhetoric, there is no way of escaping or transcending the relativistic buffeting of the mutable, the contingent and the particular to anything which is permanent, stable and final. Since the rhetorical working assumption - and all its assumptions are working assumptions - is that 'meaning' is always significance or attributed meaning, there is no index for meaning apart from the shifting sands of whatever is effective in the particular case. At its outer reaches, then, rhetoric becomes altogether unsatisfactory and inadequate, and can only throw into relief the fragility and ephemeral power of the human condition, to which it is tied, within which it operates, from which it cannot escape, and which it cannot overcome.

This, then, is the view of rhetoric as the art of persuasion in the practical world which draws the sharper division between rhetoric and philosophy. The view which sees rhetoric and philosophy as less sharply divided, differs more in its account of philosophy than in its characterisation of rhetoric. According to this view, the fundamental differences between rhetoric and philosophy are that firstly, the rhetorician's purpose is to persuade an audience to undertake a specific course of action, whereas the philosopher's arguments are not concerned with the courses of action - indeed his arguments are not relevant to specific courses of action; and that secondly, rhetorical reasoning is necessarily largely unreflective whereas philosophical reasoning is characteristically aimed at and pursues a coherent reflective understanding in necessarily general and abstract terms. Apart from these differences, which are indeed essential, rhetoric and philosophy are seen as closer, and as both more flexible, than the earlier view would allow.

According to the earlier view, one of the crucial differences that separate rhetoric and philosophy is that between rhetorical and logical reasoning. For the view which sees rhetoric and philosophy as less sharply divided, logical reasoning is not the decisive hallmark of philosophy. This view argues that the earlier picture may be accurate of logic itself, but that philosophical reasoning does not necessarily exhibit the linear character of logic and that as a picture of philosophy the earlier view is too rigid. It observes that what has counted as philosophical 'truth' has also changed over time, and that in philosophy the requirement that one argument is sufficient to demonstrate the truth of a given proposition, is conditional upon the audience's response. If the audience remains unconvinced, other arguments are typically introduced, and it may be argued that most philosophical works marshal a battery of arguments in support of a certain case. Furthermore, this view holds that philosophy does not operate with a corpus of fixed meanings but that, like rhetoric, also works with attributed meanings - in this case with those built up within the philosophical argument. In consequence, the understanding of the language used, depends upon the understanding of the particular argument developed rather than on any supposedly absolute definitions.

According to this view, one of the most important things that rhetoric and philosophy have in common is an audience. Indeed it holds that any piece of thinking expressed in a shared language, is developed with an actual or notional audience in mind, is directed towards that audience's understanding, is designed to appeal to an audience, and is intended to make that appeal effective and intelligible. To develop an argument of any kind is to enter some form of public world in which the audience's reception plays a part in the author's expression of this thinking, and in philosophy as much as in rhetoric, it holds that to pass beyond what is relevant to the argument being developed, is to argue ineffectively. One of the differences between rhetoric and philosophy here is that, in general, rhetorical argument is directed at the conviction of an audience to the presented alternative as a whole, through an appeal to their understanding which may be largely emotive, whereas philosophical argument seeks the conviction of an audience to the specific steps taken in the argument as well as to the conclusions reached, through an appeal to their understanding of those steps. In consequence, although philosophy as a public activity also takes place in a linguistic context or forum, the audience's reception is not measured merely in terms of simple assent or dissent, but in terms of their understanding of the specific connections made, and of their significance, in the philosopher's reasoning.

The other major point at which this view argues that rhetoric and philosophy are less sharply divided, concerns identification and definition in argument. It holds, firstly, that definition can also be seen as a form of identification, drawing on a framework of significant associations and resemblances, and that much argument that is acknowledged as philosophical in character, proceeds by circumstantial identifications rather than a priori definitions. In contrast with the earlier view, it holds, secondly, that identifications may, and do in philosophy, take place between things at the same level of abstraction; and thirdly that although philosophical reasoning may constantly seek to transcend the particularity of the contingent and the mutable, this does not affect its use of identification. Furthermore, this view holds that the assumptions in a piece of philosophical argument, though more reflectively held, are also working assumptions.

In sum, instead of the unbridgeable gulf between rhetoric and philosophy posited by the earlier view, this view presents an account in which there is significant common ground between the two and in which, in some respects, philosophy is closer to rhetoric than it is to logic. And while the earlier view located the difference between rhetoric and philosophy as a difference essentially in the kind of reasoning used, this view holds that the fundamental differences between them arise, rather, from the characters of the practical and reflective worlds.[5]

At this point, the second meaning of rhetoric begins to emerge. If the primary feature of rhetoric is the adaption and adjustment of ideas and considerations in the light of a purpose to inform, persuade and entertain an audience, in order to achieve a designated end in the form of a specific response, a desired choice, and a course of action, from an audience, then rhetoric may be firmly distinguished from philosophy. But if rhetorical argument is any argument which is designed to, along with other possible aims, appeal to a certain audience whose dispositions are known, then any speaker or writer essentially responsive to his audience in this way is, to that extent, a rhetorician. The second meaning of rhetoric, then, focuses upon the way in which any speaker or writer uses language to express and organise and not merely reflect his thinking.

The first thing to be noted about this meaning of rhetoric is that, in contrast to rhetoric as the art of persuasion in the practical world, rhetoric is seen here as a method of analysing utterances rather than as a property of those utterances. For when rhetoric is taken to mean the use of language, any utterance, by virtue of its being at attempt to communicate through language, is seen to contain a rhetorical structure which can be studied. In contrast, the first meaning of rhetoric provides a way of distinguishing the character of some utterances (those which are 'rhetorical') from others (those which are 'philosophical', 'poetic', or 'mathematical' etc.). In other words, the difference is between a 'rhetorical utterance' which conveys as its primary aim a stance of partiality, and 'rhetoric' meaning the (impartial) study of utterances, for what they disclose in their use of language. And it is important to emphasise that this notion does not entail a conception of ideas as 'determined' by language, and neither is the study of language seen as a 'substitute' for the study of 'ideas themselves'; any such dichotomy may be seen to rest on a false assumption, since a piece of thinking *can* only be expressed, recognised and studied in linguistic form, as a use of language. Thus, broadly speaking, 'rhetoric' here is a comprehensive name for style, and the study of a writer's rhetoric is understood as the examination of the expression of his thinking; that is, of the linguistic features, compositional arrangement, and levels of argument, which make up his use of language.

There is, then, a 'rhetoric' of any subject concerned with communicating through language. According to this notion, there is even a rhetoric of a highly abstract form of communication like mathematics, which would include the study of the conventions of mathematical argument and could explore the limits of those conventions. It may be argued that the utility of this notion of rhetoric is severely restricted in cases such as mathematics, where the language, the symbols, of communication and their conventions of usage are laid down as ground rules, and are not open to flexible use; that although mathematics retains the purpose of communicating to an audience (a first precondition for studying its rhetoric), it is denied the latitude and flexibility of *choosing* the most appropriate language (a second precondition) that characterises subjects using ordinary language. However, while the use of this notion of rhetoric may have more interesting results in the study of some other subjects, where choice in the use of language is present, the character of mathematical language does not preclude the study of its rhetoric, and a subject such as the history of mathematics, in which changes in thinking are expressed and registered in changes attributed to the meaning of its language, could usefully be undertaken along rhetorical lines.

The study of a piece of thinking through its rhetoric or use of language is essential for understanding past utterances, when the meanings and connotations of words have changed. All linguistic expressions are made in a temporal setting, and the rhetorical approach is concerned precisely with discovering rather than assuming what an author meant by what he said. Although this point may seem so obvious as not to require special emphasis, it is one to which attention is not always sufficiently paid in the study of thinking and writing of the past; C. S. Lewis' illustrations of the "dangerous" senses of words,[6] indicate the degree of attention necessary in order not to misinterpret a past author's use of language. Moreover, because the rhetorical emphasis on language "is on the social use of language, on the relation of text to contemporaneous ambience and previous tradition, an ambience and tradition by definition shared",[7] the recognition of the 'ambience and tradition' in which a past author is writing, involves the understanding of conventions of argument and uses of language which provide the student of a past text with a first level of access to a writer's meaning.

Since the philosopher, like every other writer and speaker, is concerned with communicating his thinking, he too organises language to express his thought in the most effective manner, in order both to make it intelligible to the reader and to present its coherence in the clearest way. Several implications for language and argument in philosophy follow from this point. Firstly, it follows that every philosophical argument is advocating something - a way of understanding something, and aims to convince the audience of that way of understanding it. It follows, secondly, that no philosophical argument using ordinary language can be self-evidently true, for any argument which involves choice in the use and meaning of language is open to interpretation, dispute and revision. And thirdly it follows that the language of philosophy is not 'neutral'. The language in which philosophy is conducted contains an affective dimension in common with the whole range of ordinary language. And while philosophical argument largely forgoes those words which are purely affective in scope, it cannot avoid the acutely and precisely expressive quality of language. The use of figurative language in particular, in philosophy, is considered in detail in the following chapter. At this point it is sufficient to recognise that the power of words in this sense cannot be escaped in philosophy, and that metaphor is one of the most common ways in which words capture the significance of thinking. Iris Murdoch points to the scope of this aspect of language in philosophy, as part of the province of rhetoric, when she remarks of Plato, "of course he used metaphor", and continues, "but philosophy needs metaphor and metaphor is basic; how basic is the most basic philosophical question".[8]

This point leads to the further observation that some writers also organise language in a more self-conscious manner so as to indicate an idea by utilising the resonances of the language, as well as expressing the idea through the means of language. This dimension of the use of language is also part of what is studied under the name of rhetoric.

Rhetoric as the use of language to express and organise and not merely reflect thinking, is the sense in which the term is used in the following chapters to examine Hobbes' *Leviathan*, and it is worth stressing that the aim of the inquiry is not to claim that Hobbes was a rhetorician rather than a philosopher, but that one can examine the rhetorical structure of his philosophy. Such an enterprise is especially apt in studying Hobbes, firstly because of his acute sense of and complex use of language, seen both in the precision of his words to express his thinking, and in the force of his imagery due to his self-conscious and at times poetical use of language; and secondly because at one level the argument of *Leviathan* is all about the power of words.

It remains to say something about the rhetoric of the present work. The six chapters that follow examine six different aspects of the thesis that in studying Hobbes' *Leviathan* and attempting to make sense of the work as a whole (the whole being that composed of the thinking expressed, necessarily in linear form, in the work), the study of Hobbes' rhetoric and the study of his philosophy coincide. The most general statement of the thesis, then, is that understanding Hobbes' *Leviathan* involves understanding his thinking as, at the same time, philosophy and rhetoric - as a piece of thinking which examines the conditions upon which civil society must be established and elucidates the character of the civil society that results, and as a piece of thinking which can be studied by attending to the manner in which it is expressed, in the use of language employed by Hobbes.

The relation between the chapters that follow is one of parts to the whole, each focussing on a different aspect of the subject of the thesis. The internal relations between them are not meant to be primarily narratively continuous, but for each to refer back to the central argument.

The first two chapters of the thesis are concerned with the connection between rhetoric and philosophy in general terms. The aim of the argument is to establish, firstly, that one can examine a work of philosophy through examining its rhetoric; and in chapter 2 that, secondly, the study of the use of language in philosophy involves the study of metaphor and other figurative language, and of analogical reasoning. The purpose of this line of inquiry is to set out a general account of the relations between thinking, the expression of thinking in literal and non-literal language and in different kinds of reasoning, and philosophy, as an answer to the implicit general questions raised by the approach taken in studying *Leviathan*, namely, why study a thinker through his use of language?, and why is the study of Hobbes' language relevant to understanding his political philosophy?

In the chapters following chapter 2, the connections between the rhetoric and philosophy of Hobbes' *Leviathan* are explored. The third chapter considers the effect of seventeenth-century literary criticism on Hobbes' rhetoric and his role in the critical debate that took place. Its purpose is to place Hobbes' use of language and literary views in the literary context in which they belong. In chapter 4 Hobbes' views on rhetoric and theory of language in *Leviathan* are discussed. These two chapters seek to indicate that Hobbes' interest in language should be seen in terms of his lifelong concern with questions of literary theory and practice, and the rhetorical dimension of discourse, as well as in terms of what we recognise as political philosophy. Those commentators who present an account of Hobbes' philosophy as rationalistic and scientific in temper, tend to neglect this other side of Hobbes' interest in language and so tend to misinterpret, it is argued, the significance of Hobbes' use of language in *Leviathan*.

The fifth chapter discusses the engraved title-page of *Leviathan*, in terms of the seventeenth-century tradition of engraved title-pages, and as an aspect of Hobbes' rhetoric. Like the third chapter, it aims to identify a dimension of the historical context in which *Leviathan* was composed. The considerations raised in the discussion of the engraved title-page provide important support for the argument developed in chapter 7, on the significance of the allegory in Hobbes' thinking in *Leviathan*. Chapter 5 is concerned with the manner in which, in the sixteenth and seventeenth centuries, the use of verbal language was understood as closely related to the use of other forms of expression - notably the pictorial arts - as other ways in which man constructs something through his artifice.

The sixth chapter is concerned with placing Hobbes in a third historical context, by comparing some further aspects of his use of language to express his thinking with those of Hooker in *Of the Laws of Ecclesiastical Polity*. Hooker was chosen for this comparative treatment, because he is viewed as the major political thinker of the period immediately before Hobbes in England; and as a thinker directly concerned with political thought, where Sidney and Spencer - the other two writers of the period immediately before Hobbes whose work is discussed specifically - are concerned respectively with the character and practice of literature.

In the seventh chapter, the character of the allegory of the

Leviathan and its relation to the philosophical character of Hobbes' thinking in *Leviathan* as a whole, is discussed. The examination of this use of language by Hobbes, it is argued, is the most significant for understanding his philosophy and the relation between rhetoric and philosophy in *Leviathan*.

The thesis does not aim at an exegetical analysis of the doctrines to be drawn from *Leviathan*, but at showing how the work is composed and how it forms a whole. However, some of the conclusions arrived at in the different chapters do concern matters of exegesis, and will be considered when they arise. The final chapter ties together the themes or threads of argument in the thesis; it is concerned with indicating how the different aspects of the relation between rhetoric and philosophy in *Leviathan* discussed in the previous chapters, contribute to the understanding of *Leviathan* as a whole.[9]

In his Introduction to Hobbes' *Elements of Law*,[10] Goldsmith writes, after discussing the development of Hobbes' ideas through the different texts, and the connections and differences between them, that

> *Leviathan* stands at the end of a process of revision.... And clearly what makes it a masterpiece it not its use of the organic analogy, the comparison of a state to a human body. In *Leviathan* that comparison is an infrequently used literary device. It appears briefly in the Introduction and occasionally reappears....The use of the organic analogy is part of Hobbes' stylistic polishing, just one of the many ways in which he tightened up what he said....But those qualities which make *Leviathan* great occasionally make it difficult.

Two objections to Goldsmith's remarks come immediately to mind. Firstly, he omits altogether to specify what does make *Leviathan* great. And secondly, if the "organic analogy" is one of the ways in which Hobbes "tightened up what he said", then it might be interesting to explore what was involved in this "tightening up". Furthermore, it is unclear what Goldsmith could mean by his remark, since while he is here suggesting that the "organic analogy" helps to "tighten up" the argument, he has said in the same breath that it is merely "stylistic polishing" - that is, presumably, operates at another level than that of the argument itself.

But more importantly, Goldsmith's remarks have been quoted because they present, in dramatic form, the subject of this thesis. For it is precisely towards indicating the significance of the "organic analogy" and its relation to the shape of Hobbes' philosophy as a whole, that this thesis is directed.

NOTES

1. Quentin Skinner, for instance, has examined in detail the line of argument which explores the "ideological purchase" of Hobbes' thought, in the context of the contemporary climate of debate in England.
2. Nancy Struever, *The Language of History in the Renaissance*, Princeton U.P., 1970, p113.
3. The argument here is indebted to Michael Oakeshott's *Experience and its Modes*, C.U.P., 1933.
4. Struever, *op.cit.*, p15.
5. This is a different distinction from the one used by some, mainly American, writers in the recent resurgence of interest in linking rhetoric with "communication" studies, "argumentation" and "transmission". David Johnston's *The Rhetoric of Leviathan* (Princeton, 1986) belongs either within this modern American tradition of interest in rhetoric; or perhaps more closely to the Hobbes-and-religion category since, curiously, the prominent "Rhetoric" in his title is so little explored in the substance of the argument. In any case Johnson's understanding of rhetoric bears little relation to the term as discussed in this work.
6. C. S. Lewis, *Studies in Words*, C.U.P., 1967.
7. Struever, *op.cit.*, p180.
8. Iris Murdoch, *The Fire and the Sun*, Clarendon, Oxford, 1977, p88.
9. To my knowledge, no commentator has previously explored this approach towards Hobbes. However, several writers have touched upon matters discussed in the present thesis. They include Dorothea Krook, *Three Tradition s of Moral Thought*, C.U.P., 1959; Sheldon Wolin, *Politics and Vision*, Little, Bro wn & Co., Boston, 1960, and *Hobbes and the Epic Tradition of Political Theory*, Univ. of California, 1970; Thomas Spragens, *The Politic s of Motion*, Univ. of Kentucky Press, 1973; K. R. Minogue, "Parts and Wholes: Twentieth Century Interpretation of Thomas Hobbes", and W. H. Greenleaf, "A Note on Hobbes and the Book of Job", in Department of Philosophy, Univ. of Granada ed., *Hobbes*, Granada, 1974. Michael Oakeshott's Introduction to *Leviathan*, and "*Leviathan*: a Myth", both in *Hobbes on Civil Association*, Blackwell, Oxford, 1975, have been a continual source of enlightenment.
10. M. M. Goldsmith, Introduction to the 2nd edition of Ferdinand Tönnies ed., *The Elements of Law, Natural and Politic by Thomas Hobbes*, Frank Cass, 1969, pxx-xxi.

CHAPTER 2
Figurative Language in Philosophical Understanding

Although this thesis is primarily concerned not with theories of language but with Hobbes' political philosophy, the approach taken towards Hobbes necessarily involves some discussion of the more general problems of the use of language in philosophical understanding. Even if a full discussion is not incorporated into the thesis, the background problems about language, debated by linguistic philosophers and literary theorists as foreground problems, must be considered and, in so far as they have a bearing on what may be said about Hobbes' use of language, a position with regard to these questions must be taken.

In chapters 3 and 4, Hobbes' views on figurative language and related matters are examined, and the connections with the two perspectives to which his views are related, are explored. And in chapter 7 it is argued that the significance of Hobbes' figurative language, and in particular of the allegory, in *Leviathan*, needs now to be reconstructed, to see and not misinterpret its character. Hobbes' allegory of the Leviathan, it is contended, cannot be denied a philosophical characterisation on the grounds that it does not meet present conceptions of what may count as philosophy. Notions of what may be involved in philosophical understanding have changed over time, and Hobbes' use of allegory, while if written today it might be thought eccentric to the point of being unacceptable as philosophy, must not be anachronistically confused with current canons of philosophical writing. Chapter 7 goes on to consider the allegory itself, for to be accepted as philosophical it has to be shown to exhibit that character, in the context of *Leviathan*.

In this chapter it will be argued that in terms of what is understood, in current practice also, as philosophy, the use of figurative language and analogical reasoning can be upheld as philosophical in character, and that their unfashionableness does not point to their invalidity. This line of argument is not designed to reach the conclusion that Hobbes' philosophical allegory can be identified with a potential philosophical allegory today (the obverse of the same historical anachronism), but to strengthen the case for the acknowledgement of figurative language and analogical reasoning in philosophical understanding generally.

This chapter will argue, then, that in philosophy, understanding does not entail the transmission of 'pure thought in concepts' *rather than* the communication of 'thought in language', for language organises and expresses and not merely reflects thought, and coherent meaning is not restricted to 'plain' rather than 'figurative' language. Although distinctions may be made between thought and language, and between literal and figurative language, philosophical understanding does not rest upon nor recognise only the first member of each pair, and does not presuppose that the two distinctions bifurcate the members of each pair.

Perceiving, Thinking and Understanding

The implicit aim of all thinking is understanding, and the objects of thinking are perceptions. Let us examine what this means.

The objects of thinking are perceptions, not sensations. A sensation, as Richards observes, "would be something that just was *so*, on its own, a datum; as such we have none. Instead we have perceptions, responses whose character comes to them from the past as well as the present occasion. A perception is never just of an *it*; perception takes whatever it perceives as a thing of a certain sort."[1] Perception is contextual, both in that the thing perceived already has some meaning, some minimal intelligibility within a world of familiars, and in that as perceived now the thing perceived (idea or phenomenon) inhabits a context.

Thinking is the activity of forming connections between perceptions, and of arranging and relating perceptions and connections into a pattern in which they are understood to have a coherent meaning. Thinking is an activity of sorting out, selecting, ordering, recognising, and sifting of irrelevant associations, perceptions and their connections. The mind, says Richards, "is a connecting organ, it works only by connecting and it can connect any two things in an indefinitely large number of ways. Which of these it chooses is settled by reference to some large whole or aim, and, though we may not discover its aim, the mind is never aimless." In all thinking we are choosing, and seeking to understand by identifying perceptions and connections in "the absence of explicitly stated intermediate steps".[2]

The problem of how thought is to be characterised will be considered more fully in the following section, when it will be seen to be a problem involving the relationship to be drawn between thought and language. But at this point, Iris Murdoch offers the sound advice that in attempting to characterise thought, "the choice must be rejected between logical behaviourism and the private theatre. An ontological approach, which seeks for an identifiable inner stuff and either asserts or denies its existence, must be avoided. An account of meaning which rests on a search for hard verificatory data....breaks down" for lack of evidence. The point is that it is important and necessary to think that thoughts are particular "inner experiences"; it is "a necessary regulative idea, about which it makes no sense to ask, is it true or false that it is *so*? It is for us *as if* our thoughts were inner events, and it is *as if* these events were describable" in language.[3]

Perception and thinking, then, take place in and disclose contexts of meaning. In analytical and not, it is to be stressed, chronological terms, the interaction of the meanings of separate perceptions with the meanings of the connections between them, with the meanings arising from the pattern or context in which they are placed, result in a thought which means what it means because of these interactions. Perceptions are not fundamental building blocks with fixed meanings, but are themselves resultants of previous interactions.

This interaction is the principle on which metaphor operates, for the meaning of a metaphor is not attainable without some sort of exchange between its two or more thoughts or words. The structure of metaphor is discussed in a later section, but it is important here to recognise that, as Richards shows, metaphor is not only a "verbal matter, a shifting and displacement of words", but is fundamentally an account of what takes place in thinking itself. *Thought*, he says, is metaphorical, and "the metaphors of language derive therefrom".[4] And Iris Murdoch observes that the "development of consciousness in human beings is inseparably connected with the use of metaphor. Metaphors are not merely peripheral decorations or even useful models, they are fundamental forms of our awareness of our condition: metaphors of space, metaphors of movement, metaphors of vision".[5] Thinking, then, may be characterised as a metaphor-making activity, because the resultant thought is a coherent, cohering meaning whose understanding and coherence cannot be reduced to the separate perceptions and connections which contributed to it. The meaning of the resultant thought is an understanding of the whole as whole as coherent.

Furthermore, if the aim of thinking is understanding, then understanding is analytically prior to, and a pre-condition of, the making of judgments of truth and falsity about a piece of thinking. The criteria for judgments of truth and falsity depend upon the comprehension of the degree and character of the coherence of a passage of thinking as a whole.

It is useful to distinguish philosophical understanding from scientific understanding. In science, understanding consists in accounting for patterns of phenomena which are taken to be facts, that is, phenomena whose existence and independence is seen as external to man's understanding of them. The account given of these phenomena perceived as facts, while not incomplete in itself, is seen to require verification or refutation through observation of the be-haviour of the facts. In other words, in science, understanding is taken to be only half of what is required in order to know; for understanding unsupplemented by observation would be taken to have neglected the external existence and independence of the facts.

In philosophy, understanding consists of accounting for abstract perceptions, that is, for thoughts and ideas which either correspond to no phenomena (such as 'relation', 'knowledge', 'obligation'), or to phenomena whose scientific understanding does not account for their abstract character (such as 'being'). In philosophical understanding there can be no appeal to the 'empirical verification' of science, for its reference is not to external 'facts' but to experience as expressed in thinking. Philosophical perceptions do not exist independently of man's perceiving them, and philosophical understanding cannot be supplemented by observation of phenomena taken to be external ('facts') because there are none. Thus, in philosophy the absence of 'facts' (which is not, however, to be conceived as a lack or a deficiency; indeed, it is the externalised quality of facts in science that can be viewed as a deficiency, since it creates the need of observation in addition to understanding before the perceptions can be taken to be adequately known), or less defensively, the congruence of perceptions and perceiver in philosophy, means that what is understood is also thereby known:

Thinking and Language

The only means by which thoughts can be understood by, and communicated to others, is through language. "It is little use appealing to the reader to 'consider the bare notions themselves'", Richards argues, firstly because the reader "*can* only 'collect the whole sum and tenor of the discourse' from the words", and secondly because "an idea or a notion, when unencumbered and undisguised, is no easier to get hold of....Indeed an idea, or a notion, like the physicist's ultimate particles and rays, is only known by what it does. Apart from its dress or other signs it is not identifiable".[6]

A piece of thinking can only be known through the language in which it is expressed, but the language cannot specify in advance the meaning of a thought. On the question of this double identification, whereby the meaning of thinking is identified in terms of its expression in language, and the meaning of language is identified in terms of its expression of thinking, Iris Murdoch comments that "words do not occur as the content of thought as if they were cast upon a screen and there read off by the thinker".[7] And as Ogden and Richards remark, much verbal confusion "can be traced to the superstition that words are in some way parts of things or always imply things corresponding to them".[8] Just as there are no perceptions that are fixed-meaning building blocks, so there are no words that inherently have this determinate character.

The intelligibility of a piece of thinking is dependent upon the language used to express the thought, both in that the reader or hearer must gain a minimal comprehension through the language - there being no other means through which to comprehend it - and in that, as Richards notes, "you have usually to wait till I have gone on a bit before you can decide how you will understand the opening parts of the sentences".[9] The coherence of the piece of thinking, on the other hand, depends not only on the language which expresses the thought, but also on a common acknowledgement of a set of rules of consequentiality (what can follow from what) and a common acceptance of the sort of conclusion that may count as significant. The coherence of the utterance, like its intelligibility, depends upon its contextual understanding. The evil of the common idea that there is a right or a good use for every word, Richards maintains, "is that it takes the sense of an author's words to be things we know before we read him, fixed factors with which he has to build up the meaning of his sentences....Instead they are the resultants which we arrive at only through the interplay of the interpretative possibilities of the whole utterance".[10]

Furthermore, neither consequentiality nor significance are absolute. In the history of philosophy, both what may be a consequence and what is deemed significant have changed over time. Language, taken to be a set of conventions and a repository of accumulated meanings, is also subject to change over time. The relation between thought and language may be considered to be dialectical. On the one hand, to use language is to choose, from the multiple senses in which we learn to understand words, meanings which express our thoughts, and thus to learn a language is to become acquainted with a world of meaning common to those who speak the language. But, on the other hand, the flexibility of language means in turn that the expression of new thoughts involves the extension of the resources of language in the recognition of new senses of words and the accumulation of new contextual meanings.

A vocabulary is not a rationalistic corpus of discrete meanings but a miscellaneous collection of words whose multiple meanings can only be discovered and extended in use. And a language contains no overall principle of meaning nor inherent metaphysics. A language cannot tell you what to think, or how to think. Philosophy cannot be derived from a language's meanings since a language's meanings are accumulated without regard to make all the senses and meanings internally consistent or coherent. The accumulation or corpus as a whole tells not one philosophical story but an essentially ambiguous story, or rather, witnesses the debates and doctrines of any number of philosophies, and is not concerned to tidy or organise the diversity, or to abolish vanquished meanings. In language, vanquished meanings are not distinguished from victorious ones, and meanings disappear not through defeat but from disuse, just as they appear and persist not through being 'right' but through use because understood as significant. A language is an instrument for *use*, in expressing thinking, by providing a groundwork of choices which never consumes the possibilities of thought.

It follows that the 'universal grammar', so optimistically expected by some linguists and anthropologists, could never be constructed. The essential untidiness of language, whose significance they overlooked, could only be corrected and the language systematised, at the expense of its flexibility. Secondly, the multiplicity of contexts in which words have meanings could not be accounted for. And thirdly, the idea of the 'universal grammar' assumed that words have only 'fact-stating' functions, and the underlying presupposition here, that language is a mirror of reality, was mistaken. Most importantly of all, the advocates of the 'universal grammar' mistook the character of language, an instrument whose possibilities are only found and extended in *use*, for an imperfectly realised metaphysical system, and so mistook the relation between language and thinking.

The final aspect of the relationship between thinking and language to be discussed here concerns the difference between a passage of thinking and a passage of spoken or written discourse, and the manner in which the one becomes the other.

A. C. Lloyd poses the problem that "we want thinking to be intelligible by its obedience to the rules of discourse (eg. non-contradiction). But we also want it to be something which is prior to discourse and therefore need not obey the rules of discourse".[11] However, he continues, the problem dissolves once it is recognised that there are two activities involved here. One consists of reflection, musing, pondering, speculation and recollection which may or may not involve language and which, though it is not aimless, is not structured and does not have meaning until the pattern or chain is more or less completed. The other activity consists of reflecting on the reflections, the thinking *about* which makes sense of the chain or pattern, the structuring which sees the reflection and musing *as* a chain or pattern, and thereby meaningful, and which in doing so uses language and obeys the rules of discourse. What are being distinguished here are not levels of thinking, but different sorts of accounts that can be given about a stretch of thinking. Thinking, says Lloyd, "is really being wise after the event".[12] Usually when we are interested in someone's thoughts, he explains, "we mean the results of his thinking. It is not the event but the wisdom after it that we *do* want".[13] In other words, it is not the stream of thinking we want to hear, but the abridgement of it made in the light of the significance it was seen to have when the whole of it was reflected upon, that we want.

Two consequences can be seen to follow from this characterisation. Firstly, the difference between a passage of unstructured reflection and musing and a passage of thinking *about* in spoken or written discourse, may be likened to the difference between the chronicler's relation of occurrences and the historian's account of events. Just as, as Ryle notes, "historians do not narrate extra events, over and above those narrated by chroniclers. They tell us different sorts of things - interesting things - about those same events that the chroniclers report uninterestingly";[14] so the account of a passage of thinking in spoken or written discourse presents in a context, and therefore with significance and meaning, reflections about what were, as 'inner events' unintelligible.

And secondly, the abridgement that takes place because we want the account of a passage of reflection, musing, pondering, speculation and recollection to be a history and not a chronicle - that is, to be presented as an understood - involves the employment of metaphor. As Ryle says, "we want the plot to be told in abstraction" from the detailed incidents, and to abstract is to form a metaphor.[15] In Richards' terms, "a word is normally a substitute for (or means) not one discrete past impression but a combination of general aspects. Now that is itself a summary account of the principle of metaphor....when we use metaphor we have two thoughts of different things active together and supported by a single word, or phrase, whose meaning is a resultant of their interaction".[16] Furthermore, as Iris Murdoch remarks, the character of the constituents of the perceptions that make up 'inner events', that is the language, imagery and sensations, are hardly to be distinguished at times. Again, she says, "there seems no sense in asking for a clear ontological classification. This is what thinking is like....we naturally use metaphors to describe states of mind, or to describe 'thought processes'....metaphor is not an inexact 'second best' mode of expression, it is the best possible. Here metaphor is not a peripheral excrescence upon the linguistic structure, it is its living centre....We do not 'suddenly' have to adopt the figurative mode; we are using it all the time".[17]

Moreover, if we think of thinking in this way, Iris Murdoch argues, as the activity of grasping or reducing to order our 'inner events', "with the help of a language which is fundamentally metaphorical, this will operate against the world-language dualism which haunts us....Seen from this point of view, thinking is not the using of *symbols* which designate absent *objects*, symbolising and sensing being strictly divided from each other. Thinking is not designating at all, but rather understanding, grasping, 'possessing'".[18]

Thus far, then, the discussion of what is involved in thinking and in the relationship between thinking and language, has identified two levels seen to consist of a metaphor-making activity. Firstly it was argued that connections formed in and which help to compose the materials of thinking seen as significant, are metaphorical in character. And secondly the abridging, and organising of the significances, of the materials of thinking through the expression of thinking in language, also involves metaphor and is an extension of what is already going on in thinking. This description of what is going on, in terms of the metaphor of 'levels', is perhaps misleading, since the first 'level' may already involve language, and since the description suggests separate and distinct processes. As experienced, thinking and the expression of thinking in language may more aptly be described in terms of a single process, of movement towards a greater articulation and understanding - made up of an increasing abridgement and organisation of the materials of thinking on the one hand, and of an increasingly self-conscious use of language (in the light of a notional audience) on the other.

Literal and Non-literal Language

Apart from the fundamentally metaphorical character of all thinking, where one can neither intend or not to be metaphorical, we can distinguish between literal and intentionally metaphorical meanings of an utterance. The literal meaning, "taking words in their usual or primary sense", without "allegory or metaphor" (OED), minimises the contextual influence upon a word, and shuts off all the senses and connotations of words, other than the "primary" sense. Whereas a metaphorical meaning considers one or several of the other senses and connotations of a word, and their contextual interactions, to have a greater standing or significance in the meaning of the utterance.

Richards frames the distinction between literal and metaphorical in terms of the stability of the conditions governing the meanings of words. Some words and sentences, he says, "do seem to mean what they mean absolutely and unconditionally. This is because the conditions governing their meanings are so constant that we can disregard them. So the weight of a cubic centimetre of water seems a fixed and absolute thing because of the constancy of its governing conditions".[19] But, he continues, "these words are fewer than we suppose. Most words, as they pass from context to context, change their meanings....Stability in a word's meaning is not something to be assumed, but always something to be explained".[20]

What is important about the way this distinction is framed is that it distinguishes on the grounds of how the words are *used*, and not on any grounds of inherent literalness or otherwise. For literalness and metaphoricalness do not reside in words automatically, but are attributes to be discerned in words in their particular usages, and it is in principle possible that any word may be used metaphorically. It follows that literal meanings need not refer only to objects in the 'tangible world' and metaphorical meanings only to the 'fabrications of the mind'. All that matters for a literal meaning is that that sense of the word be "usual or primary" and what characterises metaphorical meanings is the extension from the "usual or primary" sense that has been made in the use of a word in a particular context. Thus in the phrase, 'the leg of the table', the word 'leg' may be understood as a literal meaning, although it is not the original or only meaning of the word. In this way many metaphors have become, in certain contexts, literal meanings. Furthermore, a meaning may be literal and metaphorical at the same time. If a man has a wooden leg, "it is literal in one set of respects, metaphoric in another", Richards argues. "A word may be simultaneously both literal and metaphorical, just as it may simultaneously support many different metaphors, may serve to focus into one meaning many different meanings",[21] depending upon the context in which it is being used and understood.

Where are literal meanings appropriate, where do thinker and audience have the choice of taking either literal or non-literal meanings, and where is there the choice of taking both literal and one or several non-literal meanings? What, in other words, is the criterion of literal meanings? And what, if any, is the connection between literal and non-literal meanings and different sorts of reasoning? Let us consider some different sorts of thinking (which are not meant, however, to constitute an exhaustive list).

In science, the definition of terms is designed to exclude all but one meaning of a term, and to exclude the connotive force of its other possible (either dictionary or contextual) senses. While the language of science is not literal in the sense of only using the "usual or primary" meanings of words, because it employs many technical terms (either meanings which refer only in scientific contexts, or specially-coined words), it insists that only the precisely defined, fixed and absolute meanings of its technical terms are appropriate, and denies the validity of any non-literal sense to its non-technical language by excluding their significance. In Richards' terms, the meaning of terms in science is established by definitions; that is, by the specification in advance of the conditions governing meaning, such that they will remain constant in usage.

The language of the practical world is pre-eminently literal, since it is the "usual or primary" meanings of words which are appropriate to the execution of everyday transactions, whose efficiency depends in part on the ready and shared understanding of the language used by all its speakers in common. In the carrying out of everyday transactions, reflection upon that understanding and on the possible other meaning of words carries no significance and hinders the efficient, economical and effective execution of those transactions.

In politics, both literal and non-literal language is used. The "usual or primary" meanings of words like 'voter', 'election' and 'government' are used, as they are used in the practical world, without reflective understanding. These are not a technical language of politics but current literal meanings also used in other activities than politics. Non-literal language is used when technical terms are taken out of their original contexts of meaning, from fields of inquiry such as economics and law, in order to recommend a particular course of political action by investing it with the status with which the technical terms are accorded in the practical world. Non-literal meanings are also used in politics, in ideological debate, when the literal vocabulary is redefined within a different context of significance and its meaning accordingly changed. It is interesting that in politics, literal and non-literal language may be used in a single utterance.

In political utterance, the ambiguity resulting from the combination of literal and non-literal meanings, which may be seen as characteristic of political activity, is a contentious ambiguity. In ideological debate for instance, the advocate of a certain view may use non-literal meanings in order to suggest that his usage ought to be accepted as the literal usage, maintaining that 'this is how things really are'. that this is or ought to be the primary sense of this word in general currency. The detractor's ground of rejection is likely to be that the advocate's meanings are indeed non-literal since they do not present things as they really are. Thus, ideological debate is often conducted implicitly in terms of whether or not the meanings in dispute are literal or not, with each side wishing to claim literalness for his meanings.

In poetry, the combination of literal and non-literal meanings is also essentially characteristic of the activity, but is here fruitfully rather than contentiously ambiguous. In poetry the range of meanings of words and the invitation to consider literal and non-literal senses together, contribute to the total meaning of a poem, and particular meanings are understood as parts composing a whole meaning. The necessity in science to maintain the absolute predominance of one meaning of a word to the exclusion of all others, is reversed in poetry, which flourishes on the rich variety of multiple meanings and associations which words can express.

The language of historical writing is also both literal and non-literal, but for different reasons than in politics and poetry, for the historian's account of the past is concerned to avoid ambiguity, not to foster it, either contentiously or fruitfully. Apart from the use of selected technical terms imported for methodological purposes (for instance from demography and economics), and the specification of contemporary meanings (such as of religious vocabulary in the Middle Ages), the historian uses the "usual or primary" meanings of words, along with metaphors whose purpose is to make shorthand connections between the events narrated. Like science, historical inquiry seeks to provide a coherent account of evidence understood as external, and so focuses on the precision of the connections to be made; and as in science, ambiguous non-literal meanings only serve to dissipate that precision. But in history, unambiguous non-literal meanings, that is metaphors involved in using words like 'rise', 'fall', 'birth', 'growth' and 'collapse', are necessary and are accepted in general statements and broad characterisations, on condition that they are understood as metaphors designating courses of events which are or could be specified in detail from the evidence. Moreover, the more distant the meanings of the language in the historical past from the literal meanings established in the historian's language, the more the historian's enterprise will be a linguistic one, elucidating the pattern of literal and non-literal meanings employed by the historical subject. But again, the historian's own necessary use of non-literal language does not render untrue or override the possible chronicle of the course of events. For while the historian's object is to account for a course of events which a chronicle only registers, such that the historian regard the chronicle as a not-yet-understood, and such that the historian's metaphors are seen as meaningful and explanatory where the chronicle is seen as uninteresting, the metaphors used by the historian to make a coherent account of the chronicle are nevertheless understood as always capable of being translated or dismantled into chronicle form.

Contemporary logic, developed in the thirties, uses an abstract technical language, whose terms, expressed in symbols, are defined in advance of use to specify single meanings and to exclude any contextual influence whatever. The use of such a language, because it is based on definition rather than identification, can certainly not be metaphorically understood, and is only literal in the sense that the technical language of science is literal. For while both definition and identification are relational activities, involving the making of connections in thinking, the former is used to specify exact particular single meanings and to thus narrow the horizon of meaning to a single point of attention. The language of logic does not distinguish between literal ("usual or primary") and non-literal meanings in other sorts of thinking, since both are reduced, in the conversion to logical form, to the same abstract formulations of X's and Y's and their qualifying properties, one symbol to designate relation of any kind, and a small and exclusive number of connectives. The only distinction recognised in logic about the use of language is that between statements and statements about statements, and this does not, of course, correspond to the literal non-literal distinction recognised in other kinds of thinking.

Philosophical thinking begins with literal ("usual or primary") meanings, but rather than using them as they are, or inventing a technical language to supersede them, the philosopher sees them as problematic, as inviting a less conditional and more general understanding. In philosophy, literal meanings are explored and their relations with other meanings examined and expanded, until they are abstract understandings and, in a context of abstract meanings, coherent. And it is characteristic of such meanings that they operate by drawing upon the connative forces of the context in which they are understood, to a greater extent than occurs in any other kind of thinking, and in a manner peculiar to philosophy. For example, from 'freedom' in the practical world meaning 'not in prison' to 'freedom' in philosophy, calls to mind metaphors of movement towards progressively greater both height and depth - generality and specificity. The meaning of 'freedom' in philosophy is identified in terms of the linguistic context in which it is seen as most significant as the focus of a coherent whole composed of multiple meanings and associations. In this way, then, the language of philosophy is non-literal, firstly in the sense that its meanings are necessarily not "usual or primary", secondly in the sense that its meanings do not exclude contextual influence but are necessarily contextual and relational, and thirdly in the sense that its meanings cannot be known in advance but only within a particular context.

Within the sphere of philosophical language, characterised as non-literal, there is no qualitative difference between thought which utilises and builds on the connative force of meanings of words and context already established in the language, and thought which makes new connections of meaning. It follows that in philosophy, the invitation to use and extend non-literal meanings is at its most pressing, and that the difference recognised in other types of thinking between literal and intentionally metaphorical language is at its least significant, since the language of philosophy is thoroughly metaphorical even before the philosopher's conviction to either introduce or refrain from intentional metaphor takes effect. In philosophical writing and in poetry, the metaphorical character and texture of thinking are most accurately captured; their ability to support multiple meanings without dissolving into overall lack of meaning, depends upon the structure of connections which form the context. Thus from philosophy which deliberately avoids intentional metaphor to that which explicitly utilises it - as in the allegory of Hobbes, it will be argued - there is a continuum of philosophical writing which is unavoidably metaphorical.

While philosophy, like history and science, is also concerned with the precision of the connections to be made, the same stricture against the use of non-literal meanings does not follow in philosophy. The reason is found in the relationship understood between thinker and subject matter. The nature of the subject matter in history and science (in science deliberately external to the scientist, in history necessarily as-if-it-were external to the historian) presupposes that the activity of the scientist and historian is quite different from the activity of the phenomena or occurrences studied. This imposes on the scientist and historian the obligation to maintain the distinction in the account offered. Since metaphorical meanings are understood not to reside in the phenomena or occurrences, their introduction into explanation is severely restricted. This is not to be confused, however, with the scientist's and historian's activity of ordering the phenomena or occurrences into significant patterns, significant to the scientist and historian, not inherently significant, for the phenomena and occurrences have no inherent significance. The ordering and patterning and investing with significance is a methodological requirement, a feature of all thinking, the metaphor-making activity described earlier. Whereas the criterion of the language that forms an account depends upon the manner in which the subject matter is understood. In philosophy, where there are no phenomena or occurrences taken to be existing externally and independently, where the subject matter is the content of consciousness, and recognised as such, the philosopher sustains no obligation to offer his account in language other than that in which the subject matter is understood by him. Thus he draws upon and extends the metaphor-making procedure of thinking, rather than attending to something seen as external to it.

The criteria of literal meanings, then, are that firstly they are recognised, as are non-literal meanings, according to their use in particular contexts; secondly that they apply only to meanings of words taken in the "usual or primary" sense; thirdly that they apply only in utterances whose understanding excludes the connotive force of other possible (either dictionary or contextual) meanings; and fourthly that they are specified in advance. In the sense that non-literal meanings correspond more accurately to the character of thinking, and literal ones involve a narrowing down and a shutting out, it could be argued that non-literal meanings are those which come most naturally and literal ones are those which are artificial.

Literal meanings therefore attend to the meaning of each word of the utterance in isolation, in contrast to the attention to context in non-literal meanings. The context is formed by the language in which, firstly, the sentence is written, and more broadly by the language of the text in which it occurs and the discipline to which it is seen to belong. Thus, for example, if a simple sentence like 'he brought the house down', is read literally, the meaning of the sentence is arrived at by each word being understood in itself, that is defined. Read non-literally, the meaning of the sentence is arrived at by identifying each word in relation to the meaning or sense of the whole context. One of the things that each form of thinking does is to legislate for itself the scope of literal and non-literal meanings in its use of language, to specify the amount and kind of contextual significance for the meanings of words used, and when the conditions governing meaning are made in advance of their use in order to remain constant in use.

Furthermore, thinker and audience have access to a greater flexibility in the use of language, with respect to activities which are characteristically linguistic, such as politics, poetry and philosophy. That is, in activities in which the meanings of *words*, rather than the meanings of objectified things, is seen as debatable as a means of establishing the meaning of the subject matter, there is the invitation to a more flexible use of language. Two points need to be added, however, for although history is a characteristically linguistic activity, identifiable as the writings of historians, debate about the meanings of the historian's words would only serve, in general, to distract attention from the historical subject. And secondly, the flexibility of language available in philosophy is, as argued above, not so much a matter of choosing either a literal or non-literal meaning, but more a matter of necessarily utilising and extending the range of non-literal meanings.

It is not always immediately apparent when a use of language is literal and when it is metaphorical. In general, the sense of an utterance is understood without reflecting upon whether it has a literal or metaphorical character, because we are habituated to rely on the force or lack of contextual reference (and so, for instance, we easily take as literal the designation of a person's impertinent actions as 'cheeky', without pausing to note that while the etymology of the word indicates a metaphor in 'cheeky', ordinary usage indicates a literal meaning of the word, defined as 'impertinent'). But sometimes a non-literal usage is disguised as a literal usage in order to gain support for an argument - as, for example, if a political theorist asserts that 'all action is 'really' selfish'. This statement expresses the thinker's intention to extend the ordinary, literal meaning of 'selfish'. If he has to argue that all action is really selfish it is precisely because it is not commonly accepted that this is what 'selfish' refers to. The literal or ordinary meaning of 'selfish' refers to some actions in contrast to others, whereas the thinker wishes to extend its meaning from characterising particular actions to characterising action in general.[22]

Finally, it would be mistaken to think of literal meanings as prior to metaphorical meanings. Nineteenth century anthropologists who thought that the impetus to and the first function of language in primitive man was to make up simple names for objects in his surroundings, and that when his reason had evolved and he needed to express his inner life he used the same words as metaphors, have been clearly discredited.[23] The fallacy of this explanation of the development of language, lies in its assumption that primitive man felt a polarity between himself and nature which was reproduced in his use of language. It is now recognised that primitive man does not feel the need to make this distinction, and that it is characteristic, rather, of us. As Barfield comments, "nothing is easier for us, than to grasp a purely literal meaning".[24] But the current significance given to literal meanings is a comparatively recent development, and until the late seventeenth century and the beginning of modern science, "it was the concept of the 'merely literal' that was difficult",[25] for while literal meanings were recognised, they were 'merely literal' or relatively uninteresting meanings. Thus it can be seen that the meanings of the words 'literal' and 'metaphorical' have shifted over time. To illustrate the transformation of meaning that has taken place, Barfield comments that in the Middle Ages, "the phenomena themselves carried the sort of multiple significance which we today only find in symbols. Accordingly, the issue, in a given case, between a literal and a symbolical interpretation, though it could be raised, had not the same sharpness of contradictories".[26]

Thinking, Language and Reasoning

We turn now to the connections between literal and non-literal meanings on the one hand, and different types of reasoning on the other, with reference to the different sorts of thinking discussed.

The term 'reasoning' refers here to the several methods of forming and developing an argument, and it is presupposed that all forms of reasoning are designed to be meaningful or make sense. In other words, no method of reasoning could be irrational - without rationality - and all are, then, taken to be logical, that is, followable. Thus 'logical reasoning' in the sense in which it is not describing the type of reasoning used in logic, would be a tautology. Consequently, 'the logic of events' for instance, refers to the sense or meaning that a course of events have when narrated in a followable story, which is understood as the product of the historian's reasoning; and 'the logic of special relativity' refers to the understanding of phenomena established in the theory of special relativity, to the coherence of a piece of thinking. The types of reasoning discussed here may be broadly classified as either causal or non-causal. The criterion of causal reasoning lies in the necessary character of the connections by which it proceeds, and its method may be either inductive or deductive. In non-causal reasoning the connections by which it proceeds are contingent, that is unnecessitated, and its method may be either inductive, analogical or narrative.

The first thing to be noted about the classification is that there is no clearcut distinction to be made with literal meanings corresponding solely to causal reasoning on one side, and non-literal meanings corresponding solely to non-causal reasoning on the other. In part this is due to reasoning being a process (we normally speak of a chain of reasoning or line of reasoning etc.), whose character is identified more diffusely in terms of the general thrust of the argument being developed, than in terms of the particular connections made. And apart from strictly causal reasoning, an analysis of the particular connections made in a passage of argument will generally reveal the use of several methods of reasoning. Meanings, on the other hand, may be identified more specifically; even in complexly metaphorical meanings, individual words can be recognised as non-literal without having to draw the connections that demonstrate the contextual influences at work. But the lack of symmetry between meanings and reasoning is also due in part to the different sets of criteria on which the two concepts operate, such that there is no inherent reason which would lead one to expect a symmetry.

In science, reasoning is designed to provide an explanatory account of phenomena that are not only seen as related as cause and effect, but where the relation between cause and effect is taken by scientists to be a necessary one. The presupposition that the phenomena studied by scientists exist independently of man's understanding of them and exhibit regularities whose causal structure it is the scientist's business to disclose, imposes a restriction on the type of reasoning available to the scientist. For whatever the source of the scientist's explanation (and biographical accounts abound which corroborate that scientific discovery has a diversity of origins, including seemingly far-fetched analogies and allegorical dreams), his publicly communicated reasoning must be appropriate to the character of the phenomena as they are understood. And the only type of reasoning accepted as appropriate to patterns of phenomena taken to be causally related is causal reasoning; either deductive, in which effects are derived from causes, or inductive, in which causes are inferred from effects. In this scheme, particulars are intelligible only in so far as they can be subsumed under a regularity.

Reasoning in the practical world may be of different types. The criterion of reasoning here is pragmatic, both in that the choice of reasoning is decided on the grounds of its practical bearing for each particular case, and in that several different types may be used in the same passage. But in general the strictly causal reasoning employed in science will not be seen as necessary.

The character of reasoning in political activity is informed by its aim of recommending or discouraging particular courses of action and by its necessarily speculative and future-looking view of the present and selective treatment of the past. Much reasoning in politics, then, is analogical, in drawing upon comparisons between features of the present and past and the recommended future state of affairs, and between a present state of affairs in politics and that in another area, taken to be significantly comparable. Analogical reasoning is often appropriate in politics, because of the persuasive purpose to which it can be put. Arguments framed in analogical form are often compelling because of the wealth of association and connotation that they can exploit. But, as with practical reasoning, reasoning in politics is pragmatic, and other forms are used when considered to best promote a particular argument.

In poetry, as with the practical world and politics, various types of reasoning may be used, and again the criterion is pragmatic, according to what will promote the particular case. In contemporary poetry there is a school of thought in which it is largely unfashionable to use reasoning explicitly, and some poetry produced by this school dispenses with reasoning altogether, having jettisoned the meanings of words to concentrate on the associations which develop from the sounds of the words in certain combinations. This is a far more tenuous and indefinite form of structuring than reasoning. However other poetry does use reasoning, and sixteenth and seventeenth century poetry in particular was intended to develop as well as illustrate intelligible argument. The notion that reasoned thought could be expressed in poetry was unexceptionable when artful construction was not selfconsciously divorced from understanding, before poetry disassociated itself from explicit reasoning for the description of personal experience and implicit reasoning in the late seventeenth century.

Reasoning in history is neither the causal argument of science nor the pragmatic reasoning of the practical world, politics and poetry. The criterion of historical reasoning lies in the followability of the narrative understood as an account of the evidence. As with all stories, historical writing is concerned with the contingent nature of the relations between events and with the continuity of the development of events seen as outcomes. These two concerns preclude the adoption of causal reasoning and either inductive or analogical non-causal reasoning, and prescribe the use of the reasoning peculiar to the narrative form, in historical writing.

In logic, reasoning aims to furnish an account of the relation between propositions which is deductive, causal and fully certain. But a curious situation exists in logic, in that the internal consistency of a deductive argument is taken to prove its internal validity but is not enough to make it fully certain. The argument must also be able to be sustained against an infinite number of analogies with it, analogies which may disclose flaws in the argument by being common-sensibly false. Furthermore, the certainty of the argument cannot be established through inductive reasoning since all reasoning from experience is regarded as conditional and its conclusions therefore ambiguous. Thus although the argument can only in simple cases be fully certain (for an infinite number of analogies with an argument of any complexity are never exhausted), it can be proved definitely false through an analogy with it which is false. The usefulness of deductive causal reasoning is therefore limited, and analogical reasoning plays as important a role as deductive causal reasoning in logic.

It follows that the role of logical analysis in philosophy is also limited. Any piece of reasoning may be reduced to a set of propositions in the symbolic language of logic and examined to establish whether, as a piece of deductive causal reasoning, it is internally consistent. And analogies with the piece of reasoning so formulated may be constructed, to reveal flaws in the reasoning. However, even at this level the utility of the exercise is severely limited. In the first place, the reduction which must take place before logic can have anything to say, changes the character of the piece of reasoning, and this change may well involve the omission of features (for instance, assumptions and connections carried and understood in the language used) essential to the coherence of the piece of reasoning. Since the language used to express a piece of philosophical reasoning is not arbitrary but is chosen for its aptness in expressing thinking, the reduction to the symbolic language of logic entails the dissolution of the linguistic structure in which the thinking was understood. It may be argued that the thinking is equally well represented in the language of logic, and on a piecemeal basis for simple chains of argument, this may be true. But for complex chains of argument and for complete philosophical works, understood as wholes and not as collections of fragments, and expressed in the language in which the thinking is comprehended, this exercise in logic necessarily involves a loss of meaningfulness along the way. Secondly, the deductive causal reasoning of logic is only one form of reasoning, and it cannot be assumed that the presentation of a piece of thinking in this form is the decisive gauge of its legitimacy. The coherence of a piece of reasoning depends upon its conformity to the criteria recognised by that particular form of reasoning. The criteria recognised differ according to the form of reasoning employed, and it would be mistaken to suggest that the coherence of a piece of deductive casual reasoning is appropriate to the coherence of other forms of reasoning, or that it is superior to or is presupposed in them. And thirdly, the analogies constructed in logic to disclose flaws in a piece of reasoning contain a weakness which renders their application suspect. For since logic recognises only a single general term for relation and so does not distinguish between different kinds of relation, analogies which supposedly reveal flaws in the piece of reasoning are easily found, since what may be valid of one specific relation may be invalid for another.

Furthermore, logic has no means of pronouncing upon the overall legitimacy of a philosophical investigation, nor upon the validity of a complex piece of reasoning with full certainty. Because logic is a necessarily self-contained and limited abstract activity, which can take nothing given in experience as necessarily valid, and does not have available to it empirical knowledge or inductively gained confirmation or refutation, it is a supremely relativistic activity. Any proposition with which it is confronted must be assumed to be applicable potentially in some possible world (in the infinite number of worlds it must assume), and logic can have nothing to say about the argument, for instance, that all men with red hair have seven legs, beyond testing its internal consistency. Moreover, logic cannot pronounce upon the sorts of meanings or reasonings appropriate or inappropriate to other sorts of thinking, since it is only concerned with any reasoning and meanings reduced to the language of logic. It follows, then, that logic can make no pronouncement on the appropriateness of metaphorical meanings and analogical reasoning in philosophy.

Because philosophical activity proceeds from particulars seen as inadequately understood to general statements of less conditional understanding which are not regularities, and from literal meanings to those understood in a context of multiple meanings, and because the indisputableness of its conclusions depends upon the acknowledgement of the assumptions from experience which form the basis for its subsequent reasoning, all reasoning in philosophy must be characterised as non-causal. Although passages of deductive causal reasoning may appear in the course of the argument, the overall character is non-causal because of the features which distinguish this type of thinking from other types.

Within the scope of non-causal reasoning, the method used in philosophy may be inductive or analogical, but not narrative. It is part of the argument of this chapter that all philosophy uses both inductive and analogical methods of non-causal reasoning, and that their use in philosophy differs from their use in other sorts of thinking. Firstly, the abstract metaphorical character of the meanings in philosophy, described earlier, renders analogical reasoning different in philosophy than in, say, politics. In sorts of thinking where there are literal meanings involved, the identification which analogy entails can only be partial, since one of the criteria of literal meanings was that their understanding excludes the connative force of the other possible meanings and so takes only one meaning of a word. In themselves they are taken to be self-contained and unconnected to other meanings. Thus in politics, for instance, analogies may be formed through identifications between literal meanings with other literal meanings, or with non-literal meanings. But in philosophy, analogies are formed through identifications *between* non-literal meanings whose character is abstract - that is, neither specifies nor relates to any particular action. Since abstract meanings are non-literal, and so relational, meanings, they are conducive to further relational connections, and analogies made between such meanings are therefore formed through a process of *multiple* identification. This set of conditions does not apply to any other sort of thinking than philosophical thinking, and their effect is to make the analogies of philosophy far more consequential and significant than the analogies of, say, politics, in terms of the abstract understanding to be gained.

Secondly, the use of the inductive method of non-causal reasoning in philosophy differs from its use in other sorts of thinking, and the difference again lies in the abstract non-literal character of its meanings. Inductive non-causal reasoning is being used whenever the particulars of experience are organised in terms of generalities. These are understood to disclose connections between particulars (and they are contingent rather than causal connections) which thereby evoke a greater significance from the particulars than they had simply as particulars, without destroying their character as particulars. Along with analogical reasoning, this method proceeds through identification as opposed to the definitional[27] procedure of deductive reasoning. While the use of inductive non-causal reasoning in politics, poetry and the practical world is designed to give an account of particulars whose outcome indicates a course of action, its use in philosophy is not to specify courses of action (since abstract meanings cannot suggest specific actions) but to understand the particulars organised into generalities and so within an abstract contextual reference.

From this follows the manner in which analogical reasoning in philosophy can be coherent. All meaning in philosophy, once the initial assumptions are granted, is contextual meaning, and all understanding is contextual understanding. The connections which reasoning seeks to establish between the features which form the context and between each feature and the whole, results in a pattern of reasoning which may be described as a fabric of inter-related connections, in contrast with the linear pattern of connections of reasoning in logic. The precision of the connections in analogical reasoning so described, is not diminished by their non-linear arrangement, nor by their non-causal (that is, unnecessitated) character. The coherence of analogical reasoning in philosophy, then, lies in the meanings expressed being understood firstly as meaningful because inter-related, and secondly as meaningful because of the overall analogy between feature and whole that the context of meanings evokes. To reduce analogical reasoning in philosophy to linear chains of logical deduction would therefore be to lose the overall analogy between feature and whole, to reduce the connections between meanings from identifications to definitions, and so to forfeit a crucial part of the distinctively philosophical character of the coherence of reasoning in philosophy. It is with philosophical reasoning that it is most the case that one has to wait until the argument is already well advanced, before one can decide how to understand its initial stages.

Analogy

The idea of analogy, at the simplest level, is not difficult to grasp. The principle on which it operates is the recognition of an identification understood to postulate some connection of similarity between two or more things. It may refer to perceptions of objects, quantities, qualities, features, functions, ideas, meanings or of particulars, generalities, parts or wholes, realms of discourse or opposites. And it may either describe things of the same level or things at different levels.

But once one begins to examine the idea of analogy in greater detail, it becomes enormously problematic. Firstly there is the problem of drawing its boundaries; some writers have taken the view that "analogy stands as the type of all reasoning from experience"[28] and so argued that general propositions and universals are merely registers of such inference. The problem of accounting for induction appears, to these writers, to be solved at a stroke - but at the cost of its reappearance in the discussion of analogy. It has even been contended that according to Hume there is an element of analogy in *all* reasoning, on the grounds that "without some degree of resemblance, as well as union, it is impossible there can be any reasoning".[29] Thus, it is argued, "our use of any general term depends on the recognition of a similarity between the instances to which it is applied". For instance, we recognise an animal as a 'horse' by its similarity with other animals so named.[30] When the meaning of analogy has been extended this far, it is difficult to distinguish it from other sorts of connections made in reasoning, and in particular from inductive reasoning. However, if some of the territorial claims made for analogy are resisted, we can usefully distinguish between the inductive method as the "procedure of the multiplication of instances" and analogy as "the analysis of the resemblances between instances",[31] and distinguish between reasoning which employs definition and makes causal connections, and analogical reasoning which, along with inductive and narrative reasoning, proceeds by identification and makes non-causal (that is, unnecessitated) connections.

A second problem with analogy, which is related to the first, concerns the role of analogy in language. It has been argued that language furnishes a structuring of reality and that these orderings of nature are analogically related to each other, as for instance, the distinction edible/inedible becomes analogous with that of native/ foreign.[32] Indeed, it has been said that the whole structure of language and the utility of signs, marks, symbols, classification and all the other means by which we order and organise our thoughts and our thoughts in language, rests on analogy.[33] However, again there seems little point in extending the meaning of analogy so far that it cannot be usefully distinguished from anything else and so is rendered almost meaningless, for a concept which is universally applicable is applicable to nothing in particular. Thus it is important to reserve the meaning of analogy for a more specific function in language.

Thirdly, the connection of similarity in analogical reasoning has been variously understood. At one extreme, in logic, the similarity is understood to amount to an identity between the analogous statements, and at the other the similarity is understood as the most tenuous and uncertain of connections.

The fourth and most important ambiguity in the meaning of analogy is concerned with what the similarity is understood to consist in. The differences involved here are well illustrated in a comparison of the use of analogy in Plato, Aristotle and in Medieval thinkers. Analogy is originally a Greek term and its proper significance was originally mathematical. Two sorts of analogy were recognised; the arithmetic analogy, which described the equal intervals between succeeding numbers in a numerical series, and the geometric analogy, in which pairs of numbers were related in like proportions. Even before its adoption by philosophers, the concept of analogy was already ambiguous; as one writer has noted, it refers to several different mathematical phenomena. Arithmetical analogy can refer to the equi-distance between succeeding numbers, and as such says nothing about their positions; it can also refer to the position of one number, and here has nothing to do with the size of the intervals. And the same applies to geometric analogy. The ambiguity was retained in the subsequent use of analogy in other fields of inquiry, although it was the proportional analogy, characterised only in terms of like relations and saying nothing about the sizes or properties of the individual terms, that came to be regarded as the most suitable means of linking up conceptions in different fields of inquiry.[34]

Analogy is first used in philosophy by Plato.[35] Although he at times uses analogy to refer to similar general relations between kinds of knowledge and spheres of reality, to the similarity of function in otherwise dissimilar things, to indicate the character of certain concepts, and in the mathematical senses,[36] Plato most significantly speaks of concepts as analogous "in the sense that they are part of a proportion to true concepts", and what is "decisive to Plato is the relation of image to prototype" or Form.[37]

Aristotle made extensive use of analogy in biology, ethics and metaphysics. In biology his classification of animals in terms of species and genera was made according to analogies of function in organs performing similar functions in animals otherwise dissimilar.[38] The relativistic basis of analogy was also well suited to Aristotle's notion of distributive justice in ethical relations, and here he uses both numerical and geometric analogy. For Aristotle, distributive justice means "the just distribution of something to several classes or parties", not determined objectively for all but according to what is the best arrangement for the parties involved. He begins "by speaking of two persons, and two shares which are right for them. A just division is that the persons and their shares form a geometrical analogy. The shares must bear the same relations to each other as the parties. If these are equal", as in the case of two free men, then the shares will be equal, and thus form an arithmetical analogy; "if different, the shares will be different in the same proportion", as in the case of a free man and a slave. Justice "may therefore be said to be analogous, that is to each person his right proportion of gifts and shares. Both justice and analogy are therefore called a mean, in this case consisting in each receiving neither too much nor too little, but what corresponds to his value".[39] Aristotle also extends this notion to apply to other, more general, social relations.

Aristotle's designation of analogy as a mean differs radically from Plato's, for Plato understood the mean in terms of the proportion as a whole and let "the middle terms link by the two others". Whereas for Aristotle the mean depends upon the character of the individuals involved in it, for him "analogy as a mean has nothing to do with proportionality itself, but to its position between two extremes".[40]

Aristotle's most interesting treatment of analogy is found in his metaphysics. He "proceeds from the question whether the different categories - substance, relation, etc. - may be said to have the same causes", to the conclusion that "although causes and principles differ in respect of different things, they are, speaking generally" the same for all, and thus analogous. In the same way, actuality and potentiality are described as analogous causes. Analogy here refers to a general level at which "everything has the same causes. When speaking of form, matter, etc. in general as constituting some structure common to all things, they are analogously the same. But as soon as they are given concrete contents, analogy ceases and they become different in every different thing".[41]

Thus, whereas for Plato concepts are analogous in a proportion of image and Form, in Aristotle there "is no question of a concept being analogous only in relation to another, true concept; the analogous concept sums up what is common to several".[42] For example, for Plato, knowledge of God by analogy is imperfect because the analogy is drawn from the imperfect sensible world which can only express a degree of probability. For Aristotle, on the other hand, knowledge of God by analogy consists of general concepts common to God and creation, since both have properties with corresponding functions, which can be expressed in general concepts.

The ambiguity of analogy in philosophy, by which it could refer either to a correspondence through the transfer of a concept from one sphere of reality to another, or to an identification of two spheres through something common to both but realised in them in different ways according to the nature of each subject, persisted into the Middle Ages, when extensive use was made of analogy, largely for two purposes. Analogy was used to describe the relations between God and the world, through the concept of the Creation out of nothing, and to describe the knowledge of God. It was used as a "formal category" to explain the relations of God as cause to being as His effects, which was regarded as an analogy based on the likeness of effect to cause.[43]

As well as taking religiously significant notions to be philosophically significant (as when the Trinity is the basis on which the three parts of man's soul are described), the Scholastics also took notions more generally significant, such as hierarchy of higher and lower, and polarities like internal and external, and light and dark, to be philosophically significant. The structure in which ideas are placed, as well as their form and the type of relations between them, also, then, undergo an easy analogical shift. In this way, analogy moves from being a mode of reasoning employed in philosophy, to being itself the central task of philosophy, understood as an account of the essential differences and similarities between things.

The point of this section has been to examine some of the problems encountered when analogy is viewed in terms of the uses that have been made of it by different thinkers. It is hoped that the notion of analogy as a mode of non-causal reasoning, outlined in the previous section, may be seen as one way of approaching it which, while it does not attempt to resolve the ambiguities attendant on the notion (since they are not, for the most part, ambiguities arising out of a direct symmetrical conflict of meaning), has sought to express an intelligible construction of the notion.

Metaphor

Analogy refers to reasoning, and metaphor refers to meaning. The understanding of any metaphor involves analogical reasoning, but not all analogical reasoning concerns metaphors; proportional analogies, for instance, may be made where all the terms have, and retain, literal meanings, and similes express analogical connections in which only one term need be metaphorical.

The question of the role and function of metaphor in philosophical understanding may be approached through considering one of the major debates about metaphor - that concerning the character of metaphorical meanings. Some writers have argued that a metaphor always implies a comparison which can be rendered in literal terms, and that metaphor is a 'departure' from 'ordinary' language. Others have contended that many metaphors are 'irreducible' meanings, and that the distinction between 'ordinary' and metaphorical language is not found in the language itself but is a product of its necessarily shifting use. Let us consider this debate in greater detail.

Figurative language, of which metaphor is the most fundamental form, "deliberately 'interferes' with the system of literal usage by its assumption that terms literally connected with one object can be transferred to another object", Hawkes declares. The 'interference', he continues, "takes the form of 'transference', or 'carrying over'". [44] According to this view, metaphor is characterised as 'saying one thing and meaning another', and all metaphors are regarded as condensed similes such that they may be replaced by an equivalent literal comparison. The function of metaphor is confined to either "plugging the gaps in the literal vocabulary", [45] or to being "decorative additives" to language. [46] Either way, metaphor is considered as a 'departure' from the "ordinary modes of language", [47] and understanding a metaphor is seen to be "like deciphering a code or unravelling a riddle". [48]

The word 'metaphor' comes from the Greek word 'metaphora', derived from 'meta' meaning 'over', and 'pherein', 'to carry'. Hawkes infers from this derivation that metaphor "refers to a particular set of linguistic processes whereby aspects of one object are 'carried over' or transferred to another object, so that the second object is spoken of as if it were the first". [49] However, an equally plausible, interpretation of this derivation may argue that the 'carrying over' refers to a more general interaction of meanings than to the idea of pieces of disembodied luggage attached to one owner and then to another, as envisaged by Hawkes. If using language is thought of as the selfconscious articulation of thoughts which are not literal to begin with, through the choice and expansion of meanings, rather than as a set of linguistic conventions with stable and proper uses, from which "poets and over creative writers" are allowed to "deviate" by "poetic licence",[50] and which 'translates' thoughts into utterances, then the dualistic notion of metaphor propounded by writers such as Hawkes and Leech may be avoided. For behind their view of metaphor there lies the notion that language and the 'objective world' which it supposedly attempts to reflect are quite separate entities, and that literal language naturally reproduces the 'objective world' in linguistic terms and so furnishes the criterion of meaning. According to this conception, metaphor indeed fits very uneasily into the linguistic structure, and is altogether 'inappropriate' in philosophy, since 'poetic licence' has no place in the philosopher's account of the 'objective world'.

One way of overcoming the dualistic notion of metaphor is to consider, as the classical accounts of figurative language did, that the idea of decorum provides a criterion for the use of metaphor. For before the modern separation of 'objective' and 'subjective' worlds, metaphor was not relegated to a merely decorative or breach-filling role, but was understood as an essential and appropriate means of expression. And throughout the Middle Ages, the belief that the world was a book written by God which could and did mean more than it apparently said, was a fundamental metaphor affecting the manner in which individuals in Christian society understood the world. 'Meaning' was a complex matter of multiple significance, and the multiple significances captured in metaphors were recognised as arguments. In this context, metaphor had a didactic role and was considered to be grounded in logic like all reasonable discourse, and therefore was concerned with the arrangement of thought in an orderly manner.

Another way of overcoming the dualistic notion of metaphor is proposed by writers such as Richards, Empson and Black. They begin from the observation that while there is an element of comparison in all metaphor, some metaphors involve a procedure more sophisticated than simple comparison.

The comparative element in metaphor may be of several different types, as Richards illustrates: "it may be just a putting together

of two things to let them work together; it may be a study of them to
see how they are like and how unlike one another; or it may be a
process of calling attention to their likeness, or a method of drawing
attention to certain aspects of the one through the co-presence of the
other". And as he notes, "as we mean by comparison these different
things we get different conceptions of metaphor".[51] Broadly speaking, however, simple metaphors can be divided into those which
"work through some direct resemblance between two things", for
instance the 'leg' of a horse and the 'leg' of a table, and those which
"work through some common attribute which we may (often through
accidental and extraneous reasons) take up towards them both", for
example the animal 'pig' and the abusive term 'pig'.[52] In addition to
simple metaphors, Richards holds that some operate by a process of
interaction which evokes a meaning that cannot be reduced to the
individual meanings of the components, so that "an adequate
translation of their sense cannot be made by finding a ground of
likeness and asserting it in a proportion scheme".[53]

According to all three writers, the recognition of metaphor is a
function of the use of language, and its meaning depends upon the
manner in which, in its context, it is understood. Because there are
no rules of language to legislate on the meaning of a metaphor, then,
Black proposes that in this respect metaphor "belongs to 'pragmatics'
rather than to 'semantics'".[54]

Within this framework, Richards offers as a criterion of metaphor that "if we cannot distinguish tenor from vehicle then we may
provisionally take the word to be literal; if we can distinguish at least
co-operating uses, then we have metaphor".[55] Empson, however,
finds this rule insufficient; he argues that "many metaphors are
themselves traditional, and have therefore gone part of the way
towards extending the word's range of meaning",[56] that is, have
become literal usages. Empson is concerned to distinguish the
inevitable linguistic activity which goes on all the time, of making
implicit comparisons in order to describe things (for instance, in 'the
leg of the table', the word 'leg' is simply transferred, with no
particular evocation of other senses - with no real metaphorical shift
involved), from metaphor, in which we have "a feeling of 'resistance'"
to the comparison or likeness invoked. According to Empson we
respond to metaphors as opposed to 'transfers' by, as it were, "going
into higher gear, because the machinery of interpretation must be

brought into play, and then a feeling of richness about the possible interpretations of the word" or phrase is present, "so that we regard it as 'pregnant'".[57]

Empson also objects to Richards' idea of the 'interaction' metaphor and introduces the notion of "mutual metaphor" to account for metaphors in which tenor and vehicle (in Richards' terms) are transcended, and so made redundant, to become examples of a third idea which they have evoked and, which is the meaning of the metaphor. According to Empson, this type of metaphor is unaccounted for and "upsets the ordinary scheme of interpretation" put forward by Richards. In some metaphors where tenor and vehicle have equal status, Empson argues, the two ideas "do not merely illuminate one another, as in an allegory; they produce a third more general idea which reduces them to the status of examples or illustrations. The metaphor as such is destroyed....because we are no longer interested in which is the vehicle and which is the tenor".[58] Thus in Empson's scheme, there is a scale of meaning from literal to 'transfer' (in which there is no "resistance" to non-literal use), to metaphor (in which there is an awareness of "resistance" and tenor is dominant over vehicle), to allegory (in which there is an awareness of "resistance" and tenor and vehicle are on an equal footing, are mutually illuminating but nevertheless distinct), to "mutual metaphor" (in which there is again "resistance", tenor and vehicle are again on an equal footing and mutually illuminating, but are now indistinct as they collapse into a wider idea). But although Empson has distinguished three strands in Richards' conception of metaphor, Richards' main point, that not all metaphors are reducible to comparisons, remains untouched.

Black also questions Richards' criterion of metaphor in terms of vehicle and tenor, on the grounds that although Richards denies that his distinction is one between 'meaning' and 'figure or image' and asserts that the meaning of the metaphor is found in "the whole double unit",[59] his distinction is clumsy and misleading since it is so readily susceptible to this misinterpretation. And while Black and Richards would agree that a metaphor need not contain any visual or sensory image at all, and that the terms 'figure' and 'image' are therefore misleading in a description of metaphor, Black proposes a redefinition to avoid the pitfalls in Richards' terminology.

Black's redefinition distinguishes those words in a metaphor which are actually used metaphorically (the 'focus'), from those which are used non-metaphorically (the 'frame'). In simple metaphors, says Black, only one word is used metaphorically, and he gives as an example the sentence, "the chairman ploughed through the discussion". It follows, Black continues, that "an attempt to construct an entire sentence of words that are used metaphorically results in a proverb, an allegory, or a riddle".[60]

The merit of this construction, Black holds, is that the manner in which we recognise a metaphor - as a condition of the particular circumstances of the words in an utterance - is much more clearly seen. In other words, the reason for the attention to context, in understanding a metaphor, is now apparent; and it follows, says Black, that it is more illuminating "to say that the metaphor creates the similarity than to say that it formulates some similarity antecedently existing".[61]

Black's focus and frame conception of metaphor also has the advantage of making the distinction between similie and metaphor more easily discernible. A direct comparison is preferred to a metaphor, he comments, when it is "a prelude to an explicit statement on the grounds of resemblance", whereas a metaphor evokes a meaning which cannot be expressed in terms of the resemblance between a distinct this and a distinct that. To illustrate this point, Black gives the example of the " difference between *comparing* a man's face with a wolf mask by looking for points of resemblance - and seeing the human face *as* vulpine".[62] Thus the comparison in simile and the meaning in metaphor result in different understandings, through the different connections that are made between, in this case, man and wolf. In particular, the hypothetical 'as if' of similie is absent in metaphor, and this allows the connections in metaphor to assert a richer pattern of identification.

Black agrees with Richards on the question of "interaction" metaphors, and explains their operation in his own terms in the following way. The 'focus', he says, "obtains a new meaning, which is not quite its meaning in literal uses, nor quite the meaning which any literal substitute would have. The new context (the 'frame'....) imposes extension of meaning upon the focal word. And....for the metaphor to work the reader must remain aware of the extension of meaning - must attend to both the old and the new meanings together". The metaphor works in "that the reader is forced to 'connect' the two ideas" and to be aware of the literal meanings involved.[63]

One of Black's contributions to the understanding of metaphor is the distinction he makes between simple metaphors which utilise a "system of associated commonplaces", and philosophical metaphors which are "supported by specially constructed systems of implications".[64] For in simple metaphors, he argues, "the important thing for the metaphor's effectiveness is not that the commonplaces shall be true, but that they should be readily and freely evoked".[65] In the case of the man/wolf metaphor, for instance, the characteristics of wolves which are brought into play need not be strictly accurate, nor presuppose the systematic knowledge of the zoologist. The difference for philosophical metaphors is that, while as for simple metaphors it is the context of associations which helps to organise the reader's view of the subject matter in the metaphor, in philosophical metaphors it is important that the context of associations be composed of an intelligible cluster of assumptions and conceptions whose meanings may be identified.

Black draws the sensible conclusion that although the significance of "interaction" metaphors is far greater than that of simple metaphors, we cannot secure this distinction in a difference of terminology and restrict the meaning of metaphor to "interaction" metaphors, for what would we call the trivial cases of metaphor when substitution and comparison seem to adequately characterise them? The point may be met, Black concludes, "by classifying metaphors as instances of substitution, comparison, or interaction. Only the last kind are of importance in philosophy".[66]

While Richards, Empson and Black all bring valuable insights to the discussion of metaphor and all for the most part avoid the dualism whereby literal language is regarded as 'reflecting' the 'objective world' or the 'ideas themselves' and metaphor is seen as an addition or distortion, problems remain in their accounts of metaphor, where the notion of fixed meanings for metaphors tends to creep back into the discussion. These problems can be attributed, it may be argued, to the insufficient or inconsistent recognition of or attention to the extent to which both metaphorical and literal language depend upon use. The unsatisfactory elements in all their accounts arise from the rules they make, in their attempts to define when and how metaphors work, in advance of or apart from the contexts in which they are used and understood.

A simpler and less problematic account of metaphor might argue that identifying a metaphorical meaning, like identifying a literal meaning, is identifying a use of language to express thinking within a particular context. In one sense, then, all the writers in the debate about metaphorical meaning are right, for if the manner in which language is understood, depends upon the way it is used in particular contexts, then in some contexts it can be seen that a metaphor *is* used as a departure from ordinary meaning (for instance in the practical world), in others a metaphor *is* used to make a simple comparison, and in others again metaphors *are* used and recognised as irreducible meanings and are nonparaphrasable (for instance in poetry and philosophy). The problem that arises in the accounts of each of the writers discussed, however, is that each attempts to specify one or some uses as metaphorical, to the exclusion of other uses. Each writer attempts to define too narrowly the range of meanings that metaphors are used to express. Of these writers, Black perhaps goes furthest in recognising the flexibility in the use of language that metaphor encompasses, but his conclusion still reads like a pragmatic compromise rather than a positive resolution.

In sum, then, two points about metaphor need to be stressed. Firstly, the term 'metaphor' covers a whole range of extensions from the literal meaning of words. Metaphor is not the opposite of literal language, but complements it. A literal meaning is that which is recognised, in the context in which it is being used, as primary, usual, unextended; and in thinking which is concerned with the ability of language to express multiple significances, it is the least interesting way in which words can be used; and a metaphorical meaning is simply an extended meaning. In some senses it would be easier to abandon the terms 'literal' and 'metaphorical', and talk instead of unextended and extended meanings and uses of words, or of meanings which cross barriers and those which don't. But to change the vocabulary in this way would be likely to cause more confusion, in terms of general intelligibility, than it would avoid.

Secondly, a metaphorical meaning is recognised and understood *as* a use of language within a particular context. A metaphor is not *given* a meaning - it has one within the context in which it is used and understood. And the significance, or multiple significances of a metaphor, correspond to the degree of complexity of the thinking expressed in language. The more complex the context of connections, associations and significances being drawn upon a piece of thinking, the more complex will be the meanings expressed in language. The meaning of a piece of thinking in language thus depends upon what is recognised as taking place in that particular context, in terms of the relationship between thinking and language, expressed in the use made of language. It may be argued, then, that what is important is not trying to determine whether metaphors operate by comparison, substitution or interaction, but recognising that metaphor encompasses a whole range of operations and uses of language, which correspond to the degree of complexity of the thinking, the multiplicity of significances, and the degree of extension from the "usual or primary" meanings of words, being brought into the utterance, understood in use. Metaphorical language is not constructed from an existing fixed language by displacing words alone, but comes from the familiar process of expressing in language the multiple meanings and significances already composing the texture of thinking. The most important factor in the character of metaphor in language is that which comes from the kind of thinking which is being expressed. And in activities whose materials are themselves words rather than objectified things, the more significant will be the use made of language.

In philosophy both these conditions are at their most extended; philosophy, more than any other kind of thinking, draws upon and extends the metaphorical character of all thinking; its use of language is necessarily 'figurative' rather than 'plain'. Philosophy, in one sense, is all about the making and disclosing of contexts of meaning through the expression of thinking in language, more so than in any other kind of thinking. Thinking is a metaphor-making activity, and philosophical thinking is the metaphor-making activity par excellence. And the kind of metaphor which is most characteristic of philosophical meanings is that which has been called "interaction" metaphor, for that "interaction" describes most accurately the principle on which metaphor in thinking already operates. Any metaphor, any use of language which crosses barriers, may be characterised as operating according to substitution, comparison or interaction, depending on the context in which it is used. In philosophy, metaphors which are multiple meanings of pieces of thinking expressed in words, whose significances are complex and are found within the context of use, are at a premium; what occurs is not a 'double' meaning, or a 'meaning of one thing transferred to another' here, but a single whole significance which is composed of parts or aspects which can be analysed.

In conclusion, then, in this chapter three levels of metaphor have been discussed. The first refers to the meanings that emerge from the connections made between perceptions, the second refers to the meanings that emerge from the abridgement of musings etc. to thinking expressed in speech or writing, and the third refers to the meanings in an utterance that are deliberately metaphorical rather than literal. However, as mentioned earlier, it is important not to separate these three levels of meaning too much. 'Levels of meaning' is itself a metaphor and, as experienced, they merge and develop in such a way that one is not always aware of the transition from one to another. Each form of thinking legislates for itself the scope of literal and non-literal meanings, and the kinds of reasoning that are recognised as appropriate. In philosophy, more than in any other kind of thinking, the 'levels' of metaphor are least distinct, for it is the fundamental activity of thinking with which philosophy is concerned, and the power of language to express and capture the significances of that thinking with which it deals. Understanding in philosophy, then, does not entail the transmission of 'pure thought in concepts' rather than the communication of 'thought in language', for to use language is to organise and express and not merely reflect thought. The more coherent and abstract the meaning, the more it depends upon metaphorical rather than literal uses of words, and never more so than in philosophy.

NOTES

1. I. A. Richards, *The Philosophy of Rhetoric*, OUP, 1967, p30.
2. *ibid* p125.
3. Iris Murdoch, Paper 1 at Symposium: "Thinking and Language", *Aristotelian Society Supplementary Volumes*, Vol.25, 1951, p31.
4. Richards, *op.cit.*, p94.
5. I. Murdoch, *The Sovereignty of Good*, Routledge & Kegan Paul, London, 1970, p77.
6. Richards, *op.cit.*, p5.
7. Murdoch, *Aristotelian Society Supplementary Volumes*, Vol.25, p26.
8. C. K. Ogden and I. A. Richards, *The Meaning of Meaning*, Kegan Paul, London, 1923, p19
9. Richards, *op.cit.*, p49.
10. *ibid* p55.
11. A. C. Lloyd, Paper 2 at Symposium: "Thinking and Language", *Aristotelian Society Supplementary Volumes*, Vol.25, 1951, p35.

12. *ibid* p35.
13. *ibid* p61-2.
14. G. Ryle , Paper 3 at Symposium: "Thinking and Language", *Aristotelian Society Supplementary Volumes*, Vol.25, 1951, p75.
15. *ibid* p74.
16. Richards, *op.cit.*, p93.
17. Murdoch, *Aristotelian Society Supplementary Volumes*, Vol.25, p32.
18. *ibid* p33.
19. Richards, *op.cit.*, p10.
20. *ibid* p11.
21. *ibid* p118-9.
22. M. Macdonald, "The Philosopher's Use of Analogy", in A. Flew, ed. *Essays on Logic and Language*, Blackwell, Oxford, 1951, p171.
23. A. O. Barfield, *Saving the Appearances*, Faber, London, 1957, p118.
24. *ibid* p75.
25. *ibid* p75.
26. *ibid* p74.
27. In the previous chapter it was argued that definition can be seen as a form of identification. In this chapter identification and definition are distinguished, since the concern here is with how terms are *used*. In science, for instance, the scientist's belief that definitions are fixed, affects his attitude to language in general. I am not concerned, at this point, with whether or not his belief is right or wrong, but with how different kinds of writers and speakers use language.
28. G. E. R. Lloyd, *Polarity and Analogy*, CUP, 1966, p173.
29. *ibid* p172.
30. *ibid* p172.
31. *ibid* p175.
32. T. Hawkes, *Metaphor*, Methuen, London, 1972, p85.
33. G. E. R. Lloyd, *op.cit.*, p172.
34. H. Lyttkens, *The Analogy between God and the World*, Almquist and Wiksells, Uppsala, 1952, p17.
35. *ibid* p16.
36. *ibid* p18.
37. *ibid* p51.
38. *ibid* p29.
39. *ibid* p31-4.
40. *ibid* p34.
41. *ibid* p41-3.
42. *ibid* p52.
43. *ibid* p154.
44. Hawkes, *op.cit.*, p2.
45. M. Black, *Models and Metaphors*, Cornell U.P., N.Y., 1962, p32
46. Hawkes, *op.cit.*, p8.
47. *ibid* p7.
48. Black, *op.cit.*, p32.
49. Hawkes, *op.cit.*, p1.
50. G. N. Leech, "Linguistics and the Figures of Rhetoric", in R. Fowler, ed., *Essays on Style and Language*, London, 1966.
51. Richards, *op.cit.*, p120.
52. *ibid* p118.
53. W. Empson, *The Structure of Complex Words*, Chatto & Windus, London, 1951, p339
54. Black, *op.cit.*, p30.
55. Richards, *op.cit.*, p119.
56. Empson, *op.cit.*, p332.
57. *ibid* p341
58. *ibid* p347.
59. Richards, *op.cit.*, p96
60. Black, *op.cit.*, p27.
61. *ibid* p.37.
62. *ibid* p37 note.
63. *ibid* p39.
64. *ibid* p43.
65. *ibid* p40.
66. *ibid* p45.

CHAPTER 3
Hobbes and Seventeenth-Century Literary Criticism

In his Answer to Davenant's Preface to *Gondibert*,[1] Hobbes outlines his views on literary theory and practice. The significance of Hobbes' interest in literary criticism is easy to overlook, since in terms of the understanding of philosophy that now prevails, an interest in literary criticism is at most an interest in the peripheral rather than the primary concerns of political philosophy. One of the aims of this chapter is to lay the ground for the argument that Hobbes' interest in literary matters and the subject of literary criticism, is by no means tangential to an understanding of Hobbes' political philosophy. The significance of Hobbes' Answer to Davenant's Preface is not measured just in the influence on English neo-classical literary theory, accorded to it by Hobbes' contemporaries and in histories of literary criticism. More important is that the connection between philosophy and literary criticism in Hobbes' Answer, was both uncontroversially received, and was the implicit ground of the appeal his views had for contemporary literary theorists and practitioners. Hobbes' statement of his literary views is significant precisely because the very idea of a relationship between philosophy and literary criticism presupposed by him was itself unquestioned, and constitutes a shared assumption among contemporary writers on literary matters - and one which links them with the earlier approach to literary theory and practice. The situation is complicated by the way in which some modern commentators on the history of literary criticism have misrepresented Hobbes' philosophy, and this complication will be examined. The implications of this shared assumption on the character of Hobbes' political philosophy in *Leviathan* are discussed in later chapters.

Throughout the Medieval and Renaissance period, the relationship between the different forms of knowledge - science, medicine, astronomy, philosophy, theology, poetry - was cast in a manner quite different from that which has gained ground since the end of the seventeenth century and is still largely unquestioned. Put most simply, the comparison is between an outlook which viewed the various forms of learning as modes which all testified to the same overall unity in and order of the universe, and an outlook which presupposes no overall order and no inherent connection between one way of knowing about the world and another.[2] This comparison may be characterised in terms of two different commonplaces. On the one hand there is the Medieval and Renaissance assumption of the necessary correspondence between the knowing subject and what was known - the natural and human worlds forming a continuum inhabited by entities open to the same kind of intelligibility, under God's heaven. Throughout the period, it was held that the importance of salvation overshadowed the importance of, and gave meaning to and affected, all pursuits and knowledge undertaken in the temporal world. The knowledge of what was required for salvation was seen as to be found in some combination of revelation and scripture, and all other knowledge was seen in terms of this theological perspective and imperative. In consequence, such knowledge was ultimately justifiable by its being able to testify to the glory of God, and the truths it led to were seen in terms of affirming what was already known. On the other hand there is the still prevalent modern commonplace, which followed the pre-eminent authority attributed to science, of the axiomatic divorce between the subject and the object of his study. This view presupposes a discontinuous set of uninhabitable objects of study whose reality is independent of the subject. The development of neo-classical literary theory is one area which can be characterised overall in terms of a shift away from the earlier commonplace in the direction of the later. By 1650, however, piecemeal changes of emphasis had not yet amounted to a wholesale shift in outlook.

For the purposes of the present line of argument, the merits of the two outlooks are not in question. What is important here is that the two commonplaces not only cast differently the relationship between the different forms of knowledge, but that in consequence the characters of the various forms of knowledge differ also. The scope of each form of knowledge, and the sorts of questions that could be seen as relevant to it, has changed, more dramatically in some cases than others. This observation provides a caution against assuming that, for instance, the limits we ascribe to the sort of knowledge that literary theory and practice, and philosophy, are concerned with, are the same as those ascribed to them at an earlier period.

The connection that was understood to exist, throughout the Medieval and Elizabethan period, between literature and its criticism on the one hand and philosophy on the other, is then the first aspect of this subject to be examined. The substance of the connection rests in the conception of the features and postulates common to Medieval and Renaissance literature and pictorial arts (the conventions of written and pictorial expression, the significance of images, the use of metaphor and allegory), expressed in a literary theory (the understood relation between, primarily, rhetoric and logic, summed up in the prescription that literature and art mush both delight and teach) whose justification was found in the Medieval and Renaissance conception of philosophy. Compared with the modern notions of these studies, the connection is close and sustained, such that reference to literary theory cannot for very long exclude reference to philosophy, and that the understanding of the first depends upon understanding the second.

During the seventeenth century this connection and the unified approach to the world that supported it, were gradually undermined. After tracing some of the features of the transition that this connection underwent at the hands of neo-classical writers, the discussion will be in a position to describe how some aspects of Hobbes' political philosophy become fully intelligible only when seen within the context of this transition. What follows then, is an examination not of sixteenth and seventeenth century literary criticism as such, but of the bearing on Hobbes' thought of some of the postulates of that criticism.

The debate in literary criticism that took place during the seventeenth century in England, was generated by the challenge to a set of conventions concerning the scope and purpose of literature and its understanding that had been more or less uniformly subscribed to from Chaucer to Shakespeare, Spenser and Donne. In a sense the debate was a very half-hearted affair, since what was being challenged found very few defenders. But the use of the term 'debate' to characterise what took place, is warranted in the sense that a self-conscious attempt to elucidate the criteria of literary practice had never been conducted in quite this way before. In a sense, the writing that contributes to this discussion marked the beginning of literary criticism as such.

Previously, the discussion of literature - both specific pieces of literature and the rules and purposes to be observed - had been undertaken in the course of that part of the educational curriculum called the Trivium, which consisted of grammar, logic and rhetoric, as well as in philosophical commentaries and in literary works themselves. Throughout this period, poetry was not simply the dominant literary form, to be distinguished from other literary forms such as drama and prose, but was rather the general umbrella term, sanctioned by customary usage, which described and absorbed a variety of literary activities later to be seen as more divergent than broadly similar. And the discussion of poetry was understood to be the proper subject of the rhetorician, logician, grammarian and philosopher.

The rhetorician was concerned with the use of language to express and promote in an appropriate and fitting manner the 'causes' or arguments outlined by the logician, in order to convey eloquently the significant ordering of some aspect of nature or human life, through diction, figures of syntax, word order, and the tropes and figures of speech. Rhetorical handbooks had been concerned, since antiquity, with examples as much as with theory, and throughout the Medieval and Renaissance period examples were freely taken from poetry. Indeed, rhetoric had developed from the analysis of poetry and the formalising of its features. The close link between rhetoric and poetry was recognised throughout the period.

The essential difference between grammarians and rhetoricians was that instead of prescribing figures and rules in advance, the grammarians dissect and label the parts of an existing text according to a comprehensive system. However, the grammarians came closer to poetry than this classificatory function would suggest. They continued the anciently inherited conception that allegorical and etymological meanings were naturally present in poetic and other texts and deserved explication. Here the grammarians were allied to the tradition of scriptural exegesis in Medieval theology, in regarding the written word as disclosing the order and hierarchy of God's created universe, immanent with meaning; it was their job to disclose those meanings.

The discussion of poetry by Medieval philosophers proceeded through three points of connection. Firstly, like the grammarian, the philosopher was concerned with the order of the created universe, and so with the power of words to disclose that order. Secondly, the poet was properly engaged in conveying the truth demonstrated by the philosopher, through particulars which revealed it, and the philosopher in turn employed the poet's images of particulars to focus attention on the general properties and conditions they shadowed forth. And thirdly, some Medieval scholars, such as those of the Chartres school, were naturally enough, both philosophers and poets.

The major Medieval and Renaissance presuppositions about poetry are evident in and can be examined through a discussion of Spenser's *Faerie Queene*, a work which epitomises the tradition of allegorical poetry. Spenser has been chosen, rather than Shakespeare, because while both are representative, Spenser focuses attention more clearly on the allegorical features of the Medieval and Renaissance tradition, and because Shakespeare is already the subject of exhaustive critical reaction and so might not fit happily into the limited scope of this section. Sir Philip Sidney's *Apology for Poetry* is the second work to be examined, for it both expresses succinctly some of the principles of the rhetorical handbooks, and is typical of Elizabethan critical writing (as seen in writers such as Nash, Webbe, Lodge, Puttenham, Harrington and Chapman, all of whom cover roughly the same ground) which aimed to reaffirm these principles. Sidney's *Apology* also represents the nearest this tradition came to defending its principles from the challenge to them which was beginning to emerge.

Spenser's *Faerie Queene*[3] consists of six books; the first three were published in 1590 and Books Four, Five and Six, together with the Mutabilitie Cantos, were published in 1596. Each Book is structured around an allegorical core, the seeking and realising of a virtue, and the other elements in the poem are woven into and around these central foci. Overall, the *Faerie Queene* describes a quest, and as Lewis points out,[4] characteristically of quests in sixteenth century literature, it was for something not unknown, but profoundly known but temporarily mislaid, contingently and human-failingly misplaced. It was a quest for something to be regained and rediscovered, not discovered ad nuovem.

Although Spenser intended to portray in the projected twelve Books of the *Faerie Queene* the twelve Aristotelian virtues, the treatment of the six he completed (Sanctification or Holiness, Temperance, Chastity, Friendship, Justice or Concord, and Courtesy in the sense of Charity and Humility) show an equal indebtedness to the Christian opposites of the Seven Deadly Sins. The significance of the unfinished character of the *Faerie Queene* is a point that will be considered in the course of the discussion; its importance to the modern reader lies, as with other aspects of reading the *Faerie Queene*, in our initial propensity to misinterpret its significance.

Before proceeding to examine the context in which the *Faerie Queene* becomes intelligible, and the character of the poem, there is an initial distinction between allegory and symbolism which ought to be drawn, in order to prevent one source of confusion from the first. In Lewis' formulation of the distinction,[5] it revolves around the two ways that the fundamental identification of the immaterial and the material may be made by the mind. In allegory, he says, the immaterial is described in terms of what is less real, that is material things, while in symbolism the visible exists only in so far as it succeeds in imitating the real forms of things. An example of symbolism is Plato's symbol of the sun as the copy of the Good. The symbolist leaves the given to find that which is more real, whereas the allegorist expresses what is more real (the inner world) in what is less real (the visible and public world). The poetry of allegory found its greatest expression, Lewis contends, in the Middle Ages, and that of symbolism in the Romantics. It follows, says Lewis, that Dante was quite right in maintaining that there is nothing 'mystical' or mysterious about Medieval allegory; "the poets know quite clearly what they are about and are well aware that the figures which they present to us are fictions", figures of the real inner world.[6] Thus in reading the *Faerie Queene*, he says, it needs to be borne in mind that in turning to allegory, Spenser along with other Medieval and Renaissance poets, is not "retreating from the real world into a shadowy world of abstractions"; in using allegory "he is not talking about non-entities, but about the inner world, talking in fact about the realities he knows best".[7]

The distinction may alternatively be framed, in a less neo-Platonic way, in terms of allegory as moving and symbolism as static. According to this conception, symbols individually capture meaning in an image, while allegory uses symbols with multiple significances in narrative movement and interaction. Either way, the point was well understood by Medieval and Renaissance readers; they did not need to search to find the significance of the allegorical method. Indeed, this point is part of the larger one, that temporal existence and knowledge were significant not in themselves, but as pointers to the infinitely greater truth and as figures of the greater reality, of the spiritual dimension of life on earth.

Spenser's poem is related to four traditions of poetry - the Medieval courtly love allegory tradition, epitomised in the *Romance of the Rose*, the late Medieval Italian epic tradition, whose most illustrious representative is Ariosto's *Orlando Furioso*, the Homeric allegorical epic tradition, and the indigenous fifteenth and sixteenth century tradition of poetry. Spenser may be seen as the last major exponent of the tradition of courtly love allegorical poetry that began in the twelfth century in Provence. It came as naturally to Spenser as it had to Chrétien in the twelfth century, to express the struggles and conflicts caused by the heart's affections in terms of personified abstractions engaged in battles and quests. It came naturally to express the inner world in terms of actions in the outer world, because of the profound correspondence felt to exist between the two. Allegory was not a better or worse way of telling a story; it was the natural medium of poetry that expressed the inner life and its contending forces. And the characters in allegory of this sort represent not human individuals but the moods, passions and fears that are common to all individuals, distributed among personifications; in Medieval terms they were understood as instances of 'accidents' occurring in a 'substance'.

In the Italian epic tradition of Boccaccio, Ariosto and Tasso, the element of rip-roaring adventure and marvellous action-packed plot becomes predominant, and the deeper levels of allegory - the journey through and resolution of moral quandary, the revelation through the story of one's own nature placed in the ordered hierarchy of the universe - tend to fade from view. What Spenser admired in and learned from the Italian epics was their closely structured narrative form. But in sentiment and outlook the *Faerie Queene* is clearly in the tradition of English Medieval poetry.

The *Faerie Queene* is also related to the Homeric epic tradition, continuing to employ the cluster of features originally used because of their appropriateness in a culture whose primary medium of communication was the spoken rather than the written word. In a largely memorially-dependent society, Homer's epics served as a kind of cultural memory bank, encyclopaedic in scope, containing all the knowledge - of the past, of crafts, sciences and philosophy - which that society had inherited, supplemented and wished to pass on. They served as both the instrument of education and the vehicle of cultural continuity. In order to perform these functions effectively, rhetorical formulas were developed to ensure that the content was memorable and vivid to the audience, and that the epic was memorisable for the poet. These rhetorical formulas consisted not only of devices such as repetition, rhythm and dramatic structuring, but also the use of allegory - which both provides a collection of vivid images in an organising framework, a coherent structure for the effective transmission of knowledge, and a shorthand means of referring to several levels of meaning in a single passage. It is clear that in this context the poet becomes responsible in the moral education sanctioned by the society, not only because the poet is the focus of education in general, but also because the allegorical method requires for its understanding the hearer's completion of the meaning.

In the *Faerie Queene*, Spenser sought to follow the allegorical tradition established by the Homeric epics, by instructing his audience in the terms and conditions of moral conduct or, more specifically, in the private virtues of a late sixteenth century gentleman. Both Spenser and his audience understood that the meaning of the allegory depended upon their completion of its open-ended interpretations, for allegory exploits both the poverty of language and its wealth of meaning. Where no words exist to describe something, it can only be obliquely evoked and, on the other hand, sometimes there is more than one word to describe something. As one commentator has noted, Spenser "exploits this double principle in his developed allegories, where Belphoebe, Gloriana and Mercilla all refer to Queen Elizabeth, while, at the same time, Gloriana signifies two things: the Queen and glory itself....And, of course, both Belphoebe and Mercilla signify things other than the English Queen".[8]

When Spenser insists upon the serious moral instruction to be found in the *Faerie Queene*, then, he is not merely defending his art against the sceptics. He on his part recognised that morality followed necessarily from his allegorical method. Nor could Spenser's audience for their part in such a situation avoid or miss the moral dimension of the poem, for they help to make it.[9] In an allegorical poem such as the *Faerie Queene* morality is the product of language. The moral dimension of the allegory is not an optional level of interpretation, for it is written into the whole allegorical procedure. And as one writer has noted, allegory provides not the bare morality of prescription, but the "opportunity to realise, re-realise, and realise again, the full import of something we can only lamely point to by its abstract name".[10]

It becomes apparent, if Spenser's allegory is identified in this context, that the remark in his letter to Raleigh in 1590, "So much more profitable and gracious is doctrine by ensample than by rule", does not represent a statement that his primary purpose in the *Faerie Queene* was to entertain, but an affirmation of the customary principle that the poet both entertains *and* teaches. Spenser cast himself in the role of the Homeric poet, the ideal educator, offering delight and profit to the many, and a double delight and profit to the few who recognised the full import of the allegorical significance. It is ironic that while Spenser's audience appreciated his aim in the *Faerie Queene*, it could no longer generate the impact of the Homeric epic. The rhetorical situation of the poet had changed, for the practice of recording and storing knowledge in printed form had made the poet's encyclopaedic function redundant, and Spenser's poem, aspiring to Homeric proportions, increasingly struck the seventeenth century reader as extravagant.

We turn now to the character of the poem. A major problem facing a modern reader of Spenser, and indeed of all Medieval and Elizabethan allegorical poetry, concerns the manner in which his images were understood to work. Imagery is of central importance in poetry of this kind, and by focussing attention on it, we are introduced to the aspect of Spenser's *Faerie Queene* that provides the clue to its understanding.

The two basic principles which operate in the construction of images in Elizabethan poetry are that the nature of an image lies in the 'cause' of the poem, and that the relation of imagery to statement in the poem is one of means and end - a relation which does not reduce it to two separate parts in the way that the modern distinction between form and content does. When the end of poetry is spoken of, the poem is not conceived of as a meaning detached from the form in which it is expressed, but as a whole in which 'cause' is manifested in 'mode of operation'.[11] In poetry of this kind, a paraphrase cannot capture what was expressed through the imagery. The imagery cannot be discarded once one has grasped what it signifies in abstract terms, for the meaning of the poem lies in the single focus that emerges when the reader continues to reflect upon how the concept informs the image and how the image really furnishes the concept with significance. Moreover, the play of meanings with multiple references in Elizabethan poetry is not restricted to allegory proper. The prevailing theologically-centred perspective involved a whole network of analogies seen as encompassing every aspect of the universe. Minds so habituated to the multiple references of any 'particular', delighted in exploring, in poetry, the metaphors that 'particulars' shadow forth. Spenser was completely traditional in trading on this understanding, in which language (itself a 'particular' and a metaphor) is immanent with not only a meaning, but levels of analogically related meaning which generate metaphors at a stroke.

The necessity of utilising extratextual assumptions in the interpretation or completion of the poem, strikes a modern reader as odd, trained as we are in the conception of a poem as an art object which contains in itself whatever assumptions need to be made in order to understand it. But it follows from the Elizabethan understanding of poetry that the significance of the poem lies precisely in its ability to point to the ordered universe that 'particulars' figure. The principle of 'efficacy' maintained the poet's responsibility of making that significance of the poem intelligible to the reader, with the poet as the vehicle of transmission rather than as the creative artist of purely individual genius exalted in modern theory. Spenser's protestations of his unfitness for the task of writing the *Faerie Queene* without invoking the assistance of the Muses, is not a case of disguised self-praise, but a conventional expression of the poet's recognition of his limited role in the relation between poem, poet and reader.

Several criteria for the functioning of images were established in Elizabethan theory, and were strictly observed by Elizabethan poets. The most important of these is decorum or propriety, a notion which is equivocal in the abstract but of crucial importance when defined in relation to a particular poem, when the 'aptness', 'decency', 'fitness' and 'seemliness' of specific images can be judged. Decorum is a criterion not of the qualities of images but of the function they serve in the poem as a whole. It concerns the appropriateness of images to the 'height' of the cause which the poet has in mind. And the 'height' of the cause is determined by its place in the hierarchical order established in Medieval and Renaissance philosophy.

The criterion of decorum embraces the two further major principles to be satisfied in the functioning of images, 'imitation' and 'significance'. Instead of judging the significance of an image in terms of the poet's perception of the quality of his experience, as modern practice teaches, Elizabethan theory directs poet and reader to judge the significance of an image in terms of its capacity to intimate, evoke and convey ordering significances of universals. For in a world where there are agreed commonplaces, composing a whole ordered framework of interpretation of nature and the human world, the role and function of figurative language is radically altered. In such a world, images and their significances do not have to be made de novo, and a poet who attempted to do this would be regarded by Elizabethan readers as exhibiting the poverty of his understanding, not the genius of his personal creativity. The Elizabethan poet and his readers understood the functions of images as reinforcing and illuminating what is already inherent, and they delighted in the re-recognition of familiars-become-mundane that this opportunity afforded. The pleasure the Elizabethans derive from recognising particular correspondences in the world as both familiar and freshly reinvested with significance, accounts for their passion for detail in the pictorial arts and poetry. It was not the naturalistic detail of the representational painter they admired, but the interweaving of known particulars into significant designs.

Perhaps the most intractable obstacle to a modern understanding of Spenser's imagery is our modern notion that the prime function of images is the accurate rendition of the quality of individual experience. This is the simplest function images can have, but it did not particularly interest poets in the sixteenth century. The reason for their relative disinterest lies in what the Elizabethan understood by the concept of 'imitation', again a concept inherited from Medieval usage, and closely connected with 'significance' and 'artifice'. If 'imitation' is thought of in terms of exact descriptiveness - which we are taught is the representation of the real - then the function of imagery is rhetorically simple, the accurate and precise description of sense experience. However, Renaissance images are characterised by a deliberate artificiality, and not by attempts at representational accuracy. Elizabethan poets did not consider the use of artifice as making images less 'true to nature' or less 'true to life', since their object is to imitate not the visible world but the intelligible as manifested in the visible - to imitate what was significant, not what was merely visually obvious in itself. The distinction between images which offer a 'natural' or 'artificial' likeness to the visible world is not the distinction that was made; it was the ability of an image to imitate different aspects that poets see of the intelligible world that mattered. In consequence, the question of the form that the poem's 'cause' (where 'cause' refers to both the poetic subject and the poet's intention) was to take, though not assumed to be easily resolved, was neither assumed to separate the poet from 'nature', since nature was understood as "the mother of forms within the poet's mind as without it".[12] The concept of naturalness in images was far removed from the Romantic's later equation of the most natural with the most artless, and the Renaissance poet's images could be extremely and carefully artificial without being considered as not natural or merely decorative or unreal. For Renaissance poet, critic and reader all consider that "quite artless clothing is less agreeable than that showing the skill of the maker".[13] Art and artifice are very closely linked.

The explication of 'imitation' as a criterion for the functioning of images in Renaissance poetry, as the imitation of the intelligible, the significant, in an artful construct, still leaves partially unexplained the manner in which the *Faerie Queene* can be said to meet the Renaissance commonplace that what is presented in poetry must be 'like life'. On the basis of the distinction between praise for the accurate transcript of particulars and praise for the expression through particulars of the essential significance of a subject, the line between which has become blurred since the development of naturalism, we can recognise that the *Faerie Queene's* 'lifelikeness' is pitched not at a description of human behaviour but at a description of the springs of human endeavour common to all men, the inner life composed of the incessant activity of appetites and fears, moods and humours and values, ideas and reasoning, in the attempt to possess and understand the world. Lewis gives another, though related, account of Spenser's 'lifelikeness':[14]

> People find 'likeness' or 'truth' to life in Shakespeare because the persons, passions and events which we meet in his plays are like those which we meet in our own lives; he excels, in fact, in what the old critics   called 'nature', or the probable. When they find nothing of the

sort in   Spenser, they are apt to conclude that he has nothing to
do with 'life' - that he writes that poetry of escape or recreation....But
they do not notice that the *Faerie Queene* is 'like life' in a different sense,
in a much more literal sense. When I say that it is like life, I do not mean
that the places and people in it are like those which life produces.
I mean precisely....that it is like life itself, not like the products of life.
It is an image of the natura naturans, not of the natura naturata. The
things we read about in it are not like life, but the experience of reading
it is like living. The closing antitheses which meet and resolve themselves into higher unities, the lights streaming out from the great
allegorical foci to turn into a hundred different colours as they reach
the lower levels of complex adventure, the adventures gathering
themselves together and revealing their true nature as we draw near
the foci, the constant re-appearance of certain basic ideas, which
transform themselves without end and yet ever remain the same
(eterne in mutability), the unwearied variety and seamless continuity of the whole - all this is Spenser's true likeness to life.

An example may help to clarify Lewis' meaning. Several times
in the course of the *Faerie Queene*, for instance in the Wandering
Woods episode in Book I and Sir Guyon's adventures in Book III, a
character stumbles into a wood or forest which becomes progressively
more dark, overgrown and sinister. The character inadvertently
finds himself confronted by a monster, or some other manifestation
of evil, and is forced into combat. Eventually the character defeats
the evil and stumbles back out of the forest onto the clear path of his
journey. The recurrent episodes of this kind call to mind the texture
of the experience, common to all, of unwittingly wandering into a
situation full of ominous signs, the accompanying sense of forebod-
ing, and the necessity of meeting and defeating the challenge and of
restoring a more equable state. Spenser's allegorical method is well
suited to the description of this sort of 'lifelikeness', since it follows
in its method of attending to more than one level of meaning at the
same time, the character of experience itself.

Although not everything in the *Faerie Queene* is equally allegorical, or even allegorical at all, the overall allegorical structure of
the work provides the framework for its other elements. Each Book
has an allegorical core revealing the significance of a virtue; the
specific elements - adventures, set-piece battles, explicit statement,
and description - may be taken to be the expressions in practice of the

conditions associated with the realisation of the central virtue. The clue to the continuity of the poem lies in the recognition that Spenser's images are not visual. They are not successful as visual images because they cannot be reduced to pictures which remain constant. The visual picture of the images changes and shifts as the specific images employed mean now one thing, now another, according to the theme that is being developed. That is the level of continuity to which we must attend in the allegorical poem, for the images are not fixed centres of meaning, and the allegorical poet is not "talking in pictures" but developing a form of discourse. The 'levels' of allegory, then, are the different thematic questions which Spenser is exploring. The allegory was not meant to be accessible to single levels of interpretation throughout; attention was meant to focus on the treatment of the themes and their interaction and not on the abstract interpretations.

This leads to the last aspect to be considered of the *Faerie Queene* as a work in the mainstream of Medieval and Renaissance allegorical poetry, its unfinished character. There are two reasons why the *Faerie Queene's* incompleteness (Spenser having written only six of the projected twelve Books) did not disturb the Elizabethan reader in the way it disturbs modern readers and critics. In the first place, the Elizabethan audience did not approach allegorical poetry with the expectation of a close-knit unity. From the time of Homer's Greece and before, the custom was established that poems of epic proportions were recited in parts, the whole being much too long for a single recitation. The custom was inherited by the Middle Ages, and persisted well after the availability of printed versions had provided an alternative to the constraints of verbal rendition. And even with the development of printing, a work of the length of the *Faerie Queene* would take several sittings to read. Thus Spenser could anticipate a segmented understanding of his complex poem and was not expected to present a narrative with an ending in our sense. His audience would remember certain episodes and certain characters, and they would respond to the reiteration of certain themes, but they could never be expected to recall the details of his plot. Thus even if the poet constructed a careful plot, his industry would have no particular value in his rhetorical situation. Moreover, the loose *thematic* unity that the allegorical poet did impose on his work was appropriate to the allegorical character of his poem. Thus, in the second place, the incompleteness of the *Faerie Queene* did not affect its essential understanding and appreciation, since the allegory itself is open-ended in the finished work, until 'completed' by the audience. The unfinished character of the *Faerie Queene* belongs to a long history of 'unfinished' Medieval works; and although it certainly leaves many aspects of plot and allegorical meaning suspended at the end of the Mutabilitie Cantos, the arrangement of the poem into loosely self-contained Books, and the audience's appreciation of the open-ended character of the allegorical method, meant that to the extent that the audience was concerned with the incompleteness of the poem, their concern was for the loss to them of the further appreciation, of the same sort gained already, to be afforded by another six Books of the poem, and not for the lack of an 'ending'.

Although Sir Philip Sidney's *Apology for Poetry*[15] was published after the publication of the first three Books of the *Faerie Queene*, in 1595, it was circulating in manuscript form in the late 1580's and was written around 1583. The *Apology for Poetry* is significant here because while it follows the prescriptions for poetry outlined regularly in the earlier English handbook tradition, it also exhibits a familiarity with the sixteenth century critical activity of Italian theorists such as Minturno, Scaliger and Castelvetro. These theorists were concerned with assimilating to the critical tradition whose greatest authority was Horace's *Art of Poetry*, the new influences following the revival of some classical manuscripts, most notably Aristotle's *Poetics*. Sidney's *Apology* represents both the epitome of the English tradition and the most influential mediation of the Italian criticism to Elizabethan critical activity. It was quoted in the "best critical places"[16] including Puttenham's *Arte* of 1589 and Harrington's *Apologie* of 1591.

In part, its vogue may be accounted for by its immensely readable style and its unashamedly eclectic character. Unlike the earlier handbooks it was a gentleman's essay rather than a scholarly manual, and in this it showed an awareness of the emerging challenge to both the customary principles governing literary practice and the Italian contemporary synthesis. Locally, the *Apology for Poetry* was considered to be a retort to the Puritan Stephen Gosson's attack on the alleged immorality of poetry and its alleged association with 'Italianate licence' in manners and dress. Sidney puts forward a great variety of critical positions and enlists all the major traditional arguments for the value of poetry. He is, as one modern commentator remarks, "literally writing an 'apology' or 'defence'";[17] for his aim is to win the assent of the reader, by whatever argument is most likely to appeal to him, to the worth of poetry as the discipline supremely qualified to both delight and teach, and teach through delighting and delight through teaching. In other words, Sidney is affirming in explicit statement what Spenser was affirming in practice, that the criterion of the decorous relation between poetic subject and poetic means rules out any understanding of poetry that neglects its didactic aim, and as an understanding of the didactic aim, any idea that one should be able to reduce a poem to some paraphrasable message. To restate a 'poem's ideas' is simply to deny those ideas their fit and decent form, and so it is not a 'restatement' at all, but an abstraction separated from the sources of its meaning and thus also its understanding.

Sidney's *Apology for Poetry* is an attack on those who, like Stephen Gosson, want to disconnect the unity of poetry's three aims, to teach, to delight and to persuade - the third being the natural consequence of and necessary to the effectiveness, of the other two. This unity had been reiterated in all the rhetorical handbooks and freshly asserted by the Italian theorists, and one can detect in them no underlying notion of the kind that some aspects of a poem teach while others are unrelated to meaning and only delight the reader. This distinction was not made in the study of poetry, for attention to one involved attending to the other.

Sidney begins with the suitably imposing statement that poetry is the first nurse of all languages, "whose milk by little and little enabled them to feed afterwards of" other forms of knowledge, and he notes that even in barbarous countries, where there is no other developed knowledge, there is poetry. Sidney sets his frame of reference for English poetry with the assertion that the leading English poets, after whom all other followed, are Gower and Chaucer, thereby affirming the continuity between Medieval and contemporary literature. He continues the semi-historical argument with the claim of a stake for poetry in Greek philosophy, in the identification of early Greek philosophy with poetry. Even Plato, he says, was a poet, for in the "body of his work, though the inside and strength were philosophy, the skin as it were and beauty depended most on poetry". In saying this, Sidney is not referring to our modern distinction between form and content, but to the criterion of decorum which prescribed that the writer's chosen 'causes' are expressed in the language best fitted to teach and delight and whose meaning is inseparable from their expression. This claim on the authority of Plato would have been to Sidney's readers highly significant, since Plato's supposed abolition of poets from his commonwealth was commonly regarded as a obstacle to embracing his authority. And furthermore, Sidney says, history also has a poetical dimension, for it also uses poetical methods and allusions. The last strand of his semi-historical argument is that poetry was highly esteemed in the cultures of ancient Greece and Rome, where poets were identified with divines or prophets. Therefore, he reasons, poetry deserves to be esteemed in the present too, since their writers are the authors of most of our sciences; we value their endeavours in the sciences and so ought to likewise follow them in their estimation of poetry.

Sidney goes on to develop his central argument in the *Apology* - the supremacy of poetry above all other arts and sciences. He begins with an argument for poetry's supremacy on the grounds that poetry alone is not tied to nature for its subject matter, for it alone employs invention, to create another nature. This passage in which Sidney makes an inventory of the major kinds of knowledge and the way they are each tied to nature, deserves to be quoted at length, since it shows both what he regarded as the principal kinds of knowledge, in a classification differently viewed than ours, and as the relation between nature and art. And this helps to make clear the reasonableness of the relation then thought to exist between poetry and other forms of knowledge - again, a relation very different from the one commonly held in our time, but one which, in some important respects, is followed by Hobbes. Sidney says,

> There is no art delivered unto mankind that hath not the works of nature for his principal object, without which they could not consist, and on which they depend as they become actors and players, as it were, of what nature will have set forth. So doth the astronomer look upon the stars, and by that he seeth, set down what order nature hath taken therein. So doth the geometrician and arithmetician in their diverse sorts of quantities. So doth the musician in times tell you which by nature agree, which not. The natural philosopher thereon hath his name, and the moral philosopher standeth upon the natural virtues, vices, or passions of man....The lawyers saith what men have deter-

mined; the historian what men have done. The grammarian speaketh only of the rules of speech; and the rhetorician and logician, considering what in nature will soonest prove and persuade thereon, give artificial rules, which still are compassed within the circle of a question according to the proposed matter. The physician weigheth the nature of man's body, and the nature of things helpful or hurtful unto it. And the metaphysic, though it be in the second and abstract notions, and therefore be counted supernatural, yet doth he indeed build upon the depth of nature. Only the poet, disdaining to be tied to any such subjection, lifted up with the vigor of his invention, doth grow in effect into another nature, in making things either better than nature bringeth forth, or quite anew, forms such as never were in nature, as the heroes, demigods, cyclops....and such like; so as he goeth hand in hand with nature, not enclosed within the narrow warrant of her gifts but freely ranging within the zodiac of his own wit. Nature never set forth the earth in so rich tapestry as divers poets have done.

Sidney develops his distinction between nature - God's creation, including man - and artifice - man's creation, and says that in men, nature's utmost cunning is employed, for as God made man, man creates within his own world, and never so well as in poetry. And thus, he arrives at the thoroughly traditional statement, that poetry is an art of imitation whose end is to teach and delight.

The second strand in the argument for poetry's supremacy reasons that while other forms of knowledge may teach a man to know well, only poetry relates knowing well to doing well, and thereby teaches a man virtuous action, which is the highest end of knowledge. Thus all the other arts are "but serving sciences", since for instance, a mathematician may draw a straight line with a crooked heart. The two principal competitors who step forth to challenge poetry's title to be the prince over all others arts are moral philosophy and history. But on the one hand, Sidney argues, the claim of moral philosophy is discounted by the obscurity of its teaching; by its "sullen gravity" of style and its procedure by "definitions, divisions and distinctions" it can only be understood by those who already understand it, and its appeal is therefore very limited. It is interesting to note here that Sidney's argument rests on the perception that unless a piece of thinking is rhetorically successful (that is, can be understood and appreciated by the audience), its value is limited. He is not saying that what moral philosophy teaches is not the truth, but that its truths are lost on most men because of the obscurity that arises from their delivery. And on the other hand, the claim of history cannot be upheld, for although the historian proceeds by examples, they "draweth no necessary consequence, and therefore a less fruitful doctrine". Furthermore, in the teaching of virtuous action, a feigned example has as much force as a true one, and whereas poetry is singly devoted to exalting virtue, the historian is taken up also with many other - foolish, terrible - things, and so his effective (again Sidney's criterion is what is rhetorically successful) moral teaching is dissipated. Thus neither the philosopher's "thorny arguments" which set down "the bare rule", nor the historian's examples, whose meaning is equivocal, can match the poet's demonstration of the precept in the example, which is food for even "the tenderest stomachs". The poet is therefore rightly called the monarch of all the arts and sciences, for his teaching of virtuous action is the most effective, moving the emotions being "both the cause and effect of teaching". The poet not only shows the right way, "but giveth so sweet a prospect into the way, as will entice any man to enter into it".

The last major section of the *Apology for Poetry* is concerned with answering objections made against this conception of poetry. The most significant objection considered is that poetry is "the mother of lies". Sidney replies to this that the "poet can scarcely be a liar" for he "nothing affirms and therefore never lieth. For as I take it, to lie is to affirm that to be true which is false". But the poet does not "conjure you to believe for true what he writes" nor cite authorities for it, for he is concerned not with what is or is not but with what should or should not be. And in the realm of the portrayal of the conditions of moral conduct, the standard of judgment cannot be truth and falsity (for these refer to actual occurrences) but likelihood to encourage virtuous actions. In the course of this section, Sidney also answers the objection that Plato supposedly banished poets from his commonwealth, with the argument that Plato was not referring to all poets but only to those who abused poetry, and "banished the abuse, not the thing".

The main lines of Sidney's argument outline a conception of poetry held without basic modification throughout the Medieval and Renaissance period; the same conception that sustained Spenser's *Faerie Queene*. Although both works contain some characteristically individual features (notably Sidney's use of the essay form, and Spenser's amalgamation of four traditions of poetry), they adhere staunchly, through explicit statement and literary practice, to the connection between poetry, rhetoric, logic and morality which was fundamental to Medieval and Renaissance literary theory and practice.

A word might be said here about two changes which did occur during the Medieval and Renaissance period, in order to demonstrate that literary theory was not uncritically accepted, nor unreflectively received by succeeding generations, nor unanimated by debate, as its remarkable continuity of general character over the period might lead us to suspect. This continuity was due, rather, to the characteristic ability of the Medieval outlook to absorb new influences into its all-embracing framework.[18] One change is the technical one involved in the emergence of vernacular literature from Latin. This shift is responsible for the replacement of metrical, non-accentual verse in Latin by the rhythmical accented verse of the vernaculars. The rhythms of the vernacular were inductively discovered rather than proposed on the basis of a new theory, and although the effects of this shift for poetry were enormous, it was not felt necessary to explain or vindicate it in terms of a new theory. The second change was also successfully incorporated into the existing structure of literary theory. As early as the thirteenth century secular poetry was being written, and despite the potential threat that such poetry might be thought to offer to the theologically-centred Medieval perspective, its interpretation was readily absorbed into the same structure of multiple levels of meaning appropriate to theologically-inspired poetry - by simply detaching the strictly religious level of interpretation. Even Aquinas' stricture that secular poetry can only express literal meaning did not deny to secular poetry a multiple level understanding, for the term 'literal', as historians and commentators agree, "did not mean to rule out of secular poetry the range of natural metaphors and analogical meanings which are obviously there".[19] 'Literal' in this passage refers to the natural world in which temporal life is spent (or suffered), which is nevertheless understood as a divinely-created world; as opposed to direct reference to the spiritual dimension of temporal life or to that other, divine, world itself. The number of handbooks on literary matters which were written during the Medieval and Renaissance period, were not only the means through which the continuity of the general outlines of literary theory was actually effected. They also attest to the lively interest taken in literary theory throughout the period - an interest not bent on establishing the superiority of the new or novel (Medieval and Renaissance writers would have found our attitude toward 'originality' unsympathetic), but concerned with absorbing the effects of changes and with reaffirming the fundamental connection between literary theory and practice, rhetoric and philosophy, that constituted a truth about God's excellently constructed creation.

The history of literary criticism immediately following Spenser and Sidney is a story of *radical* change, with shifts in literary theory occurring which could no longer be absorbed into the Medieval and Renaissance perspective. More accurately, no concerted attempt was made to assimilate the shifts to this perspective. The history of the post-Renaissance period is an account of changes whose outcome, by the end of the seventeenth century, is the establishment of a perspective on philosophy in general and literary theory in particular, which is based on presuppositions almost entirely different from those held by the Elizabethans.

One way of introducing what may be called the seventeenth century debate in literary criticism, is to consider critical reaction to the *Faerie Queene* by such writers as Rymer, Dryden, Jonson, Milton, Digby and Davenant. For the kinds of comments made by these writers raise many of the issues involved in neo-classical criticism. Thus Thomas Rymer, while paying tribute to Spenser as "the first of our heroic poets: he had a large spirit, a sharp judgment, and a genius for heroic poesy, perhaps above any that ever writ since Virgil", considers that Spenser "suffered himself to be misled by Ariosto, with whom blindly rambling on marvellous adventures, he makes no conscience of probability. All is fanciful and chimerical, without any uniformity, without any foundation in truth; his poem is perfect Fairyland". Furthermore, Rymer says, "it was the vice of those times to affect superstitiously the allegory, and nothing would then be current without a mystical meaning. We must blame the Italians for debauching great Spenser's judgment; and they cast him on the unlucky choice of the stanza, which in no wise is proper for our language".[20]

Rymer's assessment of Spenser, written fairly late in the period we are considering, contains several points which are typical of the neo-classical approach. His tribute to Spenser combined with his denigration of the Italian influence (Rymer having conveniently overlooked the native tradition of allegorical poetry), implies an attitude which both seeks to salvage Spenser's reputation by diminishing his accountability for the alleged failures in the *Faerie Queene*, and results in Spenser's responsibility as author of the *Faerie Queene* not being taken seriously. This faintly damning praise, ignoring Spenser's express intentions, reveals the typical neo-classical attitude to Spenser, of indulgence and superiority. This point is associated with a second strand in neo-classical criticism of Spenser, their almost complete misunderstanding of his allegorical method. Rymer's identification of allegory as a vice, and even worse an affected vice, and as a method which produced not a clear meaning endorsed by 'probability' or likelihood in the visible world, but mystification and obscurity, was the estimation of allegory shared by many neo-classical writers. For them it was a 'superstitious' vice both in the sense that it is grounded in nothing more than old wives tales, pagan fears and a fevered imagination, and in the sense that the vogue for allegory was no more than the blind adoption of the fashionable. Rymer, along with Jonson and Dryden for example, could not take Spenser's intention - the revelation of cosmic truths - seriously. In consequence, the whole rhetorical mode of Medieval and Elizabethan allegory looks superfluous and inflated.

It was this rhetorical mode of the Medieval and Renaissance allegorist, appealing to the pleasure and moral sense of the many and the additional understanding of the few which, one commentator writes, "men like Jonson destroyed because they started from an utterly different position".[21] The neo-classicists emphasised not the truth the poet conveyed, but the poet as maker of an object which must be easily intelligible to the audience, and which must correspond to what is clearly probable in the visible world. The consequences of the shift from truth to poetic genius are described by Murrin. This shift, he says, in turn led to a "reappraisal of the relationship between the poet and his art. The allegorist had made the highest possible claims for the art of poetry, but he could regard himself in humble terms. In his Prologues Spenser constantly demeans his own abilities. He asks the Muses for help because his theme surpasses his own capacity. The....neo-classicists, on the other hand, reverse this relationship. They exalt the poet but....do not make any extravagant claims for his art. Poetry may mould the morals and manners of men, but it carries no cosmological message. It may exist only for entertainment".[22] Although these critics paid lip service to the notion that the end of poetry was to both profit and delight, they were by no means agreed that poetry must do both all the time, as Sidney had thought. The eventual outcome is that an art which can merely entertain has completely lost its connection with philosophy - poetry "no longer reveals to man his deeper nature".[23] But for the poet, on the other hand, "these critics made very strong claims. Poetry demonstrated one's unique accomplishments and became the medium of personal fame. The poet dazzled men by his wit".[24] It follows that "one's judgments about a poem manifest a personal estimation of the writer. The poet magnifies himself through his poetry and so achieves enduring fame".[25]

Rymer's comments on the importance of the poet attending to 'probability' and to grounding his plots in a 'foundation in truth', and his remark that in this respect Spenser's poem is 'perfect Fairyland', indicate how much the meanings of 'probability' and 'truth' have changed. Under the emerging naturalistic criterion, it is the externals of the poem, the plot and the situations, which must be true to life, whereas in the currency Spenser was using, it was the disclosure of man's essential nature in relation to his universal context, that had to be true to life. The neo-classical concern with naturalistic accuracy runs right through their conception of literature and literary criticism, and demonstrates that 'literal' now refers to the visible world alone, free from any necessary larger framework of understanding, where previously the term 'literal' had indicated the natural realm as part of the whole divinely created universe.

Milton's estimation of Spenser as "our sage and serious poet"[26] is significant in being one of the few voices raised in defence of Spenser, and thereby going against the grain of neo-classical criticism that regarded the *Faerie Queene* as a 'marvellous' fabrication. This assessment of the *Faerie Queene* contained an ambiguity which the neo-classicists show no inclination to dispel. It could be taken in the disparaging sense that the poem was frivolous in a context which now considered that poetry was a serious matter like the new science and that frivolity brought poetry into disrepute, or in the faintly-praising sense which distanced Spenser to the Medieval world and relegated consideration of him to being merely of 'historical' interest, with nothing to contribute to a 'correct' theory of poetry. Milton, whose own literary practice is in many ways an exception to orthodox neo-classical literature, differs from neo-classical writers in taking both Spenser's intention and achievement seriously.

Another aspect of neo-classical critical reaction to Spenser concerns Spenser's use of language. Ben Jonson asserted that Spenser "writ no language",[27] and Dryden, as well as upbraiding Spenser for the supposed lack of overall coherence in the *Faerie Queene*, the irrelevancy of some of its parts, his failure to finish the poem, the imperfection of his model and the inappropriateness of the stanza structure, also censures Spenser for his supposed ill choice of obsolete language.[28] The archaisms and neologisms, characteristic of Spenser's poetry, are a major point of contention among neo-classical critics. Most use it as a stick to beat Spenser with, complaining that he ought to have delivered his subject in a plain language accessible to a ready understanding, and point to Jonson's 'judicious and practicable language' as the model for poets. Sir Kenelm Digby[29] stands almost alone among his generation of critics, in perceiving that Spenser's intention, in reviving and inventing words (in a period when the size of the English vocabulary increased rapidly), was to make his language more flexible and evocative of his allegorical theme, pointing through the etymology of words to their meanings in the poem. Digby recognised that Spenser's use of language did not obscure his subject but served to express it more accurately, and thus form an analogy between the level of language itself and other levels of meaning in the poem.

Critical reaction to Spenser's language was compounded by being confused with two seventeenth century attitudes to language. The first was the movement to expunge 'inkhornisms' (latinised terms) and imported foreign, largely Italian, words and phrases. And the second, arising from the same impulse to introduce rational rules into the construction of the English language, was the attempt to standardise spelling and vocabulary which culminated in Johnson's Dictionary. These attitudes worked to predispose neo-classical critics against Spenser's use of language.

In the Preface to *Gondibert*,[30] Davenant considers that the main objection to Spenser's poetry should not be his use of "obsolete language", which has "grown the most vulgar", that is, frequent "accusation that is laid to his charge", but his argument. Davenant asserts that Spenser's "hands deserved to be employed upon matter of a more natural and therefore of a more useful kind: His allegorical Story, by many held defective in the connection, resembling, methinks, a continuance of extraordinary dreams, such as excellent poets and painters, by being over-studious, may have in the beginning of fevers". Davenant's condemnation of Spenser's allegorical argument on the grounds that its matter was not 'natural' and 'useful', is typical of the neo-classical approach. But what must also be remembered is that their attack was directed at allegory which contained what they called 'supernatural' or 'fantastic' or 'marvellous' elements. A modified form of allegory, which drew only on 'natural' elements, was 'probable' and clear and whose meaning was explicit, continued to be accepted and was used, for instance, by Bacon in the *New Atlantis* and by Dryden. Allegory closer to the tradition to which Spenser belongs was written by Milton and Bunyan.

It is important to guard against accepting at their face value the neo-classicists' self-estimation and their reinterpretation of the past, in particular of Medieval and Renaissance literary theory and practice - that which preceded their own. For while the neo-classicists appeared to condemn the earlier theory and practice wholesale, many of the same methods, usages and presuppositions (including allegory, significant metaphor and the presence of the religious frame of reference) are found in their works up to the end of the seventeenth century. The necessity of stressing this caution arises from the prevalence among modern historians of literary criticism of a too ready acceptance of the neo-classicists' own view of the matter, perhaps due to the closer affinity felt between the modern and neo-classical approaches than between the modern and Elizabethan approaches, in some respects. This tendency may be observed in three instances of neo-classical reinterpretation of the past.

Firstly, there is the assessment, shared by many modern commentators, that "before Dryden, critical prose in English is immature, and most works of criticism are patchy, mediocre and derivative. Even with work of indubitable excellence, like Sir Philip Sidney's *Apology for Poetry*, the reader is unlikely to feel, to the extent that he does with critics after Dryden, that he is engaged in a dialogue with someone who can be imagined to share precisely his own kind of interest in literature".[31] However, as has been mentioned earlier, this assessment fails to consider that English critical prose as a form only begins with the neo-classicists, that before this time literary criticism was incorporated into the disciplines of rhetoric, logic, grammar, philosophy and literature itself; that this contrast expresses the different conceptions held of literature and its relation to other disciplines; and that in consequence to measure the performance of one in terms of the principles of the other is not appropriate, however illuminating of the later attitude.

Secondly, the change of focus from poet as mediator between reader and a universal, essential truth, to poet as poetic genius, also converted the Medieval and Elizabethan understanding of 'invention' and 'imitation' into the neo-classical understanding, or misunderstanding of them as plagarism. The modern notion of plagarism did not enter into critical discussion in the earlier period; it was regarded as an ethical and social concept, "concerned with stealing another man's fame and profit. It was not a critical concept, as it has nearly become for a later age which has merged patent office legalism with aesthetic standards of inspiration".[32] The neo-classical conception of a literary work as primarily a personal expression, would have seemed to the earlier age to have put the emphasis in the wrong place. In their view, a literary work was first of all an imitation of the significances inherent in the correspondences in the world, and the poet invented his causes from this texture of meaning.

And thirdly, the neo-classical critics reinterpreted the past, and some modern historians have followed their lead, in presenting the Medieval and Elizabethan approach to literature as fundamentally defective in terms of a supposed tension between poetry and philosophy seen as running through the literature of the whole period which begins with Plato's assault on the poet in favour of the philosopher. Medieval and Renaissance literary theory is seen as having no more than papered over the cracks of this tension, and Sidney's *Apology* is interpreted as the work in which the "ancient controversy - ancient even in Plato's days - between poetry and philosophy is once more reopened".[33] Again, however, the history of the period does not bear out the claim. Medieval and Elizabethan writers did not perceive such a conflict as characterising their literature, and they insist time and again on the necessary and self-evident connection between poetry and philosophy.

The role of the Ramist reorganisation of logic and rhetoric in the development of neo-classical principles of literary criticism may be usefully introduced at this point, for while during the Elizabethan period it was understood to sustain and underline the connection between poetry and philosophy, it was also used by the neo-classicists to indicate the divorce between the two.

Ramus' educational reforms, outlined in a series of books in the middle of the sixteenth century, aimed at establishing a clearer division of labour between the parts of the Trivium curriculum, in order to re-emphasise the cooperation between the three parts. For literary theory and practice, the most important aspect of the reorganisation was Ramus' slicing off of the first two division of rhetoric, Invention and Disposition, which were also traditionally the first two divisions of logic or dialectic. Rhetoric retained and was now composed of its three further divisions, Elocution (the tropes and figures), Memory, and Pronunciation or delivery. The reorganisation was made on the grounds that the overlap between logic and rhetoric, whereby the student first learned Invention and Disposition in logic and then relearned them in rhetoric, was unnecessary, and it was intended not to divorce logic and rhetoric but to make their connection clearer. Thus the reforms did not mean that poets were no longer supposed to invent and dispose matter, but that they should learn these skills within dialectic. Nothing had changed but an emphasis.

One of the effects of Ramus' rearrangement, for poetry, was to make the logical function of images more explicit. The Ramist stressed that *all* discourse obeys the rules of dialectic; in consequence the didactic function of poetry is more clearly stated. The prescription that in a poem, images function as arguments for the poem's 'cause', must be understood in terms of the specific meaning the Ramist attributed to argument. An argument could be any word, relation, concept or image that contributed to the reasoning of the discourse. The Ramist did not consider that poetry is logically more complicated than had previously been supposed, but stressed that logic is natural to poets, as to all other reasoning men. Thus the poet was not meant to 'prove something' in every poem, but was impelled to declare reasons and causes, to examine the nature of something.

The Ramist approach makes not only poetry, but all the arts very purposeful. Again this was the outcome of the explicit emphasis they placed on the traditional conception of order, according to which it was held that men naturally seek to discover not a particular order in the universe, but a comprehension of the universe as ordered. It is within this framework that the Ramist finds particulars eloquent. For example, as one commentator notes, "a toothache is an eloquent argument for the proposition that it is better not to neglect decay, and no reasonable man is impatient when he discovers this relationship". An era which took moral law to be as natural as 'natural law' in the physical world, she continues, "was equally willing to have images point eloquently to concepts and values. That eloquence should make wisdom manifest did not seem so much a desideratum as a legitimate and universally discoverable connection".[34]

Another effect of the Ramist view, for poetry, was to stress that there is no distinction, as far as logical function in a handbook example or in a poem is concerned, between an image and a passage of 'conceptually stated' reasoning. Sixteenth century writers and audiences recognised that "poetic images which made men 'feel' and conceptual statement which made them 'think'" performed the same function of arguing a 'cause'.[35] Thus for instance the poet may look at a garden and see in it an argument for God's creation; if he then compares it to an ordered and harmonious commonwealth, he has found another argument, or ratio, or reason, or indication, for God's power. The Ramist's profound belief in and reaffirmation of a reasonable order in nature, then, stresses the common ground of rhetoric and logic in poetry. As Tuve observes, dialectic or logic is simply concerned with "orderly thinking - every man's province; thoughts placed in order, however, will demonstrate the truth of a matter without the use of other dialectical tools. Dialectic is not synonymous with disputatious 'proving'; dialectically sound statements do, nevertheless, 'prove'. Apply this to poetry - and that it should be so applied is at the very heart of the doctrine - and you have a poem that has but to examine and state, with due care for dialectical soundness in the reasoning, in order to argue the truth or advisability of something".[36]

However, the neo-classicists' reading of the Ramist reorganisation led them to an understanding of the relation between rhetoric and logic which was almost directly opposite to that current in the sixteenth century. In a sense, the neo-classicists' understanding only exploited an ambiguity of interpretation already present in the Ramist reconstitution, an implication which their disavowals could not completely dispel.

For although Ramus and his followers meant only to make a clearer distinction between rhetoric and logic, in order to stress the logical dimension of all discourse, their rearrangement could also be taken to prescribe a separation between rhetoric and logic, such that rhetoric is concerned solely with matters of style and delivery and logic is concerned, alone, with the content and structure of argument. The line between a distinction and a separation may be a fine one, and the neo-classicists, already predisposed on other grounds to rigorously separate argument and style, things and words, enthusiastically embraced this second interpretation of Ramus. Thus the Medieval and Elizabethan poets' conception, that through the conjunction of rhetoric and logic he learns to beautify his 'cause' as well as argue it, now becomes the seventeenth century poet's understanding, that through rhetoric he learns to beautify his style. Logic has become the preserve of logicians.

Once rhetoric has been set adrift from logic, and the rationale for relatively complicated figures and images in Elizabethan poetry has been lost, the advocacy of a 'plain style' in literature, representing one of the possible ways in which literary theory could change direction, becomes intelligible. The 'plain style' appealed to the neo-classicists because it seemed the means of expression most suited to their adherence to 'probability', 'nature' and utility. Their advocacy of it was also promoted by their regard for three other considerations. Firstly, the empirical scientific method fostered by the Royal Society presupposed a relation between things and words, one of whose expressions was the plain style's appropriateness to scientific discussion. Thomas Sprat's statements in his *History of the Royal Society* (1667), provide one of the clearest and most influential declarations on this subject. He says:[37]

> They have therefore been most rigorous in putting in execution, the only Remedy, that can be found for this extravagance: and that has been, a constant Resolution, to reject all the amplications, disgressions, and swellings of style: to return back to the primitive purity, and shortness, when men delivered so many things, almost in an equal number of words. They have exacted from all their members, a close, naked, natural way of speaking: positive expressions; clear senses; a

native easiness: bringing all things as near the Mathematical plainness, as they can.

The influence of the new approach to science on neo-classical literary theory, and the association between members of the Royal Society and neo-classical critics, help to account for the neo-classical adoption of the plain style in literature.

Secondly, the advocacy of a plain style by seventeenth century religious writers, especially by Puritan and Low Church clergy, was part of their more general reaction against anything hinting at 'Popish' excess, and the richly textured artifice of Elizabethan prose was tainted by association. Their attitude had a certain effect on contemporary tastes in diction, both because of the overlap of religious and literary interests in some of these writers, and through their influence on general public standards of propriety.

In the third place, neo-classical adoption of the plain style was part of the influence exercised by the authority of French neo-classicism on English neo-classical theory, between the time of Sidney's *Apology* and the beginning of Dryden's long critical career in the middle of the seventeenth century. French neo-classicism, eclipsing the Italian influence of writers such as Ariosto and Tasso for the seat of continental critical authority, insisted upon an unadorned style, and while in some other respects English neo-classical writers did not follow French principles, they welcomed the French theoretical backing for the plain style.

With Dryden, English neo-classical theory explicitly diverges from the French model and, in fact, reflects more accurately the contemporary English literary practice. Sorbiere's highly uncomplimentary remarks about English science and the English stage, especially on the question of the classical unities so dear to the French, provoked replies from both Thomas Sprat and Dryden. In his *Essay of Dramatic Poesy* in 1668, Dryden rejects the too rigid classicism of the French. While agreeing that the principal criterion for drama is verisimilitude, he argues that the imitation of human life must come through lifelikeness in the sense of the liveliness of the human passions and humours. The beauty of the French drama, he concludes, is that of a statue, unanimated by "the soul of poetry, which is the imitation of the humours and passions".

Although the tone of Dryden's comments seems to recall the Elizabethan approach, the differences between the two are more fundamental than the resemblances. Dryden's use of the term 'imitation', for example, represents an instance of the manner in which neo-classical theorists continued to employ Medieval and Elizabethan critical vocabulary, but within a changed frame of reference. 'Imitation' for the neo-classicists referred to the accurate transcription of particulars, not in order to point to their larger significance, but to record the manners and behaviour of men. 'Invention' referred not to the poet's discovery of arguments, in figures, images and statements, which suited the height of his 'cause', but to the poet's personal genius and ingenuity. And the principle of decorum, while remaining of overriding importance, no longer referred to the relation between 'cause' and arguments in disclosing a significant ordering of correspondences, but to the poet's conformity to the rules of social discourse. The interaction of 'fancy' and 'judgment' now meant not the cooperation between statement, image and graphic detail into a unity which would teach through delighting, but the application of the poet's individual judgment or discretion to the products of his individual fancy or genius. And the Medieval and Elizabethan conception of 'imagination', linked inseparably with reasoning and feeling, was replaced by an 'imagination' variously identified with 'wit' (by Dryden, for whom this faculty at one time represented the very principle of poetry) or with 'fancy'; either way, no necessary connection with reasoning and feeling together with supposed.

By the end of the seventeenth century, other changes in the critical vocabulary have also taken place. 'Probability' has replaced 'significance', 'propriety' has replaced 'decorum' and the 'plain style' has replaced 'eloquence'. The character of literature has been transformed, and so has the relation between literary theory and philosophy. It is at this point that the discussion turns to Hobbes.

The argument may at first seem contradictory, for it is contended both that Hobbes held a kind of neo-classical approach to literary theory (which does not, however, altogether tally with the view attributed to him in histories of literary criticism) and that in some fundamental respects his views link him to the earlier outlook. But the contradictory element dissolves, it is argued, once the particular character of Hobbes' neo-classicism and his position as a 'transitional' figure whose thinking is nevertheless coherent, is taken into account.

This argument sets the pattern for that developed in the following chapter and in chapter 7. In the present chapter the coherence of Hobbes' views on literary theory and practice, characterised as 'transitional', is at issue. In the next chapter, the 'transitional' character of Hobbes' views on language is examined. And in chapter 7 the discussion centres on how Hobbes' way of philosophising in *Leviathan* can be seen as a whole, and at the same time drawing upon both traditional conventions and those which were to supplant them. In each case Hobbes' thinking (understood as both coherent and transitional) is considered through his use of language. The date of Hobbes' statement on literary theory and practice, in his Answer to Davenant's Preface to *Gondibert*, and the date of *Leviathan*, provide the key to understanding the relations between the principles of literary criticism he outlines, the views he held on the relation between poetry and philosophy, his theory of language in *Leviathan*, and his own use of figurative language in *Leviathan*.

By 1650, the trends and principles outlined in the previous section had not been fully developed by neo-classical critics. On one side, the advocacy of poetry and drama which portrayed the victory of virtuous conduct in straightforwardly recognisable adverse circumstances (the 'probable') in a naturalistically accurate manner; which aimed at the explicit didactic instruction of reader or audience in the plainest terms, concerning the visible world of social morality; which observed rationalistic rules of structure to best promote this aim; and which rejected what seemed to them the 'far-fetched', the 'marvellous', the 'improbable', the supernatural, and the extravagant, was common ground among neo-classical writers. But on the other side, by 1650 some of the possible implications of this approach which were later established as neo-classical orthodoxy, were as yet unexplicit and undeveloped. Particularly important to note here are, firstly the persistence of the allegorical method, though stripped of elements earlier understood to evoke a deeper significance but now scorned as supernatural, and with its artificial character modified, secondly the continued influence that Christian moral principles were felt to exercise in poetry and drama, and thirdly the continued importance attached to a relation between literature and its criticism and philosophy, among writers who supported the neo-classical view. The rationalistic logic of neo-classical theory, which ultimately led to the complete abandonment of allegory and the devel-

opment of completely secular drama, had not yet been followed to
its conclusion.

Hobbes' views demonstrate both sides of the neo-classical
position as it stood in 1650. In the Answer he states that the work of
the poets is "by imitating humane life in delightful and measur'd
lines, to avert men from vice and incline them to vertuous and
honorable actions".[38] that the greatest 'indecency' of a heroic poem
would be "the uncomliness of representing in great persons the
inhumane vice of Cruelty or the sordid vice of Lust or Drunkenness"[39] and that "Beyond the actual works of nature a Poet may now
go; but beyond the conceived possibility of nature, never".[40] Hobbes'
antipathy towards the more extravagant expressions of literary
artifice is registered in his stern admonition that verse continued
"into the formes of an Organ, a Hatchet, an Egg, an Alter, and a paire
of Wings" is to "seek glory from a needlesse difficulty....for a man to
obstruct his own way with unprofitable difficulties is great impru-
dence".[41] The same rationalistic, neo-classical spirit, though tem-
pered by a thoroughly traditional appeal to Christian piety, is seen
in Hobbes' contention, "why a Christian should think it an ornament
to his Poem, either to profane the true God or invoke a false one, I can
imagin no cause but a reasonless imitation of Custom, of a foolish
custome, by which a man, enabled to speak wisely from the principles of nature and his own meditation, loves rather to be thought to
speak by inspiration, like a Bagpipe".[42] The role that Hobbes attributes to figurative language and imagery will be examined later.

In the orthodox history of literary criticism, Hobbes is presented
as being in the vanguard of the neo-classical movement, specifically
for his discussion of the roles of 'fancy' and 'judgment', which was
taken up by the neo-classicists as one of their guiding principles, and
more generally as being the first to outline an empiricist epistemological perspective that foreshadows Locke, which begins with the
impression of sensations on the tabula rasa of the human mind. The
shortcomings of this view of Hobbes are worth examining in some
detail, since their consideration will help to identify the transitional
character of Hobbes' position.

On the question of 'fancy' and 'judgment', Hobbes says that
"Judgment begets the strength and structure, and Fancy begets the
ornaments of a Poem".[43] The force of this distinction was twofold.
Firstly, while neo-classical writers had censured what seemed to

them the decorative extravagance of language and the fevered imagination behind the imagery and scope of earlier poetry, Hobbes was taken to have specified how and why these 'excesses' ought to be restrained. The 'error' of the previous poetry has been identified as an excess of 'fancy' due to the lack of restraint exercised by the 'judgment'. And secondly, Hobbes' prescription for the relation between fancy and judgment was seen as providing a convincing philosophical basis for neo-classical principles, because he had approached the subject from a more theoretical standpoint than that generally taken by practising poets. The passage reads:

> Time and Education begets experience; Experience begets memory; Memory begets Judgment and Fancy: Judgment begets the strength and structure, and Fancy begets the ornaments of a Poem. The Ancients therefore fabled not absurdly in making memory the Mother of the Muses. For memory is the World (though not really, yet so as in a looking glass) in which the Judgment, the severer Sister, busieth her self in a grave and rigid examination of all the parts of Nature, and in registring by Letters their order, causes, uses, differences, and resemblances; Whereby the Fancy, when any work of Art is to be performed, findes her materials at hand and prepared for use, and needs no more then a swift motion over them, that what she wants, and is there to be had, may not lie too long unespied.

In the short term, Hobbes' statement was taken up by English neo-classical theorists to fill the gap left by their abolition of the older relationship between poetry and philosophy, in which the relation between the poet and his material rested in the precepts of 'imitation', 'invention', 'eloquence', 'decorum' and 'significance'. Hobbes' definition seemed to provide the kind of alternative philosophical grounding and the kind of rational rule for poetry that was wanted. In the long term, however, another aspect of Hobbes' argument came to be regarded as more significant. The relation between fancy and judgment was later taken to indicate not so much the manner in which the two cooperated in poetry, having a common source in memory and experience, at which level they are not differentiated, but rather a clean division between subject-matter and ornament, and so the treatment of content and form as though deriving from quite separate sources. Thus Hobbes' statement was seen as significant, in the short term for restating a connection between poetry and philosophy, and in the long term for indicating an inherent and necessary split between them. As with Ramus' educational reorganisation, Hobbes' specification of the way in which fancy and judgment cooperate, sisters of one mother, in the single entity of the poem, was taken by neo-classical writers as the basis for a complete separation between and separate treatment of form and content.

Commentators on the history of literary criticism have tended to emphasise the later interpretation of Hobbes' statement. In doing so, however, they tend to confuse the influence that Hobbes' argument was taken to have, with its significance in the context of Hobbes' own writings. Thus commentators usually take the full-fledged neo-classical doctrine as representing Hobbes' own 1650 view; while the impact of Hobbes' statement is clearly evident in the works of later neo-classical theorists, commentators generally overestimate the extent to which the two are congruent. In particular they tend to foist upon Hobbes an empiricist view, which is quite foreign to Hobbes' thinking, and which is quite unnecessary for establishing the influence of Hobbes' statement on neo-classical writers.

Spingarn is one commentator who has read full-fledged neo-classical doctrine back into Hobbes' statement in the Answer. He declares that Hobbes' "antithesis" between fancy and judgment,[44]

> became a commonplace of criticism in the period of neo-classicism....
> This distinction had been suggested by the Italians of the Cinquecento, and had been more clearly indicated, as a difference in human temperament, by Bacon; but with Hobbes, who first gave it precision, it became part and parcel of English thought and was adopted by Robert Boyle, Locke, Temple and Addison. The French had for some time realised the critical significance of the antithesis, but they never formulated it so clearly as this. Throughout the second half of the century, in both countries, the two terms were placed in a sort of conventional opposition....and the clash resounds through neo-classical criticism.

And elsewhere Spingarn identifies Davenant's Preface and Hobbes' Answer as inaugurating a new period in English literary criticism; he argues both that Hobbes' philosophical approach built upon Bacon's and foreshadow's Locke's, and that the Preface and Answer introduced the principles of French neo-classicism, so influential on the literary theory of writers like Dryden and Rymer.[45]

Dowlin, while dissenting from Spingarn's view that the Preface and Answer introduced French neo-classical principles to England

(Dowlin argues much more convincingly that the Preface and Answer are characteristically English rather than French in spirit),
agrees with Spingarn in considering Hobbes "an empiricist out and
out".[46] Wimsatt and Brooks also refer to "the English empiricist
Hobbes".[47] Hobbes, they argue, provided the groundwork developed by Locke of a new epistemology based on sense experience,
which was taken up by the neo-classicists as the philosophical
backdrop of their literary theory.[48] This view is shared by yet another
modern commentator, Watson, who attributes to Hobbes a crucial
role in the "literary revolution" to neo-classicism in England, but
who in doing so merges the view of Hobbes with the later empiricist
view based on the pre-eminence of sense experience. Hobbes, he
says, is "a part of the mid-seventeenth century trend towards
empiricism in thought and clarity in style".[49]

Watson argues that a comparison of Hobbes' remarks on
metaphor in his free translation of Aristotle's *Rhetoric* of 1637, with
those in the Answer to Davenant's Preface, shows that Hobbes
changes from being an admirer of that special form of metaphor
called the conceit, a metaphor of two things which initially strike the
reader as unlikely to be related (a favourite use of figurative language of the Metaphysical poets), to being one of the first to reject it,
and so was one of the leaders of neo-classical thinking. Watson goes
on to account for Hobbes' contribution to neo-classical thinking by
arguing that Hobbes came to this position as a consequence of his
"extra-literary approach to the problems of literary style".[50] He
considers that "Hobbes' conversion to classicism and his rejection of
the poetic conceit can be traced back to his first full-time preoccupation
with philosophy in the Paris of his long sojourn from 1640 to 1651,
an intellectual world dominated by the new rationalism of Descartes
and Gassendi".[51] Hobbes' objection to the conceit, Watson comments, "is a non-literary objection",[52] an outcome of his development of the notion that language, to be meaningful, "must confine
itself to such things as can be perceived by the five senses".[53] Thus,
says Watson, Hobbes rejects as absurd terms with no grounding in
sense experience, like 'round quadrangle', and by extension the use
in poetry of metaphors which form comparisons between inherently
incomparable things. Watson concludes that Hobbes' philosophical
approach to the uses of language, which were "read and respected
by the leaders of literary fashion" in the neo-classical period,[54]

"largely irrelevant as they are to the craft of the poet, are accepted and put into effect by the poets and critics of the new age".[55]

There are three points raised by Watson's article that are pertinent to the present discussion. Firstly, along with other modern commentators, Watson confuses the description of the manner in which Hobbes' ideas were taken to apply to literary criticism, and his subsequent authority in that field, with the character of those ideas themselves. Hobbes was not a follower of empiricism and did not hold sense experience as such as pre-eminently significant. In *Leviathan*, written around the same time as the Answer to Davenant's Preface, Hobbes makes it quite plain that the basis of his 'demonstration' and the ground of his appeal to the reader is neither the inductive multiplication of instances nor the deduction of conclusions from empirical observation. Hobbes' 'resolutive-compositive' method consists of an abstract analysis of material which depends not on the empirical observation of behaviour, but on a knowledge of the consequences of human nature, which can only be based upon each man 'reading himself'. In the Introduction Hobbes stresses that "this kind of doctrine admitteth no other demonstration" than a man looking in himself to consider if he "also find not the same in himself",[56] and in the course of Leviathan Hobbes does of appeal to 'empirical evidence' to support his argument. Hobbes' distrust of conclusions drawn from the 'facts' of empirical method, is made quite clear in chapter 7 when he says,[57]

> No discourse whatsoever, can end in absolute knowledge of fact, past, or to come. For, as for the knowledge of fact, it is originally, sense; and ever after, memory. And for the knowledge of consequence, which I have said before is called science, it is not absolute, but conditional. No man can know by discourse, that this, or that, is, has been, or will be; which is to know absolutely: but only, that if this be, that is; if this has been, that has been; if this shall be, that shall be: which is to know conditionally; and that not the consequence of one thing to another; but of one name of a thing, to another name of the same thing.

And in the Review and Conclusion of *Leviathan*, Hobbes repeats that "the matters in question are not of *fact*, but of *right*, wherein there is no place for *witnesses*".[58]

Furthermore, while for Hobbes sense is the necessary starting-point, two considerations preclude the attribution of a theory of knowledge to Hobbes limited to 'such things as can be perceived by the five senses'. In the first place, Hobbes distinguishes between knowledge of God, the first cause (that He is eternal, omnipotent and infinite), from human knowledge which begins with second, natural causes, the first of which is sense. In holding this view, Hobbes successfully avoids the problems associated with the Medieval 'inborn faculties' view, and Locke's absolute tabula rasa view, in which the first cause has been banished from the argument altogether, and the ground laid for simple empiricism and the pre-eminence of sense. In Hobbes, the presence of the First Cause continues to qualify the character of natural knowledge. And in the second place, Hobbes' discussion in the first Part of *Leviathan* indicates that memory, imagination, reasoning driven by appetites and aversions, artifice, the construction of language, and the discovery of the laws of nature, are of immeasurably greater significance for the character of human knowledge and association, than is brute sense by itself. In the light of the development of the argument of the first Part, it is clear that for Hobbes it is not the physical senses, but sense as perception, that is important.

Although the evidence for the argument that Hobbes was not an empiricist, has necessarily come from *Leviathan*, since it contains a fuller account of his views, there is nothing in the Answer to suggest a different estimation. The second point raised by Watson's article follows from the same source of confusion, such that the difference between the full-fledged neo-classical view of figurative language, and Hobbes' view, is blurred. In his argument that the two need to be distinguished, Gang notes in his reply to Watson that Hobbes' strictures against terms like 'round quadrangle' were directed at scholastic philosophy, not at poetry, and that his view of language is "perfectly compatible with the advocacy of metaphor in poetry".[59] Wimsatt and Brooks also point out that Hobbes' attacks on the use of figurative language, or rather on its abuses, were directed at those who, for instance, used the pulpit to preach inflammatory opinion, and did not mean to censure its appearance in poetry, its native and appropriate place.[60]

The understanding of Hobbes' view of figurative language in the Answer lies in understanding his statement that a poet ought not go beyond the 'conceived possibility' of nature. In the Introduction to *Leviathan* Hobbes expounds a view of art and artifice as that by which man imitates and goes beyond the works of nature, which clearly shows that for Hobbes, 'artificial' and 'natural' need not be mutually exclusive, and that the 'conceived possibility' of nature embraces a much wider scope than that allowed in orthodox neo-classical doctrine, a scope which is closer to that understood by Medieval and Renaissance writers. But in the Answer too, the same relationship between nature and artifice, in man's imitation, is present. Hobbes argues in the Answer that what the poet has "of his own is nothing but experience and knowledge of Nature, and specially humane nature....For in him that professes the imitation of Nature, as all Poets do, what greater fault can there be then to bewray [than to betray] an ignorance of nature in his Poem".[61]

Hobbes' view of figurative language owes as much to the earlier approach as it does to the emerging neo-classical one, and the debt to the earlier approach may be seen as fundamental while the debt to the neo-classical approach is less significant, though more obvious to the modern reader. Like his contemporaries, Hobbes condemns the "exorbitant" fictions of earlier poets. But he attributes a more important role to figurative language than his contemporaries would accept, because the relationships he discusses between fancy and judgment, fancy and philosophy, and between 'knowing much' and 'knowing well', all rest in the cooperation and joint operation of the members of the pairs, which follows from the relationships between poetry and philosophy, and nature and artifice. The understanding of figurative language in the context of these relationships, is common ground between Hobbes and earlier writers. For neo-classical theorists, on the other hand, the role and significance of figurative language diminishes in line with the emphasis now placed on the difference between fancy and judgment, the assertion of nature and artifice as opposites, and the banishing of both artifice and philosophy from poetry.

Having defined judgment and fancy (the products of memory, which is the product of experience) as the joint begetters of a poem, Hobbes goes on to detail the relationship between fancy and philosophy. Hobbes indicates two dimensions of this relationship; man's works of artifice are the joint product of his fancy and his philosophical sense, and while sometimes these works of artifice are produced by fancy tracing the ways of philosophy, other times fancy undertakes both roles. The value of fancy comes from its "wonderful celerity" , which consists, Hobbes says,[62] not so much in motion as in copious Imagery discreetly ordered and perfectly registred in the memory, which most men under the name of Philosophy have a glimpse of, and is pretended to by many that, grossly mistaking her, embrace contention in her place. But so far forth as the Fancy of man has traced the ways of true Philosophy, so far it hath produced very marvellous effects to the benefit of mankinde. All that is beautiful or defensible in building or marvellous in Engines and Instruments of motion, whatsoever commodity men receive from the observations of the Heavens, from the description of the Earth, from the account of Time, from walking on the Seas, and whatsoever distinguisheth the civility of Europe from the Barbarity of the American savages, is the workmanship of Fancy but guided by the Precepts of true Philosophy. But where these precepts fail, as they have hitherto failed in the doctrine of Moral vertue, there the Architect, Fancy, must take the Philosophers part upon her self. He therefore that undertakes an Heroick Poem, which is to exhibit a venerable and amiable Image of Heroick vertue, must not only be the Poet, to place and connect, but also the Philosopher, to furnish and square his matter, that is, to make both Body and Soul, colour and shadow of his Poem out of his own Store.

Thus the importance of the relationship between fancy and philosophy is that together, in joint operation, they produce the works of artifice that represent the achievements of civility. Poetry, a work of artifice that is concerned with moral virtue, also depends upon this necessary cooperation; and in poetry so described, fancy takes the philosopher's part upon herself.

This passage significantly recalls Sidney's discussion of poetry in relation to other forms of knowledge, in which he concluded that poetry excels over other forms of knowledge in the teaching of moral virtue because it combines the gifts of nature and man's artifice in the most pleasing and most intelligible form. Sidney is also recalled where Hobbes contends that "the subject of a Poem is the manners of men, not natural causes; manners presented, not dictated; and manners feigned, as the name of Poesy imports, not found in men".[63] What emerges from these two statements of Hobbes', then, is a notion of poetry closer to that of Sidney and Spenser than to the neoclassicists, in which the "copious Imagery discreetly ordered and perfectly registred in the memory" of fancy and the "precepts" of philosophy combine, in a form of knowledge which teaches moral virtue through the presentation of the manners of men in fictional circumstances. Together, Hobbes' conceptions of the value of fiction in knowledge and the joint operation of fancy and philosophy in artifice, undercuts any reading of Hobbes which seeks to deny the importance of the connections in his thinking between poetry and philosophy, imagery and precepts, and nature and artifice.

Hobbes goes on, in the Answer, to argue that a poet must both 'know well' and 'know much'; these together "giveth a Poem the true and natural Colour".[64] This distinction, while related to that between fancy and judgment, is not the same as it. To 'know well' is to have "images of nature in the memory distinct and clear" which both delight and instruct.[65] And a sign of 'knowing much' is found in "novelty of expression" which "pleaseth by excitation of the minde; for novelty causeth admiration, and admiration curiosity, which is a delightful appetitie of knowledge".[66] Thus 'knowing much' also both delights and instructs. After cautioning that there are "so many words in use at this day in the English Tongue, that though of magnifique sound, yet (like the windy blisters of a troubled water) have no sense at all",[67] Hobbes identifies the use of figurative language as within the compass of 'knowing much':[68]

> From Knowing much, proceedeth the admirable variety and novelty of Metaphors and Similitudes, which are not possible to be lighted on in the compass of a narrow knowledge. And the want whereof compelleth a Writer to expressions that are either defac'd by time or sullied with vulgar or long use. For the Phrases of Poesy, as the airs of musick, with often hearing become insipide, the Reader having no more sense of their force then our Flesh is sensible of the bones that sustain it. As the sense we have of bodies consisteth in change and variety of impression, so also does the sense of language in the variety and changeable use of words. I mean not in the affectation of words newly brought home from travail, but in new and with all significant translation to our purposes of those that already received, and in far fetch't but withal apt, instructive, and comely similitudes.[69]

It is clear from the analogy Hobbes uses in this passage that the "admirable variety" of language in which a poem is expressed is to be understood, like the sounds of music and like the flesh that is sustained by the bones of the body, as an integral part of the whole - not an addition, or (separate) ornament, or embellishment. While the language of a poem may be distinguished from the conceptions expressed in it, the character of the poem - as an expression - is necessarily a combination of the two interacting. In each case, the two members of the pair sustain each other, and the character of the whole - the poem, the music, the body - depends upon the relation between the two.

Furthermore, while figurative language in a poem proceeds from 'knowing much', 'knowing well' also involves, for Hobbes, a metaphorical process, since it consists not of nature itself or facts about nature or thoughts about nature, but of *images* of nature in the memory. When 'knowing well' and 'knowing much' are both knowledge and both involve metaphor, it readily follows that both perform the double role of delighting and instructing, as Hobbes has argued.

Fancy and judgment are, for Hobbes, capacities natural to all men, and knowing much and knowing well are, for him, dimensions of the knowledge that man can cultivate through his experience and memory. Neither of these distinctions correspond to or may be reduced to our modern distinctions between 'language' and 'pure ideas' or form and content, nor to the neo-classical distinction between 'plain' and figurative language. In Hobbes' terms in the Answer, figurative language is not simply the product of fancy, but a joint product of the cooperation between fancy and judgment, the fit and apt expression of precepts judged appropriate to the subject in imagery drawn from the fund of 'copious imagery' of the fancy. And metaphor is not simply the product of 'knowing much', but is involved in both 'knowing much' and 'knowing well', such that the images of nature are expressed in the metaphors of language.

Thus Hobbes' statement that "Judgment begets the strength and structure, and Fancy begets the ornaments of a Poem", may now be understood to depend, as it did in Medieval and Elizabethan literary theory, upon a conception of poetry which was closely connected to philosophy, in which fancy and judgment cooperate together to form a poem which as a whole both delights and instructs. Hobbes' statement on fancy and judgment recalls Sidney's argument that even Plato was a poet, for in the "body of his work, though the inside and strength were philosophy, the skin as it were and beauty depended most on poetry". In both writers, reference is being made, not to the modern distinction between form and content, but to the criterion of decorum, or as Hobbes calls it in his Preface to his translation of Homer's Odysses of 1675, discretion, which prescribed that a writer's chosen 'causes' or 'precepts' are expressed in the language best fitted to teach and delight and whose meaning is inseparable from their expression. Hobbes' condemnation of words that "though of magnifique sound, yet (like the windy blisters of a troubled water) have no sense at all", as well as possibly referring to the language of the "Schoolmen", is also directed at poets whose use of figurative language obscures the connection between expression and meaning that is prescribed by decorum or discretion. And while Sidney's statement refers to 'philosophy' whereas Hobbes' refers to 'judgment', it is clear from Hobbes' consideration of the relationship between fancy and philosophy, discussed earlier, that judgment, the ability to judge the appropriateness and validity of expression to meaning and subject matter, is a prime component of what is comprehended by a philosophical sense, and is the component of philosophy most necessary for a poet to have and crucial to the writing of poetry.

Hobbes' only important departure from the earlier view comes from the limits he places on "exorbitant" fictions in poetry. And even this difference is less fundamental than it at first appears. For, in the first place, as has been noted earlier, Hobbes' restriction of the poet to the 'conceived possibility of nature' signifies a scope which encompasses the products of man's artifice, which includes the fictions produced by the "wonderful celerity" of fancy in images compounded from experience in memory, and only excludes those fictions in which the connections with experience have been lost and which are, in consequence, unintelligible to the reader. Again the importance of the poet's adherence to discretion or decorum, in the clarity of the connection between meaning and expression, is at issue, rather than the neo-classical advocacy of the 'natural' as opposed to the 'artificial'. And in the second place, Hobbes' condemnation of "exorbitant" fictions has only an indirect effect on the use of figurative language. For Hobbes, fictions come within the scope of 'knowing well', the images of nature which are expressed in the metaphors of language that are part of 'knowing much'. Thus the greater a writer's facility with language, the better his ability to express the images of nature registered in his memory; and the wider his experience, the richer his fund of "copious imagery" to express in language. It follows that in condemning "exorbitant" fictions, Hobbes is not condemning the use of figurative language but its misuse, whereby the ability of words to express meaning is abused because there is no meaning, no clear sense, but only obscurity, for them to express. Thus the object of Hobbes' condemnation is not the poet's use of his fancy, but his lack of judgment; his error is not that he does not 'know much' but that he does not 'know well'. In the Answer then, Hobbes explicitly advocates the cultivation of figurative language,[70] and his attacks on the misuse of language are levelled not at the use of figurative language as such, but at the uses which indicate that the connection between expression and meaning has been obscured or lost, due to a lack of judgment on the part of poets who do not recognise the importance of a philosophical sense in the writing of poetry.

The third point raised by Watson's article brings us back to the central argument of this chapter, that the importance for Hobbes of the connection between poetry and philosophy both accounts for his appeal to neo-classical literary critics, and identifies his thinking a 'transitional' between the earlier and the full-fledged neo-classical views.

The confusion that is evident in modern discussions of Hobbes' statement on literary theory and practice, and the consequent mis-interpretation of Hobbes' views by modern commentators on the history of literary criticism, is compounded by the nature of the appeal of Hobbes' approach to poetry to the later neo-classicists. As Watson rightly points out, Hobbes' approach to poetry is not aesthetic but intellectual; his criteria for poetry are extra-literary.[71] And it was precisely because his statement was based on philosophical rather than aesthetic or artistic grounds, that it appealed to and was taken up by English neo-classical theorists like Dryden. As argued earlier, Hobbes offered a connection between philosophy and poetry which filled the gap left by the neo-classical rejection of the Elizabethan terms of the connection between the two. In the context of neo-classical thinking in 1650, the connection presented by Hobbes seemed different enough from the earlier one to appeal to neo-classical critics, but in the light of the rationalistic theory that later emerged, in which the relation between literature and philosophy is discussed in order to establish the severance between the two, Hobbes can be recognised as holding a view which is transitional in character.

Hobbes dissented from several other neo-classical doctrines, often on grounds which again come directly from his philosophical approach. But on these points his views were not favourably received by neo-classical theorists. Hobbes also took the opportunity afforded by writing the Answer to air some of his enduring grievances, whose relevance to poetry was at best tenuous. Before concluding this chapter it is worth noting some of these points, since they demonstrate perhaps most clearly that the limits of Hobbes' neo-classicism lie precisely in the philosophical character of his interest in literary theory and practice.

In the Answer Hobbes exhibits a view of the necessarily didactic function of poetry in much stronger terms than those current among the neo-classicists. His discussion of the spiritual authority exercised by ancient poets, and their invocations of the Muses, shows a distinctly sympathetic understanding of the earlier notion of poetry, thereby going against the grain of neo-classical reinterpretation of Ancient and Medieval literary theory. Hobbes rejects the definition of poetry which equates it with verse, and sets up his own broad classification of the kinds of poetry, corresponding to Court, City and Country, with narrative and dramatic divisions in each. He pours scorn on "unskilful divines" who raise discord, fraud, tumult and controversy by their sermons, which subverts the peace of the commonwealth,[72] and attacks the "palpable darkness" of ignorance fostered by the Schools[73] - points which have little or nothing to do with poetry. Furthermore, as Spingarn notes, Hobbes "unlike his more orthodox contemporaries, does not give to the logical structure of a poem the same sort of exaggerated importance that the theorists of art for art's sake have given to the externals of style; he cares nothing for the rules which the French" neo-classicists had developed, and "has serious doubts about a fixed standard of taste".[74] Finally, with his rejection on principle of subservience to the authority of books ("the ordinary boxes of Counterfeit Complexion....not to be used without examination unadvisedly")[75], and so to neo-classical rules governing literary practice, Hobbes diverged from orthodox neo-classical thinking, and its increasingly rationalistic temper.[76]

One of the aims of this chapter has been to demonstrate that a poem like the *Faerie Queene* deserves to be taken seriously, in terms of its allegorical character and the philosophical basis of its literary presuppositions. The two main obstacles to this assessment being accepted, faced by a modern reader of Medieval and Elizabethan poetry, are the initial unfamiliarity with the sort of context of presuppositions in which such poetry makes sense, and the necessity of breaking through the neo-classical reinterpretation of Medieval and Renaissance literary practice and theory, which was largely unquestioned in the following centuries and set the perspective inherited by the modern reader. This chapter has been concerned to argue that this perspective does not do justice to such poetry, and indeed impedes an appreciation of it in terms of the understanding common to Medieval and Renaissance poets and readers. The functions of allegory are, in particular, subject to misinterpretation, since allegory assumes a conception of 'life-likeness' which the modern reader is not accustomed to bear in mind as the guide into its understanding. The purpose of this discussion will become apparent when, in chapter 7, it is argued that Hobbes' *Leviathan* contains an allegory which also deserves to be taken seriously.

During the seventeenth century the connection between literary theory and practice, and the unified approach to the world that had supported it, was gradually undermined. Seemingly unprecedented political events, religious fragmentation, and new directions of intellectual interest all appeared to call into doubt, and to be no longer capable of being absorbed by and accounted for in terms of, the older certainties. Wholesale attack in some areas and piecemeal changes of emphasis in others, together seemed to make the older truths untenable and redundant. These developments ultimately resulted in what appeared to be a wholesale transformation, from the theologically-based certainties that had sustained the older view, to the rationalistic, scientific basis of certainty in the new. And while the area of certainty had become more circumscribed, within that area its certainties seemed no less confidently assured.

The transition from the old to the new was by no means straightforward. In retrospect, the transformation that took place looks, over the long term, fairly clear-cut and simple to characterise ('scientific certainties replaced theological ones'). But such judgments are made in terms of predecessor and outcome, the two relatively settled conditions that parenthesise the period of transition, using the vantage of hindsight to select from the mass of conflicting features only those which can later be seen as significant in establishing the new perspective. The period in which the transition took place is, on the other hand, characterised by confusion, bewilderment, ferment, obscurity, a ready acceptance of some novel features combined with a resolute attachment to some older features.[77] During the period of transition, the question of *from* what *to* what was by no means undisputed, obvious or manifest.

The second aim of this chapter, then, has been to identify Hobbes' statement on literary matters in the Answer of 1650, in terms of the overall change that literary theory and practice underwent in the seventeenth century, and to indicate what is involved in calling his views 'transitional'. In Hobbes, whose direct participation in the debate comes fairly early on, one can see both the strident advocacy of new principles ('probability', 'propriety', the principle of rational rules of structure, the condemnation of the supernatural and of "exorbitant" fictions), and assumptions which belong to the understanding of poetry of the earlier outlook (the relationship between poetry and philosophy, the scope of nature and artifice, the understanding of figurative language in terms of the expression of meaning as a result of the cooperation between fancy and judgment and 'knowing much' and 'knowing well'), in a view which is nevertheless coherent in its own terms of reference. Hobbes' involvement in the shift of the criteria of literary criticism, and the significance attributed to it, are of interest here because of the bearing they have on his understanding of the relation between literature, literary criticism and philosophy, and on his own style of writing political philosophy.

NOTES

1. In J. E. Spingarn ed., *Critical Essays of the Seventeenth Century*, Volume II, OUP, 1908. Davenant's Preface and Hobbes' Answer were published together, without *Gondibert* itself, in 1650, at Davenant's suggestion. At the time, only two of the projected five "acts" of the heroic poem had been completed, and only three and a half were ever written. These first two "acts" were written by Davenant in Paris, under the close supervision which he had sought, of Hobbes.

2. Writers who have discussed the hierarchical, ordered, unified, theological and all-encompassing character of the view which persisted throughout the Medieval and Renaissance period include A. O. Barfield, *Saving the Appearances*, Faber, 1957; W. H. Greenleaf, *Order, Empiricism and Politics*, OUP, 1964; C. S. Lewis, *The Discarded Image*, CUP, 1964; M. Murrin, *The Veil of Allegory*, Univ. of Chicago Press, 1969; E. M. W. Tillyard, *The Elizabethan World Picture*, Chatto & Windus, 1960; and R. Tuve, *Elizabethan and Metaphysical Imagery*, Univ. of Chicago Press, 1947, and *Allegorical Imagery*, Princeton Univ. Press, 1966.

3. The edition used is that of J. C. Smith and E. De Selincourt, *The Poetical Works of Edmund Spenser*, OUP, 1912
4. C. S. Lewis, *The Allegory of Love*, OUP, 1936
5. *ibid* p48
6. *ibid* p48
7. *ibid* p115
8. Murrin, *op.cit.* p56
9. For example, "Spenser said Gloriana, but his audience thought of the English monarch and actually put his judgment into effect". *ibid* p65
10. R. Tuve, "Allegorical Imagery", in P. J. Alpers ed., *Edmund Spenser A Critical Anthology*, Penguin, 1969, p320-1
11. One of the best examinations of the presuppositions of Medieval and Elizabethan poetry is found in Tuve, *Elizabethan and Metaphysical Imagery, op. cit.*, which is acknowledged as a standard in this field, and in which the whole subject is exhaustively analysed with great care.
12. Tuve, *ibid* p37
13. *ibid* p66
14. Lewis, *The Allegory of Love, op.cit.* p358
15. Sir Philip Sidney, *An Apologie for Poetrie*, London, printed by James Roberts for Henry Olney, 1595, pages unnumbered.
16. W. K. Wimsatt & C. Brooks, *Literary Criticism*, Vintage Books, New York, 1957, p169
17. Alpers, *op.cit.* p18
18. Perhaps the most notable example of the Medieval impulse to absorb all comers, is found in their Christianising of the whole classical corpus. L. G. Janik, "Lorenzo Valla: the primacy of rhetoric and the de-moralisation of history", *History and Theory*, Vol. XII (1973), discusses another example of the "heterogeneous" character of "humanist culture", p398
19. Wimsatt & Brooks, *op.cit.* p150
20. T. Rymer, preface to his translation of Rapin's *Reflections on Aristotle's Treatise on Poesie*, 1674, in Alpers, *op.cit.* p73
21. Murrin, *op.cit.* p167-8
22. *ibid* p170
23. *ibid* p170
24. *ibid* p170-1
25. *ibid* p171
26. Milton, *Areopagitica*, 1644, in Alpers, *op.cit.* p62
27. Jonson, *Timber, or Discoveries*, c.1636, *ibid* p56
28. Dryden, *Discourse Concerning Satire*, 1692, *ibid*
29. Digby, *Concerning Spenser that I wrote at Mr. May's Desire*, 1638, *ibid* p58
30. Davenant, Preface to *Gondibert*, 1650, *ibid* p63
31. Alpers, *op.cit.* p17
32. Wimsatt & Brooks, *op.cit.* p179
33. Spingarn, *History of Literary Criticism in the Renaissance*, Columbia Univ. Press, New York, 1908, p271
34. Tuve, *Elizabethan and Metaphysical Imagery, op.cit.* p386
35. *ibid*, p336
36. *ibid*, p342
37. Wimsatt & Brooks, *op.cit.* p228
38. Spingarn, *Critical Essays*, Vol. II, *op.cit.* p54-5
39. *ibid* p64
40. *ibid* p62
41. *ibid* p57 Hobbes is here referring to a fashion for placing the words of a poem such that they form the oval shape of an egg etc.
42. *ibid* p59
43. *ibid* p59
44. Spingarn, *Critical Essays*, Vol. I, OUP, 1908, pxxix
45. Spingarn, *History of Literary Criticism in the Renaissance, op.cit.* p259
46. C. M. Dowlin, *Sir William Davenant's 'Gondibert'*, Philadelphia, 1934, p45
47. Wimsatt & Brooks, *op.cit.* p246
48. *ibid* p253-4
49. G. Watson, "Hobbes and the Metaphysical Conceit", in *Journal of the History of Ideas*, Oct. 1955, p561
50 *ibid* p560
51. *ibid* p559

52. *ibid* p561
53. *ibid* p560
54. *ibid* p561
55. *ibid* p562
56. *Leviathan*, ed. M. Oakeshott, Blackwell, Oxford, 1946, p6
57. *ibid* p40
58. *ibid* p466
59. T. M. Gang, "Hobbes and the Metaphysical Conceit - A Reply", in *Journal of the History of Ideas*, Vol. XVII (1956), p419
60. Wimsatt & Brooks, *op.cit.* p232
61. Spingarn, *Critical Essays*, Vol. II, *op.cit.* p62-3
62. *ibid* p60
63. *ibid* p56
64. *ibid* p63
65. *ibid* p63
66. *ibid* p63
67. *ibid* p63
68. *ibid* p65
69. *ibid* p65
70. *ibid* p60, 65
71. Although Watson's identification of that extra-literary approach an empiricist in character, has been challenged.
72. *ibid* p58-9
73. *ibid* p63
74. Spingarn, *Critical Essays*, Vol. I, *op.cit.* pxxxiii
75. Spingarn, *Critical Essays*, Vol. II, *op.cit.* p62
76. Spingarn, *Critical Essays*, Vol. I, *op.cit.* pxxxvi
77. For instance, seventeenth century scientists did not abandon a belief in alchemy; and Hobbes' own classification of the subjects of knowledge in chapter 9 in *Leviathan* includes astrology.

CHAPTER 4
Hobbes on Language and Rhetoric

In studying *Leviathan*, language and rhetoric are themes, sometimes a single theme, that recur throughout the work. This chapter is both about Hobbes' theory of language and view of rhetoric, and about one aspect of Hobbes' rhetoric in *Leviathan* - the obvious paradox that Hobbes seems to categorically argue against figurative language in philosophy, while at the same time expressing his own philosophical argument in at times distinctively figurative language. The paradox dissolves, it is argued, when the different strands of Hobbes' thinking can be seen as expressed in the different levels of argument in the text. His views on language, rhetoric and philosophy in *Leviathan* can then be understood as transitional.

For Hobbes, the question of language is crucial in the philosophical study of both man and political society. In the first chapters of *Leviathan* there is a train of reasoning in which the character of language is discussed, and which is directed to elucidating the power of words to disclose (or even, in one sense, to create) the order of the universe in which man lives.

But Hobbes' theory of language, developed in the course of the argument of the opening chapters of *Leviathan*, seems to lead to two quite different conclusions about metaphor and other figurative language in philosophy. The first concern of this chapter is to examine these two interpretations, and to consider whether they are irreconcilable.

The reading which sees metaphor as fundamental to philosophy begins with the observation that for Hobbes the discussion of language starts with sense, in the first chapter; and with the further observation that in the first three chapters he is dealing with the faculties natural to man, and then with what is acquired and increased by study and industry by the artifice of man. In chapter 1, Hobbes states that sensations produced by awareness of external objects, causes fancies in the brain and heart.[1] In chapter 2, he says that fancy or imagination is decayed sense, or decayed sense in the memory; that much memory or memory of many things is experience; and that from memory compound images are made. And in chapter 3,

Hobbes continues that trains of thought constitute mental discourse and are made of a succession of images or fancies.

It is interesting to note here that Hobbes nowhere defines a thought; thought and thinking are simply introduced into the argument. Given Hobbes' passion for the definition of terms, this absence suggests that Hobbes did not see it as necessary to separately define thought and thinking. From the context, it is clear that a thought is the same as an image or fancy. And this is the first of two points which support the reading in which metaphor is an irreducible component of philosophy for Hobbes. For if a thought is an image and if trains of thought are trains of images, then mental discourse is composed of nothing else but images and compound images formed from the memory. Indeed, chapter 3, in which Hobbes discusses trains of thought, is entitled "Of the consequence or train of imaginations", not of thoughts. The term 'image', for Hobbes, covers the whole range of perceptions and conceptions in the "brain and heart",[2] recorded in the memory, and so covers both simple and complex images, both representational and non-representational images, and both visual and non-visual images, in an undifferentiated fund. For Hobbes, thinking is pre-linguistic, and thus it follows that thinking which is philosophical, in common with all other thinking, is composed of images drawn from the whole range of the common fund. According to Hobbes' theory, then, philosophical thinking (distinguished only later from other kinds, and by its procedure, not its component elements) employs pre-linguistic images, the most significant of which, because they are the most complex, are thoroughly metaphorical in character.

The second point follows from Hobbes' explanation, still in chapter 3, that trains of thought unguided occur when there is "no passionate thought", and trains of thought guided are moved, governed and regulated by "some desire, or design".[3] Desire is motion that produces thoughts of how to reach what is aimed at, trains of thought indicating the means to achieve the object of the desire. In sum, says Hobbes, mental discourse governed by design is nothing but seeking, the seeking of the causes of effects or of the effects of causes, from within one's fund of experience; that is, fund of images. Much experience can result in prudence. And Hobbes stresses that only sense, thoughts and trains of thoughts are faculties natural to man, and all motion in man's mind is composed of these. Thinking, then, is not only entirely composed from a series of images from the memory, but is also propelled or driven by a governing passion or desire. There is a necessarily passionate element in all thinking. And there is nothing here to suggest, and no room for, a mutually exclusive distinction in Hobbes between 'pure ideas' and 'feelings',[4] or between a train of thought and a train of imagery. Ideas are compounded images - that is, metaphors - reached in fulfilment of a desire.

The significance of this aspect of Hobbes' theory, for the role of metaphor in philosophy, lies in the conclusion that the development of a specific train of thinking is a function of the particular passion governing a particular man, towards a particular object or end. The desire or design for a particular end or object precedes the development of the train of thinking by which it is reached or fulfilled. This conclusion from Hobbes' theory severely demotes the role of logic in thinking, for logic plays no part in the realm of desire, and is restricted to the secondary role of judging the validity of the connections made in the train of thinking. The object of the desire itself precedes the train of thinking, and so precedes the realm in which logic operates. In philosophical thinking, the object of the desire - which Hobbes later specifies as the desire to know - must, then, be a particular image, since according to Hobbes all desires are directed at particulars, and so the desire to know in philosophy must be the desire to know some particular thing; and philosophy, the knowledge of consequences, is an activity which takes place in the mind, whose only component elements are images. An example of the kind of image which might be the object of the desire to know in philosophy, is Hobbes' own image of the figure of the Leviathan, the single image of multiple significance, which is a metaphor. The manner in which this image may be understood to both precede and be the conclusion of his inquiry, and how this process corresponds to his resolutive-compositive method, in *Leviathan*, will be discussed in chapter 7.

Sense, fancy, imagination, thinking, memory, understanding and desire are, then, the common ground of all internal activity (both intellectual and emotional) in man, and up to this point such activity is undifferentiated. And thinking, according to Hobbes, always involves 'feelings', on two counts. For firstly, thinking is not derived from a separate line of development from the passions, but from the single source, of fancies in the brain and heart.[5] And secondly, thinking contains a passionate element - in thinking, man does not break free from the passions into a world of 'pure ideas', but is governed by his passions, for the images that compose trains of thought are propelled by "some desire, or design".

In the next three chapters, Hobbes discusses the effects of artifice on this common stock of natural faculties and motion. Chapters 4 and 5 take up the branch which deals with the cultivation of speech, reasoning and science, and chapter 6 deals with the branch concerned with specifying the passions and the forms of speech in which they, by themselves, are expressed.

In chapter 4, Hobbes introduces the notion of speech, and with it the beginning of the working of artifice, by which man's natural faculties and motion are increased and extended by study and industry. With speech - a voluntary motion - men enter a public world, and so civilisation in commonwealths, which are societies governed by contracts and peace. For this first reading of Hobbes' theory, the most important point about speech is that with speech mental discourse is "transferred" to verbal discourse;[6] trains of thought become trains of words. Speech is names and their connections, and words serve as marks and signs - marks of remembrance and signs of one's thoughts and feelings. The crucial word here is "transferred", for it indicates that the expression of thinking in language in no way alters the character of thinking. In language, men register and signify - express - their thoughts and feelings.

Hobbes then turns to consider the public character of language, for the communication of thinking - its understanding by others - requires the use of words whose significations are shared and not of only private signification. A definition, then, is the settling of the signification of a word, and definitions are the beginning of reckoning in science. Absurdity, like truth and falsehood, is the product of speech, not of thinking;[7] and reasoning (as Hobbes remarks in chapter 5, "not, as sense and memory, born with us; nor gotten by experience only, as prudence is; but attained by industry"[8]) is right reckoning in words. The two sorts of insignificant words (when meaning is not explained by the definition, and when significations are contradictory and inconstant) occur whenever words do not express meaning. Insignificant speech is defined by Hobbes in chapter 8 as "when men speak such words, as put together, have in

them no signification at all"; words "without any thing correspondent to them in the mind".[9] In other words, insignificant speech results from unclear expression of thinking, when language does not
express thinking. That the connection between expression and meaning should be clear was a major principle of rhetoric, in the tradition
of rhetorical handbook literature, summed up in the prescription of
decorum or discretion. Hobbes' view here can be understood in
terms of this tradition. And understanding, for Hobbes, occurs
when a person "upon the hearing of any speech, hath those thoughts,
which the words of that speech and their connection were ordained
and constituted to signify";[10] that is, when the shared meaning of
words express the meaning of thinking.

It becomes apparent in chapter 5 that the brunt of Hobbes'
attack on insignificant and absurd speech, is directed against the
Schoolmen, who speak of 'immaterial substances' and 'free will',[11]
which, according to Hobbes, signify self-contradictory conceptions
and so are non-sense or nonsense.

In chapter 6, Hobbes takes· up the branch of man's internal
activity which is concerned with the expression of the passions in
speech - when what is to be expressed in language is not a train of
thinking propelled by a passion, but the character of a passion itself,
a train of words which express the passion itself. He divides the
passions into those of sense and those of the mind; both prudence
and science belong to the second kind. Hobbes discusses the desire
to know as one form of passion, and thereby reaffirms the importance
of the passionate element in all thinking and utterance. And he
comments that speech of deliberation of the passions "differs not
from the language of reasoning, save that reasoning is in general
words; but deliberation for the most part is of particulars",[12] thereby
reaffirming the common stock from which reasoning and deliberation
develop.

In sum, according to this reading, there is nothing to suggest
that philosophical thinking expressed in language overcomes or
escapes its basis in images and metaphor. The constituents of all
thinking are images, and language simply "transfers" thinking into
words. Thus it follows that while some images are properly signified
by and expressed in literal words ('man', 'horse', 'table'), other
images will be properly signified by and expressed in figurative
language. Two examples of the second kind might be the simple

image of reasoning as "the light of human minds",[13] and the word "Leviathan" to express the meaning of the complex image or thought in the mind, of a particular type of commonwealth, where the word 'commonwealth' by itself does not express what is meant by the image or thought. Since Hobbes does not distinguish between images and thoughts, and since 'images' covers conceptions, some of which are properly expressed in literal and others in figurative language, the use of figurative language in philosophy is valid, according to Hobbes' theory, whenever the meaning of a conception in the mind is best and most clearly expressed in this manner.

The second reading of Hobbes' theory of language leads to the conclusion that figurative language has no place in philosophy at all. It begins by noting Hobbes' condemnation of metaphor at several points in the course of the first chapters of Leviathan. In chapter 4 for instance, Hobbes writes that it is one of the abuses of speech to "use words metaphorically; that is, in other sense than that they are ordained for; and thereby deceive others".[14] And in the same chapter, after arguing that the names of the virtues and vices are inconstant, since their meanings are different for each person, Hobbes continues, "And therefore such names can never be true grounds of any ratiocination. No more can metaphors, and tropes of speech: but these are less dangerous, because they profess their inconstancy; which the other do not".[15] In chapter 5, Hobbes remarks that one kind of absurdity refers "to the use of metaphor, tropes, and other rhetorical figures, instead of words proper. For though it be lawful to say, for example, in common speech, 'the way goeth, or leadeth hither, or thither'; 'the proverb says this or that', whereas ways cannot go, nor proverbs speak; yet reckoning, and seeking of truth, such speeches are not to be admitted".[16] Later in chapter 5, after the comment that the "light of human minds" (sic) comes from reason and science, Hobbes says, "And, on the contrary, metaphors, and senseless and ambiguous words, are like 'ignes fatui'; and reasoning upon them is wandering amongst innumerable absurdities; and their end, contention and sedition, or contempt".[17] In the following chapter, Hobbes discusses the point that scholastic philosophers consider there to be no motion in appetite and says, "but because some motion they must acknowledge, they call it metaphorical motion; which is but an absurd speech: for though words may be called metaphorical; bodies and motions can not".[18] And in chapter

8, while Hobbes considers that in demonstration, counsel and all rigorous search for truth, an apt similitude is allowed, he continues that, "But for metaphors, they are in this case utterly excluded. For seeing they openly profess deceit; to admit them into counsel, or reasoning, were manifest folly".[19]

Hobbes' seemingly unconditional condemnation of metaphor in these passages, is qualified by noting several initial considerations. Firstly, the first condemnation in chapter 4 refers to the abuse that corresponds to the use of speech "to show to others that knowledge which we have attained, which is, to counsel and teach one another".[20] In this context, it is clear that the abuse consists in the obscuring (rather than showing) of that knowledge which we have attained, by the ambiguous or equivocal use of words. Several of Hobbes' other condemnations of metaphor can also be understood to refer to the deliberate or accidental ambiguous use of words, which cloud the meaning and expression of thinking.

Secondly, not all Hobbes' remarks about metaphor are condemnatory. In chapter 7 for instance, he says that "Afterwards, men made use of the same word [conscience] metaphorically, for the knowledge of their own secret facts, and secret thoughts".[21] This statement is not made as a condemnation of the way in which metaphor operates, but just as a statement of what happened, to which Hobbes does not take exception. And in chapter 8, Hobbes praises the ability to coin "new and apt metaphors", that those with the prized intellectual virtue of discretion have.[22]

In the third place, Hobbes distinguishes, in the quotation from chapter 6, between words and the perceptions of things they describe, and says that metaphor refers to the former but not the latter. His condemnation is directed at the use of the word 'metaphor' to describe "motion", not at its validity to describe the use of certain words.[23]

Fourthly, in the quotation from chapter 8, Hobbes distinguishes between 'similitudes' and 'metaphors', and allows the former a place in "demonstration, counsel and rigorous search of truth". By the word 'similitude' Hobbes might mean either similie or analogy, but either way the blanket condemnation of figurative language is diminished.

Furthermore, against Hobbes' condemnations of metaphor, must be placed the rich variety of metaphor and other figurative

language, which occurs in Hobbes' own use of language in *Leviathan*.
One explanation of this discrepancy might be that Hobbes was
unaware of his own use of language, but this is highly unlikely in
view of his concern with the theory of language, and the careful and
apposite use of language evident in Hobbes' own practice in the
writing of *Leviathan*. A second explanation might be that Hobbes
considered that his attacks were directed at an object of abuse of
which his own use of figurative language was not culpable. This
explanation gains support if all Hobbes' condemnations of metaphor
are taken to refer to either the ambiguous and equivocal use of words
(whether deliberate or accidental), which may reasonably enough
be called an abuse, or to the words used by the Schoolmen which are,
according to Hobbes, self-contradictory or nonsensical, or perhaps
to both these sources. Hobbes' antipathy towards scholastic philosophy is openly declared by him, and an attack on their vocabulary
is an obvious polemical weapon for him to use. And it may be argued
that Hobbes' own use of figurative language in *Leviathan* avoids both
these sources of "abuse".

These considerations do not, however, altogether absolve
metaphor from the pointed condemnation that Hobbes heaps upon
it. [24] And as well as these open censures of metaphor, there is also a
line of argument in Hobbes' theory of language which works against
any acceptance of metaphor in philosophy. According to this line of
argument, in chapter 5, the conclusions of reasoning reached by the
methods of geometry are "indisputable", [25] and the wisdom of science (which includes philosophy), when it follows the method of
geometry, is "infallible". [26] Since there is no place for metaphor in
geometry, there can be no place for it in philosophy either. Moreover, by defining philosophy as the knowledge of consequences, the
consequences of words in reasoning, Hobbes suggests that there can
be no philosophy before the artifice of speech and reasoning have
been established, that philosophy itself is a work of artifice rather
than part of the natural human condition, and that in being based
upon the definitions of words rather than the images of thinking
philosophy somehow enters a world of certainty.

However, when this argument is examined more closely, it is by
no means clear that metaphor need necessarily be denied in philosophy. In the first place, if the force of Hobbes' argument here is
against the equivocal use of words in reasoning, which renders the

reasoning uncertain by the obscurity of the meaning of its terms, then a metaphor whose meaning is not equivocal is not subject to this objection.

In the second place, Hobbes assumes that the subject-matter of philosophy is of the same kind as geometry. But whereas geometry is concerned with concretely representable angles and figures, philosophy is concerned with conceptions whose concrete expressions (in conduct) do not provide the kind of intelligibility required. The understanding of 'obligation' for Hobbes, for instance, depends not upon the observation of particular concrete actions, but on an image or thought in the mind, through which particular concrete actions become intelligible. It may be argued that geometry involves the same procedure, but the difference on the question of representational reference remains.[27] Thus metaphor may be appropriate to the description of images in philosophy while not, in this sense, to the angles and figures of geometry.

Thirdly, it may be argued that the analogy Hobbes uses between reasoning in geometry and reasoning in philosophy leads him to overestimate the role of strict deductive argument and to underestimate the role of other reasoning in philosophy. Reasoning as the addition and subtraction of parcels from cause to effects or effects to causes may characterise arithmetic, and geometry.[28] But the development and characterisation of a philosophical perspective may suffer if reduced to the single simple piece of argument found in arithmetic.

It is clear, in chapter 5 of *Leviathan*, that Hobbes wants to argue that the reasoning of science and philosophy leads to certainty because the words involved are all definitions, in contrast to the reasoning in prudence and opinion, where definitions but also "inconstant" names tainted by personal preferences (since, for Hobbes, what an individual calls good and bad cannot be generalised) are involved. The appeal for Hobbes of "the clarified world of mathematics"[29] is enormous. But in pursuing this argument, Hobbes seems to have overlooked the earlier part of his own train of thinking, whereby mental discourse is composed of images, is propelled by a desire or design, and is simply "transferred" into verbal discourse - all of which undermines the kind of certainty Hobbes wants to claim for reasoning in philosophy. It may even be argued that Hobbes' argument here can only be upheld at the expense of saying that there is no such thing as philosophical *thinking*, since for Hobbes thinking is pre-linguistic and philosophy is a product of speech.

Fourthly, Hobbes accounts for reasoning itself in terms of a metaphor of arithmetic, and his account of the knowledge which is philosophical is based on a metaphor of arithmetic and geometry, a procedure seemingly precluded by his argument. And finally, even if the argument for philosophical reasoning on the geometric model could be sustained, the aspect of Hobbes' theory whereby trains of thinking are propelled by a passion or desire towards ends which are particular to each man, effectively diminishes the necessary quality of a piece of reasoning, due to the element of each man's affective part in it.[30]

In sum, Hobbes' condemnations of the ambiguous use of words in the "search of truth" points to an object which fully deserves censure, and if all his strictures are taken to refer to this object, then the two readings of his theory need not lead to incompatible conclusions, for metaphor need not be ambiguous. But in order to reach this measure of reconciliation, the line of argument in Hobbes' theory which sees reasoning in philosophy on the model of geometry, and so banishes metaphor, has to be discounted. And, whatever the problems with that line of argument, its presence in Hobbes' theory cannot be denied.

One way of accounting for the divergent conclusions about metaphor in philosophy which follow from Hobbes' theory, may be to say that his thinking is incoherent, self-contradictory and inconsistent. However, it might be enlightening to consider instead the reasons for the divergence of the conclusions.

Although the role of metaphor in philosophy may seem an important feature of Hobbes' theory of language, in view of the number of his remarks about it and the space he devotes to images in the earlier part of his theory, it may be argued that the burden of his argument is elsewhere. For the overall force of Hobbes' thinking in his theory of language is clearly directed not at the language of philosophy, but at the very use of language in a public context. And in terms of this consideration, the argument which underlies the second reading of his theory of language begins to look highly significant. For what Hobbes is perhaps concerned with primarily, in his discussion of language, is the rhetorical effect of speech in civil society.

What is most important for Hobbes overall is not language, but speech. It is speech, spoken language in a public context, that represents the real watershed, for Hobbes, between the natural and artificial, between private and public,[31] and between the conclusions of prudence and those of science. In the Introduction to Leviathan God is said to have created the world by his *word*,[32] rather than by his thought or his intention, and at the end of chapter 15 Hobbes emphasises the significance of speech in the spoken word, for law. He says, "law, properly, is the word of him, that by right hath command over others";[33] this is distinguished from the laws of nature which are properly only the "dictates of reason", "conclusions", or "theorems". In law, as in other matters where the distinction between private and public is important, it is the *spoken* word which is crucial. The significance of this watershed, for Hobbes, lies in that, according to his view, it is the confusion of the private with the public and of opinion with truth, that is the source of major instability in civil society. Language is no more than the instrument, by which mental discourse is transferred into spoken discourse. It is the act of speaking, as a public action, that makes language significant for Hobbes, and from this point of view language itself is not for him of primary interest. Hobbes' theory of language has, then, a dual purpose - to indicate how words express thinking, and how speech affects men in the public world of civil society - and on the question of the role of metaphor, Hobbes' two concerns, governed as they are by different sets of considerations, lead to different conclusions.

The difference between the two readings, in other words, lies in that the first emphasises the connection between thinking and language, and the second stresses the connection between language and speech in the public world. For the second reading, the end of chapter 3 of *Leviathan* marks a watershed of crucial significance, while for the first reading nothing changes at this point other than that mental discourse is "transferred" into spoken. This difference can also be seen in the two ways that the word "ordained" may be understood in Hobbes' statement in chapter 4, that understanding occurs when a person "upon the hearing of any speech, hath those thoughts which the words of that speech and their connection were ordained and constituted to signify".[34] This may refer to the way an individual expresses thinking in language, where "ordained" means 'meant or intended by this speaker to signify'.[35] Or it may refer to the acknowledgement of the public character of a language, that its users recognise shared meanings which are not private but public meanings in common amongst users, and that to use language entails the observance of public rules and the acknowledgement of a public authority. If a man wishes his utterance to be understood, therefore, he must use language according to the publicly ordained meanings of words. And while any theory of language can be expected to take account, in some way, of the two aspects which affect its use - the individuals who use and enrich and change it, and its public and shared character - it is interesting that with Hobbes these two aspects operate not in concert but counter to each other.

The difference between the two readings is supported by the observation that Hobbes' condemnations of metaphor occur only from chapter 4 onwards - only when he begins to speak about the public and artificial world of speech, only when he introduces the notion of speech as a function of the public world and artifice, only after the transition from thinking to speech. The first reading, then, emphasises that part of Hobbes' theory which considers the natural faculties of man, where thinking is mental discourse composed of images and propelled by a desire, before artifice in the form of speech is introduced. The second reading emphasises Hobbes' concern with the power of speech to sway men's minds and passions, and instigate action disruptive of peace and stability, by abusing the publicly ordained meanings of words.

Thus, on the one hand, Hobbes holds that speech is no more than the transference of mental to spoken discourse, which leaves untouched the validity of unambiguous metaphor in philosophy, as outlined in the first reading. And, on the other hand, Hobbes holds that speech is a dangerous weapon of enormous power, whose abuse represents an abuse of authority, and whose use by citizens in public must therefore be restricted as far as possible to literal, that is authoritatively-ordained, meanings of words.

In the light of this argument it follows that, firstly, the object of Hobbes' attacks on metaphor is indeed those uses of language whose rhetorical effect determines their significance, and which are therefore abuses - such as the ambiguous use of words, the use of inconstant names, and the use of metaphor to intentionally deceive an audience and incite disruptive action. And secondly it follows that both readings of Hobbes' theory of language can be found in, and can co-exist in, his argument, according to whether attention is focussed on the role of metaphor in philosophical thinking expressed in language, or on the rhetorical effect of speech in civil society.

The consideration of Hobbes' theory of language thus brings us to the question of rhetoric, firstly because his concern with speech, the act of speaking, rather than with language, is a rhetorical concern; and secondly because Hobbes' stress on the passionate element in thinking has rhetorical consequences. For however important words are for Hobbes, the passions are more so. When Hobbes says, for instance, at the beginning of chapter 17, that "covenants, without the sword, are but words, and of no strength to secure a man at all",[36] he is pointing to the weakness of speech when a man's passion directs him to another object, and is arguing that the only way to control a man's passion - ultimately - is by the exercise of power in physical force. And it may be noted that Hobbes' conception of man differs from Aristotle's here, not in man's ability to use reason, but in the force of his passions. For Hobbes, men use reason to support their feelings of discontent with civil society; reason is a double-edged weapon, because it is at the service of the passions.[37]

The way in which thinking never escapes or transcends the passions, for Hobbes, is thus seen at two levels in *Leviathan*. For firstly, thinking itself, and so the grounds of philosophical reasoning, is always driven by a passion. And secondly, when the subject of the inquiry is man, as it is in civil philosophy, it is the purpose of philosophical reasoning to establish a framework of civil association in which the most powerful feature - men's passions - is harnessed; and to present a line of reasoning that appeals to this strongest feature by promising deliverance from that most terrible of fears, the fear of violent death, through appeal to the fundamental desire for self-preservation. For Hobbes, the recognition of that passion (and of the passions in general) as the basis on which civil association must rest, is expressed both in his notion of commonwealth, and in that his powerfully evocative account of the destructive potential of the passions is the basis of his appeal to convince each man who reads *Leviathan*. Hobbes appeals most strongly not to the reader's 'reason' but to his passion of fear; and he offers deliverance not through reason, but through the passion for self-preservation and felicity.

In chapter 25, Hobbes uses the potent metaphor of fire to indicate the danger to civil order that follows from the connection between the passions and speech, when he says, "For the passions of men, which asunder are moderate, as the heat of one brand; in an assembly are like many brands, that inflame one another, especially when they blow one another with orations, to the setting of the commonwealth on fire, under pretence of counselling it".[38]

Two initial points, then, may be made about Hobbes' concern with rhetoric in *Leviathan*. In the first place, his discussion of the passions, language and speech, indicates that he recognises the affective element in the use of language and its affective effect - the language is characteristically affective as well as being a medium of knowledge in prudence and science, and that it both arouses and is propelled by the passions as well as being able, at the same time, to lead to understanding. And secondly, Hobbes' concern with rhetoric, focussed on the connection between the passions, language and speech, is a thoroughly traditional concern. His attacks on the abuse of language may be understood to express not the modern rationalist's preface to a promise of deliverance through 'Reason', but the customary sensibility which grounded the body politic in the passions of men.

Thus rhetoric can be seen as central to Hobbes' political philosophy. And in terms of *Leviathan* as a whole, Hobbes' concern in developing a theory of language is, by indicating the significance of artifice, to be in a position to argue that in the world created by man's artifice there is an overwhelming need for a public authority, to firstly legislate on the meanings of words (to prevent the state of anarchy which would follow from the unchecked proliferation in public of private meanings, and the consequent loss of communication and understanding); and to secondly legislate in disputes between different reasonings, as well as between different judgments of good and evil. Hobbes argues in chapter 5 that "no one man's reason, nor the reason of any one number of men, makes the certainty ....When there is a controversy....the parties must....set up, for right reason, the reason of some arbitrator, or judge, to whose sentence they will both stand".[39] This is a fundamental level at which public authority is needed. And in chapter 6, Hobbes argues that good and evil are not absolutes, but are judgments made from the appetites and aversions of men towards and away from particular objects, which vary with different men. There is therefore a necessity to establish an arbitrator or judge, to set down rules of good and evil - either in the person of a man where there is no commonwealth or, in a commonwealth, from the 'person' that represents it.[40] Thus it is clear from Hobbes' discussion firstly, not only that reasoning and deliberation are analogous, but that the notion of authority is introduced not in chapter 16 of *Leviathan* but in chapters 5 and 6. The connection between the passions, language and speech, forms the pattern for all the arguments Hobbes later develops in *Leviathan* about the need for public authority in all aspects of civil society. Thus, secondly, the significance of Hobbes' argument in the first chapters only becomes fully apparent in the second Part of *Leviathan*.

The discussion of the features of civil society in the second Part, revolves around the relation between man and the artificial man that men have made and compose. Just one example of this constant point of reference occurs in chapter 21 where Hobbes considers "Artificial bonds, or covenants" in the following terms:[41]

> But as men, for the attaining of peace, and conservation of themselves thereby, have made an artificial man, which we call a commonwealth; so also have they made artificial chains, called civil laws, which they themselves, by mutual covenants have fastened at one end, to the lips of that man, or assembly, to whom they have given the sovereign power; and at the other end to their own ears.

But the central point in the relation between man and the artificial man of Leviathan is established in the last few chapters of the first Part, when Hobbes discusses obligation and authority. In chapter 14, Hobbes describes obligation as the transferring of a right.[42] And the final chapter of the first Part, which operates as a prelude to the discussion of civil society as well as pin-pointing the analogy between man and the artificial man of *Leviathan*, is that in which Hobbes explicitly considers the character of authority, the right of him to whom others have 'transferred' their right and so established the bond of obligation. In the argument of chapter 16, then, Hobbes' train of thinking proceeds from a 'person', to 'natural and artificial persons', to 'actor', to 'author', to 'authority', and so to 'covenants by authority' which bind the author but not the actor. And from this central notion of authority, the major themes in the discussion of civil society itself - sovereignty, civil rights and duties, power, the generation of the commonwealth, civil liberty, and civil law - may be seen to radiate.[43]

It is interesting to note that in Hobbes' discussion of obligation the vital word 'transferred' reappears, and that in his discussion of authority the crucial words are 'artifice', 'words' and 'actions'. Just as the significance of language, for Hobbes, lies in the 'transferring' of mental to spoken discourse, and in the actions that follow acts of speech, where speech is made by man's artifice, so the significance of authority lies in the "words or actions"[44] done by an artificial person representing many natural persons through the 'transference' of rights. The connection is yet closer, for it is through the artifice of authority that the danger of chaos inherent in the use of speech is to be overcome, for Hobbes.

But as well as setting the pattern for the centrality of authority in the argument of the second Part of *Leviathan*, Hobbes' concern with the rhetorical effects of speech in civil society itself remains an important theme in his discussion of the features of civil society.

Hobbes' attitude to rhetoric itself is twofold. On the one hand, rhetoric is described by Hobbes in chapter 9 as a science,[45] one of the consequences of speech in company with poetry, logic and jurisprudence, all of which form a subdivision of natural philosophy. And in chapter 8, Hobbes discusses the differences between the various disciplines according to the rhetoric appropriate to each, in terms of a balance between the categories of fancy and judgment. Furthermore, in his free translation of Aristotle's *Rhetoric*,[46] Hobbes closely follows the analytical approach of the original and the neutral attitude adopted by Aristotle towards the subject; and Hobbes' discussion of the variety of the passions in chapter 6 of *Leviathan* resembles those in Aristotle and the tradition of rhetorical handbooks. And in the preface to his translation of the *Iliads and Odysses of Homer*, Hobbes discusses the rhetorical qualities appropriate in heroic poems and, he says, "indeed in all writings published".[47] In the Review and Conclusion of *Leviathan*, Hobbes again expresses the thoroughly traditional prescription that rhetoric and dialectic should work together:[48]

in all deliberations and in all pleadings, the faculty of solid reasoning is necessary: for without it, the resolutions of men are rash, and their sentences unjust: and yet if there be not powerful eloquence, which procureth attention and consent, the effect of reason will be little.

And, he continues,[49]

So also reason, and eloquence, though not perhaps in the natural sciences, yet, in the moral, may stand very well together. For wheresoever there is place for adorning and perferring of error, there is much more place for adorning and preferring of truth, if they have it to adorn.

In chapter 25, furthermore, Hobbes demonstrates an acute awareness of the demands of the rhetorical context in which an utterance is made:[50]

where a man may lawfully command, as a father in his family, or a leader in an army, his exhortations and dehortations, are not only lawful, but also necessary, and laudable. But then they are no more counsels, but commands; which when they are for execution of sour labour, sometimes necessity, and always humanity requireth to be sweetened in the delivery, by encouragement, and in the tune and phrase of counsel, rather than in harsher language of command.

Finally, the last paragraph of Part 3 of *Leviathan*, Hobbes explicitly recognises another aspect traditionally considered under the name of rhetoric, the context of meaning in which utterances should be understood:[51]

For it is not the bare words, but the scope of the writer, that giveth the true light, by which any writing is to be interpreted; and they that insist upon single texts, without considering the main design, can derive nothing from them clearly; but rather by casting atoms of Scripture, as dust before men's eyes, make everything more obscure than it is; an ordinary artifice of those that seek not the truth, but their own advantage.

On the other hand, Hobbes is much preoccupied in *Leviathan* with the dangers for the stability of civil society, inherent in the rhetorical effects of language. The direst consequences have, and may again, follow from the wrong uses of words and names in speech. Hobbes' attacks on the insignificant and nonsensical speeches of the Schoolmen and on the absurd speeches of religious preachers to epitomise error in philosophy and theology following from lack of attention to right naming, are not just based on philosophical grounds for, in an association that reveals the profoundness for Hobbes of the connection between language and political stability or instability, he attributes rebellious speeches due to wrong naming as one of the major causes of the Civil War.[52] The connection between language and civil stability or instability forms, for Hobbes, a continuum, with anarchy or the state of nature at its extreme limit. Hobbes attaches enormous importance to this state of affairs, in *Leviathan*; indeed his theory can be seen as directed towards an answer to the question, 'how can the degeneration of the commonwealth and the return of the state of nature be prevented?'

Hobbes' answer is to underpin his relativistic view of reality, truth and meaning (which are functions of names not of things), with an absolute notion about the process of naming, according to which although the names chosen are arbitrary and reflect no higher or deeper rationality, once a set of names has been chosen (by the sovereign) and agreed to (by those who use language), their meanings are fixed and the world they not merely describe but also define is absolute. Hobbes is led to a view of language which seeks to find in language itself the means of eliminating the instability of the world by harnessing its relativistic power to a fixed set of names. Hobbes identifies the rhetorical effects of language in speech as the cause of instability in general, and thus naming (in his sense) as the fundamental remedy. In particular, he locates in speech the cause of, and in 'right naming' the cure of, that threat of civil war, endemic to the condition of men in commonwealths, which haunts the pages of *Leviathan*. Thus Hobbes is led to seek to abolish rhetoric altogether, to abolish the dangerous effects by abolishing the cause. This he does in the fixed absolute meanings of words in definitions - fixed by an act of authority.

In terms of his own theory of language, then, Hobbes' argument here is propelled most strongly not by the desire to know that characterises philosophy and science, but by a fear (ultimately the fear of violent death) and the corresponding passion or desire (to protect, make invulnerable, defend, guard and preserve).[53] Language is made a solely benign instrument by restricting its uses, fixing its meanings, congealing its scope - that is, by abolishing the whole range of its rhetorical effects. Thus the attacks on the speeches of the Schoolmen and others are significant on two different levels. They serve not only the philosophical purpose (whereby Hobbes holds that language is the means of expressing the meaning of thinking), but also the political purpose (whereby Hobbes holds that unrest and civil war may be prevented by censoring the public propagation of errors in speech) with which Hobbes is concerned.

Thus, while Hobbes describes rhetoric as one of the sciences that is concerned with the consequences of speech, he also seeks to abolish it.[54] Although Hobbes closely follows Aristotle's analytical treatment of rhetoric, he does not share the conviction held by the tradition of political thought following Aristotle, that the civil condition is identified by political discourse, that civil society entails that its members, as civies, relate to it in terms of persuasion, based on choices, rather than force. According to Hobbes, the persuasive aspect of political discourse is the very thing that threatens the continued existence of civil society; in his scheme, language in speech has become anaesthesised. However, this is not the whole of the matter; Hobbes remains tied to the Aristotelian tradition by virtue of seeing the issue of language in speech as at the centre of the political stage. Hobbes remains within the tradition in so far as he rejects the specific Aristotelian connection between language, speech and political life, without dismissing these things (and the passions behind them) as the fundamental categories to be accounted for in a political philosophy.

Hobbes' twofold attitude to rhetoric corresponds to his earlier recognition that language provides man with the means of expressing his thinking, but also provides the means for abuse. The latter consequence of the artifice of speech is cured by the artifice of authority. With respect to rhetoric, the solution Hobbes proposes is more drastic, the abolition of the rhetorical effects of speech altogether.

In the previous chapter, Hobbes' treatment of fancy and judgment in his Answer to Davenant's Preface to *Gondibert* was discussed. Fancy and judgment are terms which also play an important part in Hobbes' discussion of language, rhetoric and philosophy in *Leviathan*, and so deserve to be considered here.

Hobbes gives two accounts of fancy and judgment in *Leviathan*, one of which is similar in many respects to that provided in the Answer, the other of which is quite different.

In the Answer, fancy and judgment are portrayed as natural faculties. Fancy's value lies in its "wonderful celerity" and it consists of "copious Imagery discreetly ordered and perfectly registred in the memory". Judgment is the ability to judge the appropriateness and validity of expression to meaning and subject matter, a prime component of a philosophical sense. Fancy and judgment are born together of experience and memory - fancy provides the ornaments and judgment provides the strength and structure; using fancy the poet places and connects, and using judgment he furnishes and squares his matter.

In chapter 8 of *Leviathan*, Hobbes discusses fancy and judgment along similar lines. Fancy and judgment come under the heading of the intellectual virtues (and all virtues are comparisons) which are abilities of the mind that are praised and valued and desired by men, and are also called "good wit", although "wit" also refers to one particular of them. There is both natural and acquired wit; the former is gained from experience alone, and consists of "celerity of imagining" ("swift succession of one thought to another") and "steady direction to some approved end". Natural wit, furthermore, consists of comparisons in the seeing of similitudes and differences. Those who excel in seeing of similitudes are said to have a "good wit", which means a "good fancy"; those who excel in seeing differences and dissimilitudes are said to have a "good judgment", in judging, distinguishing and discerning. Fancy without the help of judgment is not commended as a virtue; but the latter is commended of itself without the help of fancy.[55] After discussing the roles of fancy and judgment in poetry, history, orations, pleadings, and demonstration, counsel and rigorous search of truth, Hobbes concludes that "where wit is wanting, it is not fancy that is wanting, but discretion. Judgment therefore without fancy is wit, but fancy without judgment, not".[56] Acquired wit, as one might expect, is that gained by "method and instruction", that is, reason, "grounded on the right use of speech, and produceth the sciences".[57]

In the course of the argument of chapter 8, Hobbes begins to veer towards another view, as the balance between fancy and judgment is eroded by the increasing pre-eminence accorded to judgment. But the connection between the two still rests in their interdependence. By Hobbes' second account of fancy and judgment, they are discussed not together but separately, and the connection between them is much less close. Fancy is defined in chapter 1 as decayed sense, in the memory, and is also called imagination. And judgment is defined in chapter 7 as "the last opinion in search of the truth of past, and future", the "resolute and final sentence of him that discourseth".[58] Judgment, moreover, is analogous to the function of will, the last appetite in deliberation of good or evil. In mental discourse the counters are opinions, which are thoughts; in deliberation (mental discourse of the passions themselves) the counters are the passions simply, towards and away, appetites and aversions, concerning good and evil. The two operations - mental discourse and deliberation - which are internal motions in man, are not only analogous, but are composed of the same motion. Hobbes says, "that which is alternate appetite, in deliberating concerning good and evil; the same is alternate opinion, in the enquiry of the truth of past, and future". The analogy extends therefore from between appetite and opinion, to between will and judgment, and to between the "chain of appetites" in deliberation and the "chain of opinions" in doubt.[59]

According to this second account in *Leviathan*, the relation between fancy and judgment is quite distant. And while in the Answer fancy and judgment are faculties natural to man, born of experience and memory, in this second account in *Leviathan* fancies are images, the fundamental building blocks in the heart and brain, that make up memory, not born of it; and judgment is neither an image nor a faculty, but simply a name given to the last opinion, which has a character no different from any earlier opinion but has a special name because of the place it occupies.

However, there is also an implicit argument in the first Part of *Leviathan* for the role of a natural judgment as a faculty of man. And, at the end of chapter 5, Hobbes speaks of "natural judgment",[60] which had not been introduced into the account earlier, unless it be taken to mean the wisdom of prudence from experience, under another name. From the context of chapter 5 this reading seems likely. It follows, however, that judgment is now of considerably greater significance than the chapter 7 description of it as merely the last opinion would suggest.

These two accounts of fancy and judgment in *Leviathan* can be seen to correspond to the two epistemological views on which Hobbes draws in the work. But while in some respects the first account is traditional and the second relatively novel, in other respects it is the second which follows the Medieval inheritance and the first which is unorthodox. Hobbes' first account follows the rhetorical tradition of Classical and Medieval writers in that fancy and judgment are faculties natural to man which cooperate in the construction of all the products of civilisation through man's artifice; while his second account, in which fancy and judgment are not directly related and in which judgment operates in a realm much more significant for philosophy,[61] expresses a view which was later developed into an approach that superseded the Medieval orthodoxy. But Hobbes' first account can also be seen as unorthodox, insofar as judgment begins to assume, in the discussion in chapter 8, a primacy that tends to displace the Medieval balance; while his second account can be seen as thoroughly traditional in the explicit connections that are made between judgment in mental discourse and will in deliberation. In the analogy that Hobbes draws, reasoning used in the "search of truth" is analogous to that used in deliberating good and evil.

Hobbes' views on language and rhetoric in *Leviathan* have affinities both with the traditional approach, which in the middle of the seventeenth century was still accepted as authoritative, and with the 'new scientific' approach that later claimed the mantle of orthodoxy; and since his theory as a whole may be characterised not as a pedestrian attempt to juggle disparate insights, but in terms of an imaginative grasp of the possibilities in the scope of his subject matter, Hobbes' thinking deserves to be called 'transitional' rather than incoherent.

The two sides of the transition may be described by drawing out from the whole those aspects of Hobbes' thinking which follow the inherited and the relatively novel approaches. On the one hand, then, his views that thinking is composed of trains of images propelled by a particular and particularised desire, that rhetoric has (following Aristotle) in itself a natural value, that the discussion of rhetoric involves the recognition of the passions as the basis on which a commonwealth must be established, that philosophical thinking is expressed in images such as that of the 'Leviathan', and that fancy and judgment are natural faculties which co-operate to produce the fruits of civilisation, may all be understood in terms of the traditional framework of understanding. On the other hand, Hobbes' views that speech is properly defined in terms of the publicly ordained definitions of words, that rhetoric should be abolished, that philosophy is the knowledge of consequences and whose conclusions have the certainty of those in geometry, and that fancy and judgment are divorced, with judgment of crucial importance in the reasoning of philosophy and fancy irrelevant to it, are all views which were later developed to help compose the 'scientific' approach to knowledge in the eighteenth century.

However, in terms of Hobbes' theory of language, speech and rhetoric in *Leviathan*, the two sides of this transition are expressed at different levels of his argument. Insofar as Hobbes explores the character of philosophical thinking, its expression in language and the discipline of rhetoric, his understanding may be placed within the context of the Classical and Medieval inheritance. But where Hobbes is concerned with the stability of the commonwealth and the threat to it which he sees arising from the oratory of the discontented, it is from arguments of the second kind that he draws his prescriptions. Hobbes' use of the relatively novel views he puts forward is not to expound modern methods for philosophy as such, but to underline the political conclusions to which he is committed. In consequence, while the views on the 'modern' side of the transition were later significant more for the way in which philosophy was conceived than for political thought, in *Leviathan* these views are used by Hobbes for the primary purpose of supporting an argument for the absolute authority of the sovereign in a commonwealth composed of 'passionate' men.

NOTES

1. In the *Elements of Philosophy, The First Section* (Molesworth, *op.cit.*, Vol. I, p91) of 1655, Hobbes makes it plain that philosophy begins not with sense as a merely physical phenomenon, but with perception as a psychological phenomenon. Confusion arises since both forms of inquiry about man's senses begin with the same subject matter, but the way they are viewed is different for each inquiry. Evidence in *Leviathan* to the same reading was discussed in the previous chapter.
2. *Leviathan*, p7. All page references to *Leviathan* are to the Oakeshott edition, Blackwell, Oxford, 1946.
3. *ibid* p14.
4. For Hobbes, the difference between 'thinking' and 'feeling' seems to be that thinking is a reflective activity that takes place in the 'brain and heart', whereas feelings (whether caused by external or internal sensations) are nonreflective and immediate 'motions' in the 'brain and heart'. But Hobbes does not spell out the difference.
5. And Hobbes does not say that those in the brain give rise to 'thinking' while those in the heart give rise to 'feeling'.
6. *Leviathan*, p18.
7. A view which places Hobbes firmly in the Nominalist tradition. L. G. Janik, "Lorenzo Valla: the primacy of rhetoric and the de-moralisation of history", *History and Theory*, Vol. XII (1973), p389-404, provides an absorbing account of another exponent of this view.
8. *Leviathan*, p29.

9. *ibid* p51.
10. *ibid* p24.
11. *ibid* p27.
12. *ibid* p38.
13. *ibid* p29.
14. *ibid* p19.
15. *ibid* p25.
16. *ibid* p28.
17. *ibid* p30.
18. *ibid* p32.
19. *ibid* p44.
20. *ibid* p19.
21. *ibid* p41.
22. *ibid* p44.
23. Hobbes' distinction between metaphor which applies only to words, and images which apply to our perceptions of things, thus differs from my use of the word metaphor to describe not only words but also complex images. The difference rests in that Hobbes sees thinking as pre-linguistic, a view to which I would not want to subscribe.
24. In Part 3 of *Leviathan* Hobbes mentions metaphor a number of times (p257, p260, p264, p266, p269, p271, p274, p298, p299, p304, p347). However, the distribution of condemnatory and neutral comments is fairly even. The reference in Part IV (p415) can be taken either way; those in Part II (p167, p169, p183, p233, p238) are again divided between condemnatory and neutral remarks.
25. *Leviathan*, p27.
26. *ibid* p26, p30.
27. In general, Hobbes is committed to the view that general words are names of words and names only. But at this point he tends towards the view of the Schoolmen, that such words actually represent 'things'.
28. It may also characterise what later became the governing conception of logic. But Hobbes' notion of philosophy cannot as a whole be assimilated to the modern conception of logic.
29. Iris Murdoch, *The Fire and the Sun*, Clarendon, Oxford, 1977, p75. The reference is to Plato, but is also appropriate to Hobbes.
30. In the *Elements of Philosophy*, Molesworth ed., *op.cit.*, pxi, Hobbes even calls the rules of philosophy "the opinions of private men".
31. The significance of this distinction for Hobbes' philosophy will be discussed further in chapter 7.
32. *Leviathan*, p5.
33. *ibid* p105.
34. *ibid* p24.
35. In line with Hobbes' statement in chapter 4 that the general use of speech is the personal one of serving as 'marks' of remembrance and 'signs' of one's thoughts and feelings, *ibid* p19.
36. *ibid* p109.
37. *ibid* p111 "Thirdly...."
38. *ibid* p170-1. It is interesting to note that in this passage, the effectiveness of Hobbes' use of language is enhanced by the economical technique of moving from similie to metaphor.
39. *ibid* p26.
40. *ibid* p32.
41. *ibid* p138. The significance of the language in which Hobbes describes the relation between man and commonwealth at points such as this one, is discussed in chapter 7.
42. *ibid* p86.
43. I do not want to suggest, however, that *Leviathan* is 'about' authority. This matter is discussed in the final chapter of the thesis.
44. *Leviathan*, p105
45. *ibid* p54-5.
46. Molesworth, ed., *op.cit.*, Vol. VI. Written perhaps in 1637, but published with two fragments on rhetoric posthumously in 1681 . It includes some passages from Aristotle's *Poetics* as well as from the *Rhetoric*.
47. Molesworth, ed., *op.cit.*, Vol. X. Written in 1677.
48. *Leviathan*, p460
49. *ibid* p461.
50. *ibid* p168.
51. *ibid* p396.
52. And in *Behemoth* (completed in 1668 and published in 1682), Hobbes contemptuously

calls that forum of public speech, a 'democratical assembly', "the goddess of rhetoric".
Molesworth, ed., *op.cit.*, Vol. VI, p250

53. This, incidentally, puts Hobbes' own discussion in the class of deliberation rather than reasoning, according to the terms of chapter 6 of *Leviathan* - of which he may or may not have been aware.

54. Since on this level Hobbes identifies rhetoric with all the errors of speech.

55. *Leviathan*, p43.

56. *ibid* p45.

57. *ibid* p46.

58. *ibid* p40.

59. *ibid* p40.

60. *ibid* p30.

61. the realm of 'reasoning.'

CHAPTER 5

Hobbes and The Engraved Title-Page of *Leviathan*

The engraved title-page[1] of *Leviathan* is regarded by most readers of Hobbes as a curiosity, a quaint but insignificant appendage to an otherwise serious discussion (however interpreted) of the generation, nature and characteristics of civil society. However, in the intellectual context in which Hobbes wrote and published *Leviathan*, the presence of an engraved title-page indicated neither a descent into the nursery nor into formally engaging but trivial embellishment, but was recognised as an integral part of the work's interest and enjoyment to the reader. Many of the engraved title-pages of this period are composed of complex images and allusions drawn from a thorough knowledge of the classics, Medieval Christian thought and contemporary intellectual currents, as well as from a knowledge of the work which the title-page prefaces. Such title-pages were designed by the author of the work, and translated into pictorial form by the engravers, and were addressed to the learned, whose appreciation of the manner in which learned sources had been used to convey the significance of the overall design, would be both intellectual and aesthetic. These title-pages are both instructive and entertaining, and their value lies in the content, the author's contribution. Where aesthetic and intellectual requirements conflict, it is the latter which prevail, resulting in some compositions which are, aesthetically, over-burdened but intellectually pleasing. The presence of an engraved title-page in a work like *Leviathan*, then, was not an anomaly in that period, but one of its characteristic features, an example of the interdependence of visual emblem and verbal expression in sixteenth and seventeenth century culture and thought.

Publications which were printed with engraved title-pages in the period c.1590-1690, cover the whole range of thinking expressed in language on cultural, intellectual and topical subjects, from official and government publications, programmes for ceremonial occasions such as the opening of parliament or the launching of ships, to religious books and bibles, scholarly treatises and monographs on a wide variety of subjects from the alleviation of deafness to scientific and philosophical questions, atlases and travel books, translations of classical texts, poetry, drama and literary criticism, to the broadsides distributed by both sides during the Civil War to spread news and propaganda. Examples of the popularity of allegorical engravings among scholarly works are found in the title-pages of Francis Bacon's *Instauratio Magna* (1620) and *Of the Advancement and Proficience of Learning* (1640), Burton's *Anatomy of Melancholy* (1618), Hooker's *Of the Laws of Ecclesiastical Polity* (1662), Browne's *Religio Medici*, and several of Hobbes' works.

The significance of the allegorical character of the engravings was understood to depend upon and correspond to the 'height' of the subject treated in the work. Their purpose was more than simply decorative and illustrative; the engravings functioned both to express in pictorial allegorical form the author's view of the major themes of the work and the relations between them, and to honour the author and his work. During the hundred years or so in which the convention of engraved title-pages flourished in England, the presence of a decorous and appropriate engraving in a scholarly work was considered as a dimension of the author's argument in the work, the complex images requiring a literary rather than an aesthetic interpretation to be understood. The manner in which this convention was practiced reminds the modern reader of the connection felt to exist between the verbal and pictorial arts, and between literary and pictorial understanding on the one hand and philosophy and science on the other - both aspiring to confirm the same order of significances - in the sixteenth and seventeenth centuries. The visual symbols of the author's thinking, chosen and designed as its most fitting emblems, constituted not a second language as it would in our modern understanding, but part of a single language in which to express one's thinking and argument.

Engravers working in England and Europe during this period can be divided into master craftsmen and hack workers. Master craftsmen generally operated on a freelance basis, either commissioned by authors directly or sometimes by wealthy patrons, and rarely worked directly for publishers or booksellers.[2] Some master engravers also became, after about 1600, print-sellers, keeping a stock of designs and portrait plates (especially of royal portraits) which booksellers could draw upon for use as the need arose. Hack workers were usually employed directly by publishing firms to provide engravings for title-pages, frontespieces and decoration for pages of print, for whatever was to be published. Engravers of both types could be called upon to do any sort of illustrative work - not only decorative ornaments and allegorical pictures, but also maps, natural science illustrations and scientific diagrams. Expertise in composing representations for artistic, decorative and scientific subjects was not differentiated as they are today. The common stock of iconographical symbols and images drawn upon by engravers for works on any subject, reflects the understood relation of all subjects to the same shared order of ultimate meaning. In general, of those engraved title-pages which still exist from this period, those which are anonymous are usually of inferior quality and can be attributed to the hack workers, whereas those which are signed are usually of superior quality and are acknowledged as the work of master craftsmen.

The responsibility for the designs of engraved title-pages lay in differing degrees with the three or four parties involved - author, publisher, artist and engraver. Where hack workers were used to execute the design, the responsibility lay generally with the publisher in consultation with the author, who would provide the engraver with verbal instructions. Where master craftsmen were involved, the components of the design were generally specified by the author in greater detail, to be arranged harmoniously by the engraver. In some cases, a sketch of the title-page would be made by an artist commissioned by author or publisher, and executed by an engraver, but most master craftsmen were artists as well as engravers. The author was likely to take a greater interest in the visual presentation of his themes and subject, and so employ a master craftsman to his taste, the more important the detail and accuracy of his thinking in graphic expression seemed to him, and the more he was prepared to pay for it. C. le Blon, a master engraver, executed the title-page for Burton's *Anatomy of Melancholy* directly for Burton himself, for instance, "in the course of friendly relations in London and Oxford", and Charles I's *Eikon Basilike* (1649) and Francis Bacon's *Advancement of Learning* (1640), both had engraved title-pages made to their instructions by William Marshall. Marshall was also commissioned by George Wither to engrave a title-page for his *Emblemes* (1635), but on this occasion the author's instructions were not followed. In consequence, the title-page is accompanied by verses explaining that the artist has not carried out the author's intention, but that nevertheless the design has been allowed to stand for the entertainment of readers.

In most cases, the authors were not themselves artists, and so their specifications would be literary rather than both literary and artistic. But two points indicate that, in general, the author's contribution to the design of the title-page, outweighed that of the engraver. Firstly, the engravings nearly all bear the signature of the engraver as 'sculpsit' or 'fecit' rather than 'inventor', alluding to their less important role in the making of the engraving. And secondly, the literary character of the engravings (the wealth of learning conveyed by the symbols and images, and required in order to understand them), especially in the engravings of master craftsmen, points to the principal importance of the author's contribution to the design.

The convention of engraved title-pages drew its inspiration from several, all predominantly literary, sources - from the tradition of emblem books which also flourished during this period, from the tradition of devices designed for those of noble rank, from Medieval allegory, and from a particular interpretation of Egyptian hieroglyphs. The traditions óf emblems and devices were closely linked and were not always distinguished in the sixteenth and seventeenth centuries. Both were concerned with the metaphorical relationship between visual picture and verbal expression, and to a large extent drew on the same sources of imagery and symbol. Both also aspired to achieve a fine balance in their works between indicating and obscuring a hidden meaning, by the juxtaposition either of learned references in visual form to teach a commonplace, or of commonplace images to indicate a learned source. In this way, their meaning would be beyond the comprehension of the vulgar, but afford the audience to whom they were addressed the pleasure of discovery. But while devices were commissioned and designed individually to have a personal application, contained two parts - a picture and a motto, and were concerned with a personal aspiration, declaration, vow, ambition or preoccupation, emblems had a more general application, contained three parts, were designed in collections, and were concerned with moral, philosophical, amorous or political themes of general interest.

Of the four main sources of inspiration for the convention of

engraved title-pages, that of the emblem books was the most important and extensive. Each emblem was composed of a picture or
'description', a verse or 'interpretation' and a moral application or
'motto', and its three parts contribute equally to the meaning of the
emblem. More accurately, the meaning of the emblem is meant to be
gained by reading each part of it in the light of the other two parts -
each part, on its own, remains unintelligible. The reason is not only
that the meaning is deliberately not made explicit in each part, but
also because emblems work by making equations (parallels and
connections) which produce the allegorical meaning, rather than by
making identifications, the characteristic procedure of straightforward allegory. Emblems use stock images which carry different
significations depending on which others are used with them, and
how they are treated and developed. The meaning of the emblem
depends on the particular equation that is made in the juxtaposition
of stock images. The moral allegorical force of the emblem is generated
by the images through the particular equation.

The most famous English emblem books were by Francis Quarles
and George Wither, both published in 1635. Neither of them engraved
their own 'descriptions' but, like other emblem makers, employed
engravers (who also engraved title-pages) to execute the designs
they had specified. Although the emblem books strike the modern
reader as ponderously didactic, and the mottoes in particular seem
laborious and heavy-handed, it is worth remembering that the
response of the seventeenth century reader was quite different. For
him, the pleasure and interest of the emblem books (as with other
books) lay, not in confronting novel ideas or in aesthetic appreciation alone, but in observing in the ingenious presentation, and use
of Classical, Medieval and contemporary learned references, and so
reinvesting with significance, the correspondences in the moral
order of the universe.

The tradition of Medieval allegory and the interpretation of
Egyptian hieroglyphs both invested the appreciation of emblematic
imagery in engraved title-pages with a greater moral and philosophical force. Allegory had long been recognised as a means of
pointing to the continuity between the natural, human and divine
worlds, and so of drawing out the potent moral significance of
human actions. And although the widespread conception of
hieroglyphs in the sixteenth and seventeenth centuries, as arcane

symbols with transcendental and occult significance, is not supported by historical evidence, it augmented the appreciation of emblematic imagery of contemporary men.

The appeal to the sixteenth and seventeenth century mind of emblem books and engraved title-pages cannot be regarded, then, as an isolated phenomenon. The conceptions of imitation, artifice, and correspondences between the levels of the natural, human and divine order, which account for their appeal, were also expressed in emblematic decorative detail in domestic and ecclesiastical architecture, household furniture and decoration, painting, embroidery, jewellery, medals, dress, education, the shields and banners used in war, and the development of the publisher's device. And all these, as well as the imagery devised for splendid pageants, weddings, funerals and other ceremonies, provided further sources whose appeal was both visual and intellectual, for the design of engraved title-pages.

Burton's *Anatomy of Melancholy* provides a good example of the hybrid of emblem and engraved title-page. While both are principally composed of references to learned sources, draw upon a common stock of imagery, and are addressed to the same, learned, audience, the emblem forms an equation between its three parts, while the engraved title-page serves as the prelude to a sustained argument, and so is not a general statement of a moral or philosophical precept detached from the work which it prefaces, and its learned references are closely related to the themes of the work. In the *Anatomy of Melancholy* the engraving, composed of a set of compartments containing the major images of Burton's subject, is accompanied by the verses or 'interpretation' characteristic of emblems.

The death of William Faithorne, the last English engraver of any distinction, in 1691, effectively marked the end of the engraved title-page convention. Over its hundred years of popularity, engraving in England had always been dominated by continental craftsmen and followed the trends in the field established in Europe. Fine quality engraved books on all subjects continued to be published in England, but these were increasingly restricted to the wealthy. The decline in the convention involved several circumstances. To some extent, the popularity of engravings featuring complicated architectural facades, allegorical scenes and sets of compartmentalised images, was superseded by a taste for simpler engravings containing portraits.

And to some extent, the decline of the convention can be attributed to the form having reached the limits of its initial aesthetic conceptions and not developing beyond them. By 1691 the master craftsmen working in the heyday of the convention, c.1630-60, had died. Their apprentices were in general less imaginative, and no new inspiration informed their work. Many of the later engravings are tamely derivative, their treatment of the styles and elements stale. Also, since the popularity of engraved title-pages was essentially a European phenomenon, its decline on the Continent heralded a decline in England too. On the practical level, the introduction of cheaper sources of paper and mass production in printing and binding, meant that the cost of the hand-made engravings and technical problems involved in incorporating them into the books increased, relative to those of the new methods. Engraved title-pages became a luxury reserved for those who were prepared to defray the extra expense involved in hand printed and hand bound books. Furthermore, wars and economic recession resulted in a general decline in printing standards; and religious dissension and government censorship led to the development of printing monopolies, which then did not have to heed demand for improved quality. Finally, and perhaps most importantly, the popularity of engraved title-pages depended upon the currency of the outlook that considered the natural, human and divine worlds as forming a hierarchical order instinct with correspondences, and viewed the writers and artists as 'imitators' whose works afforded the double (or rather single) focus of visual and intellectual pleasure and interest. By the end of the seventeenth century this outlook had lost currency; engraved title-pages and emblem books no longer held the same significance, and they ceased to be published, except in children's books.

The most common design or layout for engraved title-pages in the first thirty or forty years of the period in which the convention flourished, was the architectural facade. Its popularity was due in part to the importance of architecture in sixteenth century art forms, in part to its connection with the interest in classical antiquity, in part to its usefulness as an immensely adaptable format for structuring the contents of the title-page, in part to its implication that the book was a monument to the fame of the author and his work, and in part because of the appeal of the graphic arts which represented architectural forms and allegorical statues not as architectural reality but as deliberately illusory and artificial.

In the 1620s and 1630s, other forms of overall layout design appeared and quickly gained in popularity - the title-page which is a single allegorical scene, the title-page divided into geometric compartments, and the title-page whose dominant motif is a simulated three-dimensional scrollwork or cloth of honour. But the different overall designs were not rigidly separated and, in particular, modified features of the architectural design continued to be extensively used in other overall designs.[3]

The wealth of imagery and symbols used within these overall designs was drawn from various sources. Obelisks, inscribed tablets and tombs, classical statues and medals, figures of classical heroes and other symbols drawn from the history and writings of the Greeks and Romans, recalled classical antiquity, and were particularly appropriate in title-pages to translations of and commentaries upon the classics. Title-pages animated by classical gods and goddesses, nymphs and satyrs, and fabled beasts might preface works on classical mythology. The features of Christian life - ecclesiastical architecture, Old and New Testament characters, robed monks, saints and angels, imagery suggesting the Devil, haloes, figures in prayer, the Paschal Lamb, the cross, and imagery associated with God such as the bright shining ray of light from heaven, the eye of God and the right hand of God (symbols in keeping with the prevailing Protestant prescription on anthropomorphic representations of God) - were used in title-pages for Bibles and theological books but also, like the other sources of imagery, had a wider application. Imagery associated with nature and the natural world included animals, fishes, birds, plants, trees, parts of the human body, metals, precious stones, the heavenly bodies and the seasons. Medieval allegory provided symbols such as walled cities, knights, princes on horseback, and moral imagery from real or legendary lore of the natural and animal world, such as the piety of the pelican, the constancy of the turtle-dove, the fidelity of the sunflower, the chastity of the ermine and the wholesomeness of marjoram. Medieval allegory also provided personifications of the Virtues and Vices, cardinal and theological, which are properly expressed in anthropomorphic form because they signify, both concretely and allegorically, moral qualities, properties and attributes of man, types of character, humours and passions. Sources of topical imagery included the representation of Queen Elizabeth in the figure of Britannia; and maps, projections, globes, mechanical, nautical and medical instruments, and the celestial sphere, express the intellectual excitement surrounding the geographic discoveries and advances in astronomy and other sciences, as well as being appropriate for books on these subjects.

Portraits also figured prominently in title-page engravings, and served to advertise the author, honour his work and connect him with the themes portrayed in the engraving. An added tribute to the portrait of the author or to a central figure in the title-page, could be indicated by architectural features, swags of cockleshells, marine creatures, garlands, fruiting branches and clusters of bay leaves. The use of the Hebrew and Greek alphabets and of Latin, in engraved title-pages, served several purposes. They protected the significance of the content from the yes of the vulgar, and enhanced the effect of awe which an unfamiliar alphabet was meant to convey. They also, by employing the authority given to the written word in a literal representation of words in visual form, provided another level at which authoritative associations and connotations were conveyed, as in references to classical texts in Latin inscriptions, and to religious authority in Christian references in the Hebrew Tetragrammaton. The use of geometry, as in the figure of a triangle enclosed in a circle, carried the same significance.

The primacy of intellectual over visual authority in engraved title-pages, results from the author's invention preceding and dictating the pictorial design of the engraver. The kind of pictorial form in which the author's intellectual conceptions and references were seen to be fittingly expressed, was allegorical representation. Thus the allegorical character of the engravings, congenial to contemporary readers in any case, was also a result of the procedure by which they were generally composed.

Two aspects of the allegorical character of the images and their combination in the overall designs of the engravings, then become clear. Firstly, while the significance and purpose of the engraving is understood in terms of its expression of the author's themes and the scope of his subject, the choice of imagery and symbols was not limited to what was historically accurate. A combination of elements from different sources was not thought incongruous, since in the view of sixteenth and seventeenth men and women, the whole of history and of the natural and human worlds, provided images which pointed to the divinely-ordered universe, which expressed the moral character of that universe, and through which human thinking was and could be further organised. Thus figures of contemporary noblemen, Roman centurions, and an unkempt woman depicting Nature, may happily co-exist in a landscape containing a walled Medieval city, with cherubs and the Tudor rose arranged among the clouds, without at all being intellectually incoherent. And secondly, not only did the elements of the composition not need to be historically consistent, but the elements themselves need not be naturalistically accurate either. The sunflower with a face, the six-breasted queen, the man composed of countless smaller men, grotesque monsters and fantastical birds, are only some of the more obvious examples of images in these engravings that need to be read allegorically. Indeed, even where each single element in the engraving is, by itself, naturalistically accurate, the conjunction of elements indicates an allegorical meaning. The allegorical significance of the engraving is found in the image presented by the whole as well as in its separate images and symbols.

Several of Hobbes' works apart from *Leviathan* [4] were published with engraved title-pages. The title-page of the translation of Thucydides (1629), engraved by T. Cecill, is in the mainstream of the convention, using predominantly classical elements to indicate the subject of the work; but it is not conspicuously imaginative in execution. The title-page of the translation of Homer's Iliads and Odysses (1677) is similarly classical and unexceptional. *De Cive*, however, bears a more interesting title-page. The first edition of *De Cive* (Paris 1642) has an elaborate engraving by 'Math. F.' depicting in three female figures the major features and virtues of civil order, Religio, Imperium and Libertas - who also represent the three sections of the book. The engraving is divided horizontally, and heaven and hell are portrayed behind the figure of Religio surmounting a scene of religious battle in the top part of the engraving. Below, the figures of Imperium holding a dagger and a pair of scales and of Libertas holding a bow and arrow, stand on pedestals flanking the cloth of honour bearing the title and a quotation from Proverbs. Behind Imperium and Libertas, scenes depicting civil peace and war in the state of nature are portrayed. The second edition of *De Cive* (Amsterdam 1647) has a reduced copy of the 1642 engraving, and differs in some of the detail. A further edition of Amsterdam 1647 features an engraving with a different design, in simpler lines with sparse background and detail, but again depicting Religio, Imperium and Libertas, clothed in classical robes and bearing the symbols of their names, with Religio again taking precedence by her position in the top section of the engraving.

The title-page of the *Philosophical Rudiments* (1651) was engraved by Vaughan, copied from the Latin Amsterdam edition of 1649. As with *De Cive*, the engraving is dominated by the three figures of civil order and, in particular, by Religio who is seated on top of a pedestal which bears the title and Hobbes' portrait. Dominion and Libertas stand on either side. In an earlier state of the engraving, the title begins 'Philosophical Elements' and the names of Religio etc. are not inscribed on the plate. The history of this engraving demonstrates that sometimes (though it was on the whole uncommon) the same plate was used for different works. Thus, a third state of this engraving, with a different portrait, is found in L. de Montalte's (Pascal's) *Les Provinciales* (1657), and a fourth state of it is found in Lipsius' *War and Peace Reconciled* (1672). The conception of the three figures, their arrangement, and the accompanying detail, in the title-pages of *De Cive* and the *Philosophical Rudiments*, because of the aptness and accuracy of the references they make to the works and to other intellectual sources, strongly suggests that they were Hobbes' invention.

The *Elements of Law* (1640), and *De Corpore* (1655) and *De Homine* (1658), both published in London by Andrew Crooke, have title-pages engraved with decoration but no allegorical scene. The *Opera* (1668) appropriately bears an engraved frontespiece with Hobbes' portrait, engraved by William Faithorne. However, none of the engraved title-pages of Hobbes' other works approach the engraving of *Leviathan* in invention or skill in execution.

It may be thought that the absence of an engraved title-page in *Behemoth* requires some explanation, since it is, after *Leviathan*, the work of Hobbes which most explicitly calls for an allegorical understanding. However, the reason is quite simply found. No genuine edition of *Behemoth* was published in Hobbes' lifetime. William Crooke published it in a collection of 1682, and by this time the convention of including engraved title-pages in scholarly works was becoming less and less common.

The title-page of *Leviathan* is exceptional in several respects - in the imaginativeness and originality of its central figure, in the wealth of detail expressed in its images and symbols, in its striking use of symmetry, and in its skilful execution. Only the last of these aspects can be attributed to the engraver. The others represent departures from the usage of the common stock of imagery and designs established in the convention by 1651; departures whose significance would be unfamiliar to an engraver, and whose design requires a thorough knowledge of Hobbes' philosophy in *Leviathan*.

The conception of a human figure made up of countless smaller figures, is unique to *Leviathan* in the history of this convention of engraved title-pages. An Indian miniature painting of the seventeenth century in the Victoria and Albert Museum, shows an elephant composed, on close inspection, of lots of different animals - monkeys, birds and other jungle creatures. And this conception is not unknown in other iconographical traditions. But in the engraved title-page convention of this period, the closest similar design is in the title-page of Drayton's *Poly-Olbion* (1612), in which the flowing robe of the central figure (the mythical Albion, representing England in the personification of Queen Elizabeth) is embroidered with the geographical terrain of the land of 'Great Britaine', showing the variety and richness of its hills, rivers, trees, castles and towns. But here the design definitely indicates that the landscape is embroidered onto a garment (though suggesting their significance by forming the clothing of Albion), whereas in *Leviathan* the figure himself is composed of smaller figures,[5] such that the smaller figures could (notionally) not be detached from the whole larger figure, without thereby dismantling the central figure himself. Thus what is indicated in *Leviathan* is an indissoluble connection between figure and components, while in *Poly-Olbion* the connection between ruler and who or what is ruled over is far less integrated (for Albion could notionally take off her robe and still remain queen).

The symmetry of the title-page of *Leviathan* is unusual on two counts. Firstly, most of the engraved title-pages in this convention are rectangularly symmetrical, formally so in those composed of a set of compartments, and informally so in those depicting allegorical scenes. But in *Leviathan* the upper half of the engraving is triangularly symmetrical, with the crown of the central figure forming the apex of the triangle. The second point concerns the scale of the elements in the engraving. In general, the relative sizes of the images and symbols expresses their relations with one another and their relative importance. Sometimes the elements are naturalistically proportionate, but often the most significant are depicted as proportionally larger. There are one or two instances of human figures towering above the landscape, apart from *Leviathan*, but it is an uncommon design. But what makes the scale of elements remarkable in *Leviathan*, is that the engraving combines the allegorical picture design with the set of compartments design, thereby dividing the engraving in two. The relation between the elements is thus much more sophisticated, since what is indicated is that the figure of Leviathan both stands on the foundations of civil and ecclesiastical institutions, but is also independently sovereign above them.

It is worthwhile describing the title-page of *Leviathan* in some detail, in order to substantiate the claim that it is built upon intellectual rather than simply decorative images, which points to its design being Hobbes' invention rather than the engraver's.[6] In the top section of the horizontally divided engraving, the human figure of Leviathan towers above a landscape of hills enclosing a valley. He holds aloft the sword of temporal power and authority in one hand, and grasps the crozier of ecclesiastical power and authority in the other. He wears an imperial crown to emphasise his supreme power and authority in the commonwealth, which is already indicated by his size. His body is composed of countless small figures of men dressed in different styles to indicate the variety of different ranks. These men are portrayed in the act of making the covenant which establishes the commonwealth, by uniting themselves into one person and so creating the sovereign. The quotation across the top of the engraving is from Job, where the story of the Leviathan whale is found, and reads "there is no power on earth which can be compared to him". On the hills and in the valley below Leviathan, the ordered, industrious and peaceful life within the commonwealth is in progress, under the protection of the sovereign.

In the lower part of the engraving, there are five compartments on each side, directly under the sword and crozier, and in the centre a richly fringed cloth of honour bears the title and author's name. The left-hand compartments contain scenes and symbols of the principal matters over which the sovereign exercises temporal rule.

The first compartment contains a castle on a hill, the symbol of civil and military power. The second contains a coronet, a symbol of the 'titles of honour' bestowed by the sovereign. The third contains a cannon, a symbol of effective warfare and a reminder that military equipment could only be manufactured under license from the sovereign. In the fourth compartment the tokens of war are pictured, over which the sovereign has absolute command. And the fifth compartment contains a scene of warfare, indicating the sovereign's sole right to make war. The resemblance between the appearance of the conflicting armies suggests that it is not a civil war.

The right-hand compartments show scenes and symbols of the principal matters over which the sovereign exercises ecclesiastical rule, which correspond to those concerned with civil rule on the left-hand side. This is emphasised by the parallels between the different sizes of the compartments. The first compartment contains a church, which is the symbol of religious life and which Hobbes defines in *Leviathan* as not only 'Christ's house' but also as a company of men of Christian religion united in the person of one sovereign. The second compartment contains a bishop's mitre which is, for Hobbes, one of the titles of honour ecclesiastical, matching the coronet on the left, given by the sovereign. The thunderbolt in the third compartment is the traditional symbol of excommunication which, Hobbes argues in *Leviathan*, is a right not of the Pope but solely of the civil sovereign. The fourth compartment contains a pair of horns, a trident and three forks. From the inscriptions it is clear that these represent the weapons of logic - the horns of dilemma; the three prongs of the syllogism; spiritual and temporal disputes, over both of which the sovereign has absolute public authority; the terms of scholastic philosophy signified by the fork inscribed 'real' and 'intentional'; and the forms of adequate proof signified by the fork which reads 'direct' and 'indirect'. The fifth compartment contains a scene showing a disputation in progress. This indicates the sovereign's sole authority to organise official debates on theological issues and to prescribe the official doctrines and public observances of the religion of the commonwealth.

It is interesting to note that the largest compartments contain the tokens of war on the left, and the instruments of logic which symbolise speech and reasoning on the right - both matters over which the sovereign has a right to public obedience and subjects have an obligation to observe.

One of the differences between the engraved title-pages of this convention and emblems, was that the three parts of the emblem formed an equation in which the significances of the emblem lay, while the title-page contained the pictorial expression of the themes and scope of the work which followed it. It is apparent that, in line with this general practice, the description of the title-page of *Leviathan* involves an understanding which goes beyond what is immediately intelligible in the pictorial representation. The title-page is made up of images and symbols of complex intellectual conceptions, and a knowledge of the work is required in order to understand them and the significance of their particular organisation in the title-page.

In *Leviathan* the Introduction fulfils the functions of a bridge between the title-page and the verbal argument of the work - setting out in verbal language the overall conception to be detailed in the discussion to follow, and explicitly emphasising the significance of the relation between the pictorial expression of the title-page and the verbal expression of the four Parts of the work. The Introduction contains the most comprehensive verbal imagery to be found in the whole work, and in it Hobbes makes explicit the meaning of the central figure and the two sets of compartments of the title-page. The images of the title-page are not only related to the later discussion, as in "that great Leviathan called a Commonwealth, or State, in Latin Civitas, which is but an artificial man"; the verbal imagery of the Introduction is extended beyond what could be shown in the title-page, and again its significance in the later discussion indicated, as in the explicit relations drawn between the parts of the artificial man (artificial soul, artificial joints, heart, nerves, wheels) and his qualities (strength, health sickness, death), and the parts of civil society (sovereignty, magistrates and other officers, rewards and punishments, law) and its character (wealth and riches, concord, sedition, civil war). The verbal image of the Leviathan in the Introduction, like the visual image in the title-page, is of an artificial man who holds sway over the civil and ecclesiastical Commonwealth, who contains in himself the qualities of a mechanical construction produced by the art and artifice of the men who compose him, and of a natural, organic being with "life and motion". The significance of *Leviathan* over *De Cive* and the *Philosophical Rudiments*, as the most mature exposition of Hobbes' political philosophy, is demonstrated in the title-pages as well as in the verbal arguments of the works. The pictorially and intellectually complex image of the integrated, single figure of Leviathan, expresses the conception of sovereignty, and of the character of the relation between sovereignty, authority, obligation and power, that is fundamental to Hobbes' political philosophy, in contrast to the three separate figures of Religio, Imperium and Libertas which figure in the title-pages of the earlier works.

The engraver of the title-page of *Leviathan* has always been described as anonymous in bibliographical sources and in works on Hobbes in English. In the light of the evidence advanced, from the practice generally followed in the design of title-pages in this convention, and from the knowledge of Hobbes' political philosophy required to design the title-page of *Leviathan*, which points to the principal role of Hobbes' contribution over that of the engraver in the invention and design of the title-page, the attribution of a particular engraver is not of crucial significance. However it is interesting that Corbett and Lightbown[7] argue convincingly for a definite attribution to the French engraver Abraham Bosse.

The connection between Hobbes' works, and their publication with engraved title-pages, is not necessarily the rather arbitrary one, that engraved title-pages were the fashion of the day, and so Hobbes' works feature them. This assessment underestimates both the significance of the convention in general, and the importance of the title-pages of Hobbes' works, especially that of *Leviathan*, in particular. The connection between the pictorial expression of the title-page and the verbal expression of the argument of *Leviathan* - the kind of intellectual understanding that the title-page requires - is the same as that found in other examples of scholarly works in the convention. The connection between the title-page and the argument of *Leviathan*, and the manner in which Hobbes uses verbal imagery and other metaphorical language in the development of his thinking in *Leviathan*, demonstrate that Hobbes' philosophy is deeply informed by the Medieval and Renaissance understanding of the continuity between the natural, human and divine worlds, which the emblem tradition and the convention of engraved title-pages both presuppose.

Hobbes' notion, presented in the Introduction of *Leviathan*, that as nature is the art of God, by which He made and governs the world, so man imitates nature, and in his art imitates nature's most excellent and rational work, man, in the civil commonwealth, has most often been seen by commentators on Hobbes as providing a quite new assumption in political philosophy - of man's ability to construct a civil society within the terms immediately available to him, in his reason, will, and physical strength. This is taken to be an individualistic conception, in so far as it dispenses with the requirement of a necessary involvement by or collaboration with divine will, or in accord with the weight of tradition or custom. However, this individualistic reading is only one of the interpretations that may be made of Hobbes' notion. Another reading, which views Hobbes in terms of the context of his intellectual background rather than as a 'precurser' of Locke and seventeenth century rationalism, takes as its starting point the meanings that words such as 'nature', 'artifice', 'imitation' and 'art' had in the late sixteenth and early seventeenth centuries.

Italian literary theorists in the sixteenth century drew upon classical Greek aesthetic theory and Christian theology, to argue that "the beautiful in art is identified....with the beautiful in nature. All the technique of art has for its purpose the imitation of nature, as nature has for its end the imitation of God".[8] The notion of the relation between the natural, human and divine worlds as both hierarchical and correspondent, that this argument presupposes, is also presupposed in English Renaissance thought, and in Hobbes. It is expressed in the title-page of *Leviathan* in the figure - a conception unique in this convention - of Leviathan shown as both a living man and as an artificial body composed of men. The figure is thus a strikingly literal image[9] of Hobbes' conception of the commonwealth as an artificial man, formed by the covenant by which men confer their natural power and right upon one man who bears their persons. The commonwealth is a unity in one person who is both natural and artificial. And the same notion is expressed explicitly, following the title-page, in the Introduction of *Leviathan*, where the term 'artificial' carries, not our meaning of 'superficial' or 'second-rate', but the combination understood in the late sixteenth and early seventeenth centuries of construction, a making and an organising and a composing which is both aesthetically pleasing and functional, by man according to and developing from, the very best models possible - those given by God in nature. Nature is here seen as an endless source of examples and instruction by God for the proper (correct, appropriate and decorous) way to go about things, in practical sciences, arts, thinking, and human conduct. The construction of civil society, which is a living mechanism, as much as the construction of instruments to measure the movements of the planets or the construction of paintings and poems, should and does follow the examples of nature. In this way, then, Hobbes' philosophy has written into it the postulates of late sixteenth and early seventeenth century metaphysics and epistemology, and the presence of an engraved title-page in *Leviathan* which exhibits these postulates is an appropriate expression of this shared view.

The significance of the engraved title-page of *Leviathan* is found not only with respect to the context of late sixteenth and early seventeenth century thought; it also expresses Hobbes' answer to the major preoccupation of seventeenth century political theorists, the nature and character of the state. Throughout the Medieval period, political theorising focussed upon the political entity of Christendom, but with the decline of the authority of that entity, the subject of political theorising became the emergent European state. Hobbes was characteristic of seventeenth century political thought in his concern with explaining the generation of the commonwealth, accounting for the authority ·of its sovereign, and delimiting the scope of those who (if at all) were entitled to question that authority. But unlike the theorists of the later seventeenth century who followed a rationalist approach, Hobbes' philosophy employs the understanding of the older view in the service of the new political entity. In the engraved title-page of *Leviathan* and in the discussion that follows it, Hobbes' answer is vividly and uncompromisingly expressed. Because men both *make* (by their artifice) the Leviathan, civil association, through covenant with each other to set it up, and *compose* (in their natural bodies) the Leviathan, the commonwealth, there can be no other source of authority than the indivisible sovereign they have constructed and form.

NOTES

1. The presence of at least part of the full title of the book, with or without publisher's imprint, constitutes a title-page. An engraved design which is emblematic or merely decorative, possibly containing a portrait, but without the actual title of the book, is called a frontespiece.
2. Many publishers in the seventeenth century were also booksellers, and vice versa. It must also be remembered that many books were circulated in unpublished, manuscript, form.
3. Examples of title-pages from the period, including those from some of Hobbes' works, are found on pages 226-237.

4. Published by Andrew Crooke, a leading publisher and bookseller of his day, in 1651. Andrew Crooke dealt largely in plays, and he also published the first authorised edition of Sir Thomas Browne's *Religio Medici*. William Crooke took over his father's publishing firm after the death of Andrew Crooke in 1674.

5. Curiously, the *Catalogue of Engraved Title-pages* (Prints & Drawings Room, British Museum), the definitive catalogue in this subject, in its description of the title-page of *Leviathan*, says that the "garments worn" by the Leviathan figure are covered with small figures. All other major sources say that Leviathan himself is made up of these small figures. In particular, in the authoritative volumes of Colvin, Hind and Johnson, which draw on the Prints & Drawings Room catalogue, all describe the Leviathan figure in the latter manner, but without indicating their divergence from the Prints & Drawings Room catalogue.

6. The content of the description is not a matter of controversy. The following account draws on the work by M. Corbett and R. Lightbown, *The Comely Frontespiece*, Routledge & Kegan Paul, London, 1979, which contains the best description of the title-page of *Leviathan*.

7. *ibid* p221-2.

8. C. D. Thorpe, *The Aesthetic Theory of Thomas Hobbes*, Russell & Russell, New York, 1964, p61

9. And so conforms to Hobbes' view of the kind of 'fictions' that are permissible, as outlined in the Answer to Davenant's Preface to *Gondibert*.

CHAPTER 6
Hobbes and Hooker

Hobbes' *Leviathan* and Hooker's *Of the Laws of Ecclesiastical Polity* invite comparison on several different levels, and the present treatment does not attempt to be exhaustive. The argument which follows takes as its starting point several features of comparison in the rhetorics of the two works, and through these considers the ways in which the enterprises of the two writers, and the thinking expressed in their works, seen through the rhetorical structures they chose, disclose points of significant similarity and dissimilarity which lead to a greater understanding of both works. One of the arguments of this chapter is that the claims made for the 'modern' character of *Leviathan* by some twentieth century commentators must be modified, both in scope and in character - in scope in the light of Hooker's treatment of various aspects of political philosophy, and in character in the light of the altered significance that the attacks on Hobbes' work by many of his contemporaries have in consequence.

A comparative treatment of the works of two thinkers should, perhaps, be prefaced by some cautionary remarks, since comparison in the history of ideas is fraught with methodological difficulties. The use of comparison in the history of ideas has been subject to considerable methodological debate, and its abuses outlined at length, such as to make a full account of them here unnecessary.[1] It may be noted, however, that one of the main lines of criticism has been directed at those working in the field of the history of ideas who assert that they are engaged in 'philosophical' as opposed to 'historical' reflection, and consider that comparison is a self-evidently legitimate tool requiring no reflection upon its own conditions.[2] Against such historians of ideas it has been argued that, consequent upon the two sorts of reflection being demonstrated as necessarily complementary in this field of inquiry, the tool of comparison must be used only to the extent that historical evidence supports the kinds of connections it makes and the kinds of conclusions it wishes to draw from them.

The strongest argument in favour of the use of comparison to study thinkers in the history of ideas is that it is simply a species of a necessary and unavoidable part of thinking itself. For all thinking involves trains of thought or argument (an argument simply being a developed train of thought towards a specific end) whose progression rests on connections made.[3] And it may be argued that connections in thinking are comparisons seen as significant. If it is accepted that the making, or rather the perceiving, of connections is a necessary and characteristic part of the human activity we call thinking, and if it is acknowledged that in studying one thinker in the history of ideas, one is engaged in attempting to make the kind of connections that lead to the formulation of an intelligible account of some aspects of that thinker's work, it follows that the formal tool of comparison between thinkers - that is, using comparison as the overall rhetorical structure of an argument - cannot be judged, a priori, as illegitimate.

The conclusion of this line of argument is that the methodological problems involved in the use of comparison in the history of ideas may resemble a minefield to be picked through carefully, rather than a set of obstacles fruitlessly beseiged.

The conclusions drawn from comparisons between thinkers, in the history of ideas, are likely to be most tenable, firstly when the historical contexts of the thinkers are the same or closely related, and secondly when they are concerned with the same mode of discourse about a subject. In the case of Hobbes and Hooker, it may be argued that they are closer on both these counts than would be supposed on a reading of much of the literature on Hobbes. The difference between the publication dates of the *Laws* and *Leviathan* is only the difference between the publication of works in the 1930s and those published today. And Hooker's work was well-known in the first half of the seventeenth century. Although Walton's "Life"[4] may be regarded as of limited reliability, because of the evident partiality of his account, there is evidence in the "Life" and in the publication history of the *Laws* that Hooker's work was widely read throughout the decades following his death. The *Laws* was much admired by James I, Charles I and Charles II; it was quoted by Charles I in a parliamentary debate, and much maligned by the various factions of 'Separatists', even in 1664. And the stories of the burning of Hooker's notes, the emergence of various corrupt copies of the later Books after Hooker's death, and the transmission of his papers through the libraries of various high ranking members of the Church and Government, all suggest that the importance of Hooker's ideas was a subject of lively interest in the period 1603-1669 as well as during Elizabeth's reign. These considerations suggest, then, a greater commonness of context between Hooker and Hobbes than is often acknowledged.[5] And on the second count, it will be argued that Hooker's work is a work of political philosophy in the same sense that we understand Hobbes' *Leviathan* to be.

The comparison of Hooker's *Laws* and Hobbes' *Leviathan* begins with an examination of the titles of the works, and this introduces the discussion of the general structures of the works and their use of language. The manner in which the whole of each work is divided and composed, and the kind of relationship between the parts, will be a constant point of reference in the argument. And the way in which discussion of rhetorical considerations constantly becomes discussion of the meaning of what is written, is one of the points that this chapter seeks to demonstrate. The strands of rhetoric and meaning in the argument are collected into a set of conclusions at the end of the chapter.

The words in Hooker's title upon which we focus attention are "laws", "ecclesiastical" and "polity", and the term formed by the words "ecclesiastical polity". As Hooker explains at the beginning of Book I, he was prompted to write about law by the activities of those who "openly reprove supposed disorders of state",[6] by those whose criticism of the country's laws reveals not simply the desire for the reformation of specific laws, but a fundamental contemptuous disregard for the necessity of the rule of law itself as the basis of human societies. Hooker then links this 'argument by refutation' for the necessity of law, to two further propositions about law; firstly that "the law whereby the Eternal himself doth work" is that "which giveth life unto all the rest", and secondly that all things "do work after a sort according to law", since "all things that are, have some operation not violent or casual".[7] That is, there is an aspect of all things and their actions that have a regularity and are subsumed under law - firstly under the Eternal law divine, and secondly under the Eternal law of the universe which God has set down. The second Eternal law comprehends nature's law, the physical laws of the universe which goven the behaviour of things in so far as they are "natural agents"; the law celestial, by which angels are ruled; the law of reason, which binds creatures in so far as they are "reasonable";

divine law, that which God has revealed in Scripture; and human law, that man makes to govern his public conduct. Man is subject to several kinds of law, according to the different aspects of his being. The conjunction of these three propositions about law thus make it clear from the start that Hooker is concerned with the nature and character of laws, their several kinds and relative status, as they operate in *human societies.*

Hooker is here restating the complex sixteenth century conception of law, as that which creates the ordered universe in which man lives and of which man is a part, where order means both a hierarchical ordering or regulated arrangement of all things, and the establishment and maintenance of order or peaceableness between things, and which is created by God as First Cause, upon whom all else depends. In this context of thinking, then, it follows that Hooker's interest in law is not only theoretical but is anchored to his interest in man as a political being. Man's ability to improve upon nature, by artifice, is very important to Hooker,[8] and in this his view is thoroughly orthodox. According to Hooker's conception, the significance of law lies in the manner in which it operates to connect the two most important concerns of man - his life on earth and his relation to God. For Hooker it is thorough the operation of law that man can most readily understand the connection between these two concerns.

The meanings of "ecclesiastical' and "polity" follow from this conception of law, "ecclesiastical" referring to the activities of that body of men who implement the laws derived from the divine law from their offices of authority in human societies, and "polity" referring to a set of political arrangements for a group or society of humans. "Ecclesiastical polity", then, describes the kind of human society that the conception of law requires and entails, the set of arrangements for human society, whose ordering, and in which the individual obligation to order, rests on the recognition of God as the creator of all order and law.

In Book III, where Hooker considers the laws governing ecclesiastical polity, following his discussion in Book I of law in general and in Book II of the scope of divine law in scripture in the human world, he says of the term "ecclesiastical polity",[9]

> Which word I therefore the rather use, because the name of Government, as commonly men understand it in ordinary speech, doth not comprise the largeness of that whereunto in this question it is applied. For when

we speak of Government, what doth the greatest part conceive thereby, but only the exercise of superiority peculiar unto Rulers and Guides of others? To our purpose therefore the name of Church-Polity will better serve, because it containeth both government and also whatsoever besides belongeth to the ordering of the Church in public. Neither is any thing in this degree more necessary than Church-Polity, which is a form of ordering the public spiritual affairs of the Church of God.

The initial impression that is conveyed in this passage may be that ecclesiastical polity refers to the public arrangements of the church, notionally quite distinct from those of the temporal government, implying a division between church and state into two separate areas of authority in the society. This impression may be considered as gaining support when in Book V Hooker comments, "So natural is the union of Religion with Justice, that we may boldly deem there is neither, where both are not",[10] and "Seeing therefore it doth thus appear that the safety of all estates dependeth upon religion; that religion unfeignedly loved perfecteth men's abilities unto all kinds of virtuous services in the commonwealth".[11]

However, this impression gives way to another reading in the light of two considerations. Firstly, the comments in Book V must be viewed in their context as arguments from natural reason which confirm what the Christian already knows, that the same (Christian) criteria knowable through natural reason inform all kinds of public arrangements. And secondly, the passage from Book III must be read in the light of Hooker's conception of law in general, such that while all law derives from God and so must necessarily concur, different offices are maintained in the public arrangements of the whole polity for the exercise of the different kinds of law. Thus although the divine law governs the ecclesiastical polity and positive law governs the strictly temporal affairs of citizens, the two kinds of law remain extensions of the prior law, and the two kinds of arrangements are extensions of the one public body which is a "Church-Nation" (to use Lewis' term[12]), and are both represented on earth in the sovereign. As Hooker says in Book VIII, "there is not any man of the Church of England but the same man is also a member of the commonwealth; nor any man a member of the commonwealth, which is not also of the Church of England",[13] and "within this realm of England....one society is both the Church and commonwealth".[14]

The mistake which is written into the first impression of the passages from Books III and V, lies in a failure to take into account the grounding of all law, for Hooker, in an ultimate divinely-created law.

One of Hooker's objects here is to argue against the antithesis, subscribed to by the Puritans, in the world man lives in, between what is created by God and is divine, and what is 'merely' made by man and is therefore human. For instance, Hooker argues that certain powers are given to princes by human right in the social contract, but princes also hold them by divine right. Explicit divine injunction in Scripture is part of the rule or law that governs man, but another part is nature, a law no less God-given, but which is rational, accessible to human reason. Thus for Hooker there is one polity which, viewed in its aspect of divine law in scripture is a Church, and viewed in its aspect of divinely-derived natural and human law is a Nation. Therefore there can be no division between church and state, since the authority of these two extensions of the polity comes ultimately from the same source. "For every good gift", as Lewis comments, whether by way of revelation or reason, Grace or Nature, Church or commonwealth, "comes from the same source".[15] Hooker never envisaged, Lewis continues, the situation of our own time or of Hobbes', when sects of Christians live side by side with atheists in a commonwealth; Hooker "still hopes that the divisions between Christians will be healed (IV.xiv.6) and the basic assumption of his thought is the unitedly Christian nation in which Church and State, however defined, are in fact 'the selfsame multitude' (VIII.i.2). Nations are churches organised for the conduct of their temporal affairs; churches are nations organised for the conduct of their spiritual affairs".[16]

In Hooker, the dualism between flesh and spirit, nature and supernature, man and God, always immanent in Christian thought, is at its least separated. With the aid of his graduated and ordered hierarchy of law, Hooker describes a universe which, so far as man is concerned, is connected at each point by the double binding of natural reason and divine will.[17]

In the phrase "the laws of ecclesiastical polity", then, the meanings of the words refer to and entail each other; for given Hooker's understanding of law, the polity, to be properly ordered, must comprehend an ecclesiastical polity; and the polity, for Hooker, presupposes not simply law but a hierarchy of several sets of arrangements of law of the kind he describes. The use of the plural "laws" in the title, rather than "law", expresses the significance for Hooker of all law which affects man being anchored in God and directly related to Him. Furthermore, by recognising that man is subject to several kinds of law, Hooker acknowledges the importance of human positive law in his treatise, confirming that his work is about man rather than either religion or law in the abstract. If a label is to be given to his work, then, it may be called political philosophy as justly as anything else. For in the context of thinking in which Hooker works, one cannot talk about man for very long without considering the religious dimension of man's life. In the context of much twentieth century thinking, in which the consideration of man as a social or political being does not need at all to involve a discussion of a religious dimension, his work might be considered as theology or theological legal philosophy; in the context of late sixteenth and early seventeenth century thinking, it is indisputably political philosophy, since one of the focuses of his attention, the character of government and politics understood by the Elizabethan settlement, revolved around the issue of the kind of relation between the authority of divine law in scripture and the authority of human law in the sovereign that existed in the commonwealth, the issue centring on the ecclesiastical structure of the Church. The combination of emphases that have led to the conclusion that Hooker's work is a work of political philosophy, are felicitously expressed by Hooker in the penultimate paragraph of Book I:[18]

> Thus we see how even one and the selfsame thing is under divers considerations conveyed through many laws; and that to measure by any one kind of law all the actions of men were to confound the admirable order, wherein God hath disposed all laws, each as in nature, so in degree, distinct from other.

The examination of Hooker's title cannot conclude without a word about the significance of the first word, "of". By the use of this qualifying "of", Hooker illustrates one of the main points he is at pains to expound in the course of his work, that the nature of God (eternal, oneness, immanent, omnipotent, inscrutable, Absolute and transcendent) and the nature of man (human, tied to the natural world, and whose capacity for understanding and explanation are defined by the limits of being an imperfect creation and only a part of a whole), qualify the achievement of all man's human endeavours to account for the whole. Hooker, then, is using this convention to acknowledge the limits placed on him in an attempt to write a definitive treatise on a subject which, by its nature, can only be partially known by any man. The word "of", then, serves several purposes - it is a decorous profession of humility and a tribute to God's supreme knowledge, a reminder to his readers of their equally limited understanding, and a warning to his adversaries about their, as he contends, arrogant claim to know more than any man can know. While the qualifying "of" is found in many sixteenth and seventeenth century and earlier works, and serves in them to emphasise or point to the un-final and indefinite character of human knowledge in the light of God's absolute knowledge, its use by Hooker is more significant. For him, this common usage also reinforces his own argument against the Puritan writers. So in using the convention, Hooker is drawing upon the traditional attitude of humility to God in the service of his argument against the Puritans. The qualifying term in parentheses in the title of the preface to the *Laws*, in which Hooker rehearses the main arguments of the work - "A Preface to them that seek (as they term it) the Reformation of the Laws and Orders Ecclesiastical in the Church of England" - serves the same purpose.

Both Hooker's and Hobbes' titles set up a configuration of words which revolve around and reinforce one focal word - in Hooker's title it was "laws", in Hobbes' it is "Leviathan". Whereas in Hooker's title all the words make reference to the focal word directly, or take their most important meaning from that reference, the structure of Hobbes' title is more complex. Firstly there is the division between "Leviathan" and "the matter, forme" etc., whereby the word "or" sets up the two parts of a mirror image, a something and its mirror image. But which is the something and which the mirror image? Since "Leviathan" comes first, it should be the something, since mirror images cannot exist without something of prior existence being brought before them. But because "Leviathan" is a word which is being used as a metaphor or image, with the remainder of the title elucidating it, it may be thought that "the matter, forme" etc. is the something and "Leviathan" the mirror image. However, this results in the mirror image having been formed before the something was brought before the mirror, which is unsatisfactory. The result, then, is a nice ambiguity in which "Leviathan" and "the matter, forme" etc. are interchangeable as the something and the mirror image, which in turn has the effect of merging the two, cutting down the grounds of making distinctions between them in terms of literal and metaphorical meanings.[19]

The division between "Leviathan" and "the matter, forme" etc. is, furthermore, a perilous one, for the weight of the second part threatens to dissolve the division between parts of a whole and result in a title, "Leviathan", and a subtitle, "the matter, forme" etc., which relegates it to an inferior status.[20] This, however, does occur, since the word "Leviathan" on its own does not convey enough explicit meaning to the reader to serve as an adequate title, when he first picks up the work. However, once the work has become familiar, it is usually known simply as *Leviathan*. That is, when the meaning explicitly laid out in the rest of the title has been absorbed, the single word "Leviathan" is enough to organise and carry that meaning. In other words, before the work is read, "Leviathan" can only be identified as a metaphor whose meaning is not altogether self-explanatory (though the currency of biblical references may make it intelligible to the reader *as* a metaphor), and which needs the rest of the title; but after the work has been read, the need to distinguish between metaphor and literal words loses the significance it had, and fades. The remainder of the title has now become an understood, already incorporated into the first word, "Leviathan", and so the need to use it falls away. It becomes redundant because it adds nothing to what the first word already says, adds nothing to the meaning that is not already contained in the meaning of the single word "Leviathan". And it is worth remarking at this point that this process does not rest on some cunning trick of Hobbes', nor on some undemonstrated assumption of the present writer, but shows rather that Hobbes is using to the full the ability of language to express thinking.

The most important word in the rest of Hobbes' title is "commonwealth", which is the general word signifying in general terms the scope of Hobbes' inquiry, "Leviathan" being a particular of it. In the body of the work, the word "commonwealth" occurs far more frequently than the word "Leviathan", since Hobbes is concerned with specifying the features of a particular kind of commonwealth, understood as a whole as "Leviathan", and with distinguishing this commonwealth from other kinds. "Commonwealth" is a fifteenth century word referring to the state or common weal or matters of general or public good or welfare.

The remainder of the title forms two accompanying qualifications, which are of different sorts. The first qualification, "the matter, forme and power", describes the three elements in an abstract analysis of a commonwealth, and are for Hobbes species of the three dimensions of any inquiry - from what is it made?, what shape or structure does it have?, and what drives or propels it? (or, what is the nature of its motion?). The second qualification concerns the kind of commonwealth that can be identified. Thus the first qualification analyses a commonwealth into its constituent elements, and the second composes the identification of a commonwealth as a unity. This of course, illustrates the method Hobbes is at pains to outline and use in his work.

There is an element of ambiguity in this second qualification, since "ecclesiastical" and "civil" can be seen as either complementary or as alternatives. The ambiguity arises from whether the set of words to be understood after "commonwealth" is "which is both" or "which is either". The difference is made more explicit if we imagine whether a comma may be understood after "commonwealth" or not. If a comma is understood, then the qualification may be read as to "a commonwealth, both ecclesiastical commonwealths and civil commonwealths". If the comma is not understood, then we take the commonwealth to be "a commonwealth which is both an ecclesiastical and a civil commonwealth at the same time". Since there is no comma marked, the weight must fall on the second reading.[21] However, the element of ambiguity is not thereby dispelled altogether, since the words which would conclusively resolve it (and only then could it be conclusively resolved) are not inserted nor unequivocally implied in the title.

The ambiguity of the phrase "commonwealth ecclesiastical and civil" arises partly from the qualification coming after rather than before the central word. Had the title read "an ecclesiastical and civil commonwealth", the meaning would be quite clearly that the two parts of the qualification complement one another, and that there is one kind of commonwealth under discussion, not two kinds. There are, however, two reasons why the qualification should succeed rather than precede the central word; the first is a rhetorical consideration and the second a historical one. Firstly, then, had it preceded it, the stress on the word "commonwealth" (the second most important word in the title) would have been somewhat dissipated, by distancing it from the focal word of the title, to a position which could not be further removed, thus affecting its direct relation to the word "Leviathan". Thus the structure of the title has a balance in its present form that would be lost by putting this second qualification before the central word (and the threat of the title-subtitle arrangement increased). And secondly, the use of this syntactical arrangement, whereby adjectives and other qualifiers can succeed the noun they refer to, was quite common throughout the period.[22] This form follows that used in Latin which, in the seventeenth century, was still the universal language of scholars, and influenced English syntax as well as English vocabulary.

Furthermore it may be noted (as matters of rhetoric become matters of the meaning of thinking) that this element of ambiguity in the phrase "commonwealth ecclesiastical and civil", arises in the work itself, and persists throughout it. In consequence, the relation between religious and strictly temporal matters, or the significance of theological considerations in civil matters, is not unequivocally drawn out by Hobbes in the work. By "commonwealth", Hobbes means a "state, in Latin Civitas", which is created by "the art of man" for his own "protection and defence".[23] "Ecclesiastical" refers to the activities of the Church or "Ecclesia", which is defined in Chapter 39 as "one person" which is "a company of men professing Christian religion, united in the person of one sovereign, at whose command they ought to assemble, and without whose authority they ought not to assemble".[24] And "civil" refers to the overall character of the commonwealth, in a manner such that once the criteria of a commonwealth have been outlined, the adjective "civil" is already understood and becomes redundant. The ambiguity now arises, both in what is said and in several elements of the rhetorical structure of the work. On the one hand, firstly Hobbes does *not* say that "civil" describes the activities of the state as opposed to the ecclesiastical activities of the Church, and[25] a writer with Hobbes' passion for definition and distinctions may be expected to have made this distinction if that is what he meant. And secondly Hobbes *does* argue that a knowledge of civil duty has a religious dimension in a knowledge of the laws of God, that thirdly the obedience of subjects to sovereign is conditional on the laws of God, and that fourthly "God is king of all the earth by his power".

However, on the other hand it can be argued that the first point loses its force when it is recalled that for Hobbes a commonwealth is above all a "one person" represented by the sovereign whose power is indivisible, so that a distinction along these lines is already ruled out of court, and the other points are so hedged by qualification by Hobbes as to make them carry, in part, quite different connotations. The second and third points occur in the passage at the end of the second Part which reads,[26]

> ....that a commonwealth, without sovereign power, is but a word without substance, and cannot stand: that subjects owe to sovereigns, simple obedience, in all things wherein their obedience is not repugnant to the laws of God, I have sufficiently proved, in that which I have already written. There wants only, for the entire knowledge of civil duty, to know what are those laws of God. For without that, a man knows not, when he is commanded any thing by the civil power, whether it be contrary to the law of God, or not: and so, either by too much civil obedience, offends the Divine Majesty; or through fear of offending God, transgresses the commandments of the commonwealth. To avoid both these rocks, it is necessary to know what are the laws divine....Whether men will or not, they must be subject always to the divine power.

Although the central point of this passage is that the laws of God are necessary to a knowledge of civil duty; that is, that the consequences which follow from God's power cannot be excluded from consideration in an examination of the character of a commonwealth, the qualifications Hobbes makes to this clear statement, and in particular the positing of offense to God and to the sovereign as equals, both "rocks to avoid", present a picture in which God and his laws have been given a cramped and limited position, and in which the force of the argument has been turned on its head, making consideration of God's laws conditional upon those of the civil sovereign. The qualifications which surround the fourth point also work to diminish the force of God's laws in civil commonwealths, for Hobbes says "God is king of all the earth by his power: but of his chosen people, he is king by covenant",[27] and:[28]

> But where God himself, by supernatural revelation, planted religion; there he also made to himself a peculiar kingdom....and thereby in the

kingdom of God, the policy, and laws civil, are a part of religion....

The connotation here is that in ordinary commonwealths, those not created by God by the planting of religion in supernatural revelation, the scope of the influence of God's laws on a knowledge of civil duty is not crucial at all. And while Hooker also distinguishes between a direct theocracy, based on divine positive law, and an ecclesiastical polity where God's word is interpreted by natural means by the king in convocation and parliament, Hobbes seems to go a step further. For the presence of divine law is clear, in Hooker's ecclesiastical polity, whereas Hobbes insists, in chapter 12, on speaking of religion *only* in terms of how it is understood by natural reason, which, while innocently in keeping with his method of developing his argument at this point, has the rhetorical effect of suggesting that *only* the conclusions of natural reason are or can be relevant.

The elements of the structure of the work that promote this ambiguity between a distinction which may or may not imply a separation, in "commonwealth ecclesiastical and civil", all work to suggest a sharper division that Hobbes explicitly draws in his argument. Firstly, in the second Part Hobbes discusses extensively the issues relating to the generation and constitution of a common-wealth; and with the exception of the treatment of religion in terms of natural reason in Chapter 12 in the first Part, only introduces religious considerations in the third Part, thus giving the impression that they are an addition, something tacked on to the already constituted commonwealth. In the Introduction too, where Hobbes lists the matters to be discussed in the description of "the nature of this artificial man" or commonwealth, the bald statement "Thirdly, what is a Christian commonwealth", immediately after the stress that Hobbes has placed on "Secondly....", has the effect of accentu-ating the distinction between a commonwealth and a Christian commonwealth (even if it is only meant as a methodological distinc-tion) and the autonomy of the constituted commonwealth before religious considerations are introduced into the argument. The detail which Hobbes provides in "Secondly, how, and by what covenants it is made; what are the rights and just power or authority of a sovereign; and what it is that preserveth and dissolveth it", for whatever reason, in contrast with the curt "Thirdly, what is a Christian commonwealth", works rhetorically to diminish the value of the third Part.

Furthermore, while Hobbes, in characteristic fashion, begins the second Part with a *definition* of commonwealth, the third Part contains no definition of a Christian commonwealth. This is an important matter, for Hobbes sets great store by the power of definition. In general, whatever is important to him, he defines, and in one sense, a reading of the first and second Parts of *Leviathan* involves the reader swinging from definition to definition. This is particularly true of the first Part, where the rhythm of the prose is dictated by the sequence of definitions, which act like beacons, as points of attention in the continuity of the argument. The development of the argument depends upon, in part, the connections between the definitions and, in one sense, what is important in the first and second Parts can almost be identified in the construction of a list of these definitions. For Hobbes it is in the definition of a word's meaning that its truth resides. Definition thus has the power to bring something, and the truth about it, into being. And definitions are, for Hobbes, absolute; once a word is defined, its meaning is exactly stated and remains true through all contingencies. Thus the absence of a definition at this point has the rhetorical effect of diminishing the status of the term in question and of casting doubt upon the notion of a 'Christian commonwealth'.

Instead, Hobbes begins the third Part by stating that the main 'principle' of Christian politics is the word of God delivered by prophets, and immediately follows this with the argument that natural reason (already used exclusively to derive the rights of sovereign power) is not to be discarded, since this is the only unequivocal tool of understanding man has, and is to be used to consider religious matters as well.[29] Hobbes' approach to the subject of Christian commonwealth, tied as it is to what has gone before, thus makes it clear to the reader that a Christian commonwealth depends for its very existence (not only methodologically but in practice too, the rhetorical structure of the work affirms) on the prior existence of a (civil) commonwealth. Furthermore, even the one new 'principle' that is introduced at this stage - the word of God delivered by prophets - confirming that a Christian commonwealth contains a dimension not found in the discussion up to this point, is diminished in value by the mediation at the crucial point of men, in the figures of prophets, who are therefore subject to a civil sovereign; and by the mediation of language, in the words spoken by the prophets, which is also subject to a prior master, natural reason.

Hobbes' "commonwealth" and Hooker's "polity" both suppose a set of political arrangements for the ordering and order of human societies, public arrangements of law defining obligation, duty, sovereignty and rights, which cover every aspect of man as a social being. And for both writers, the kind of commonwealth primarily under consideration is identified in general as that in which divine law is mediated through the civil sovereign. Thus far the similarities between their subjects are significant and central. But what is also notable is that their conceptions are reached from opposite directions - Hobbes' from the nature of man and Hooker's from the nature of the divinely created hierarchy of laws. This section concludes by considering what effect this has on the initial similarity.

In one sense, the difference between Hooker and Hobbes at this point is not that one comprehends a greater and the other comprehends a lesser role for religion in 'civil' society. For both, the notion of religious considerations in discussing the character of (civil) society is a foregone conclusion, an undeniable fact. The issue for both writers is the prospect of the fragmentation of religious authority, and so ultimately for all authority, leading to the utter disordering of society and the advent of civil war, that the autonomous groups of elders proposed by the 'Separatists' and 'Independents' would bring. As Hooker argues,[30]

> sith the kings of England are within their own dominion the most high, and can have no peer, how is it possible that any, either civil or ecclesiastical person under them should have over them coercive power, when such power would make that person so far forth his superior's superior, ruler and judge?....till better reason be brought, to prove that kings cannot lawfully be exempted from subjection unto ecclesiastical courts, we must and do affirm their said exemption lawful.

But whereas Hooker argues against this prospect largely by defending the ecclesiastical hierarchy of the Church, as an institution which custom and natural reason and Scripture (largely by its silence) all support, Hobbes argues against this prospect primarily by attempting to show that all authority and therefore religious authority too, must rest with the sovereign if a peaceful commonwealth which God would approve is to survive. The difference between Hooker and Hobbes here, thus revolves around their different conceptions of natural reason. For Hooker natural reason comprehends the testimony of custom and tradition, as a dimension of that same ability which men exercise in the present to organise their affairs in an orderly way consonant with God's will and laws. Hobbes at times seems to endorse this view, for instance in his approval of the monarchical history of England. However, in the first Part of *Leviathan* especially, he also argues that custom and tradition cannot be relied upon as evidence of the use of natural reason. Man's natural reason is here described as an essentially private matter, unaffected by any external considerations, and understands the need for a unified authority in civil society because the train of reasoning that leads to this conclusion is, for him, indisputable.

Other aspects of the structures of the *Laws* and *Leviathan* also provide a means of entering the discussion of the patterns of significance in the undertakings expressed in the two works, that is, from rhetoric to meaning. It may be noted, first of all, that Hobbes begins with the statement, in the Introduction, that the procedure of his argument rests on the proposition "read thyself",[31] know your own heart. This analytical statement contrasts with Hooker's; he begins with the statement, in the first chapter of Book I, that he has endeavoured "that every former part might give strength unto all that follows".[32]

While statements of procedure were a convention in sixteenth and seventeenth century works, the statements chosen by Hobbes and Hooker are not arbitrary, and it is worth exploring their character. The appropriateness of their statements is more obvious in Hobbes than in Hooker, since Hobbes' concern with methodological matters in general is more explicit. The methodological questions to which his resolutive-compositive method, his statement of procedure and his abundant definitions are answers, not only frame his arguments but also enter into the substance of the arguments explicitly, particularly in the first chapters of the first Part. But it is no less important to Hooker. Two examples will serve to show how Hooker's argument is built up, the later building upon and dependent upon the former, so that his argument accumulates in a manner which, in the best rhetorical tradition, looks natural.

In Book V Hooker considers in detail the nuts and bolts of both his theological doctrine and his view of the Church of England, its practices, customs and ceremonies. Towards the end of the Book the whole discussion merges into one about Church office holders and their powers. This is again a nuts and bolts matter, but also lays the ground for the discussion in Book VI of the powers of ecclesiastical jurisdiction and who should properly hold them. In this way Hooker introduces a highly contentious argument while making the movement of the whole discussion of the Laws fluid and natural-seeming, such that when the controversial question is explicitly posed in Book VI, the answer has already been laid in foundation in Book V.

The second example comes in Book IV, chapter iv, where Hooker says that the Puritans "do not disallow only those Romish ceremonies which are unprofitable, but count all unprofitable which are Romish; that is to say, which have been devised by the church of Rome, or which are used in that church and not prescribed in the word of God".[33] Hooker's argument at this point has a strong force in its own right, but a very much stronger force when we consider that Hooker has already argued convincingly earlier[34] that in things indifferent (that is, in some of the outward forms of the Church, as distinct from the doctrine of Christ which can only be found in Scripture and is not subject to change by man), man may alter the outward forms according to time, place, custom and circumstance, without changing anything vital to Christian faith and doctrine; and that God approves such alterations, which help man to faith in God by making external forms more convenient, so that man finds them acceptable. Hooker argues that the path to truth ought to be made convenient and beautiful, that this does not change the truth, but enhances it. He is here reaffirming the important Medieval and Renaissance view, most famously stated by Sidney, that truth and beauty can and ought to be one; which is both a philosophical and rhetorical principle.

In this way, then, Hooker's statement of procedure is expressed in the development of his argument, becoming at the same time a rhetorical and a methodological principle. And, as Lewis remarks,[35]

> the *Polity* marks a revolution in the art of controversy. Hitherto, in England, that art had involved only tactics; Hooker added strategy. Long before the close fighting in Book III begins, the puritan position has been rendered desperate by the great flanking movements in

Books I and II. Hooker has already asked and answered questions which Cartwright and Travers had never considered and which are fatal to their narrow scripturalism.

Lewis' comments point to the way Hooker's arguments characteristically develop, and their pattern conforms to that to be expected from his statement of procedure. While Hobbes and Hooker employ very different approaches to the structure of their own arguments, they also indicate that they both recognise a common rhetorical tradition.

The late sixteenth and early seventeenth century was a time when literary style was being developed for the English language. Before then, most scholarly and literary work was written in Latin, and while this practice persisted throughout the period such that Latin was still the language of scholars (and it may be recalled that several of Hobbes' works were written in Latin and that Hooker's *Laws* was translated into Latin), schoolboys were taught to speak and write it fluently, and education still focussed on the Latin classics, the move toward expression in English increased in this period. It followed that syntax and other grammar, rhythm, meter, accent and rhyme all had to be adapted from what was appropriate in Latin to what was appropriate in English, in both verse and prose. Hooker and Hobbes represent two answers to this problem, both superb in their way. Hooker uses, largely, Latin sentence structure etc., but in a way that in his use sounds mellow and gives his argument a memorable fluidity, while in most other writers attempting the same thing, it sounds contrived and leaves meanings at times obscure, wrongly accented and incoherent. Hobbes uses a new style for English prose which, while characteristically terse and short, by the profusion of imagery that his 'plainness' supports, avoids the traps to which some of his contemporaries succumb, of being either unrelievedly austere and tedious or uncontrollably convoluted.

Hooker's and Hobbes' statements of procedure, "that every former part might give strength unto all that follows" and "read thyself", as well as indicating the principles of their rhetorical structures in their works, also provide an entrance into the significance of their central preoccupations. Hooker's whole discourse is on law, and is addressed to the general question, 'what is the nature and character of law in a polity or commonwealth which is both a

Church and a Nation?'. And he takes as his starting point the nature or "cause" of law. While in the course of his argument Hooker does also deal with other notions - sovereignty, obligation etc., which we would consider under the head of Political Philosophy - his introduction of them, and treatment of them, and reason for dealing with them, all stem directly from their relevance to his central preoccupation, and the naturalness with which these other notions seem to emerge attests to the skill of his artifice. Hooker is not intent on writing a full-scale political philosophy, and that his work does nevertheless result in one, is due to the comprehensiveness of his central focus and its implications.

Hobbes, on the other hand, sets out with the intention of accounting for the whole, and so his focus is the whole commonwealth of which law is a part or aspect. For Hobbes, the central focus is the kind of civil society or commonwealth that the word "Leviathan" comprehends, seen as a whole or integrated composition, and therefore composed of parts which can be analysed. The very concept of composition demands, for Hobbes, a reciprocal conception of analysis, and so Hobbes' work builds from an analysis of the first secondary cause, sense.

The difference in statements of procedure, then, is expressed not only in the difference in the characters of their focuses of attention, but also in their general methods of approaching a subject, Hobbes identifying the simplest element analytically and abstractly considered, and reconstituting civil society from there, and Hooker jumping in with what is there. But there is also an important similarity between them. For Hobbes 'civil society' and for Hooker 'law', both constitute a 'system' of mutually supporting parts, as are the arguments elaborating them. The result is that Hooker has written as comprehensive a political philosophy as Hobbes, since his discussion of law involves him in the discussion of the other major categories, with law as the central point from which civil society hangs together. In Hooker, then, society follows from law, whereas in Hobbes, law in the sense that matters most to him, follows from society. That this is so, is expressed in both writers in both their explicit arguments and in the rhetorical structure of their arguments.

The effect of this difference between Hooker and Hobbes on their political philosophies is an interesting one, and can be seen in the arguments of the two writers on the generation of "politic societies". In Book I, chapter x, in the context of his argument that man's natural reason teaches him the laws to live by, Hooker says,[36]

> The laws which have been hitherto mentioned do bind men absolutely even as they are men....we are naturally induced to seek communion and fellowship with others. This was the cause of men's uniting themselves at the first in politic Societies, which Societies could not be without Government, nor Government without a distinct kind of Law from that which hath been already declared. Two foundations there are which bear up public societies; the one, a natural inclination, whereby all men desire sociable life and fellowship; the other, an order expressly or secretly agreed upon touching the manner of their union in living together. The latter is that which we call the Law of a Commonwealth, the very soul of a politic body, *the parts whereof are by law animated, held together,* and set on work in such actions, as the common good requireth.

Both Hooker and Hobbes belong to the tradition of political thought which considered it crucial to account for the generation of political societies, and that did so through the mechanism of a social contract or covenant, which sets up a distinction between men in a state of nature, with only the laws of nature to guide them, and men in civil society governed by positive law. Hooker goes on to argue that positive law must be consonant with and an expression of the laws of nature, as does Hobbes. They differ in that, for Hobbes the state of nature was a state of perpetual war from which the fear of sudden death forced men to follow the path indicated by the conclusions of natural reason, the law of nature to seek commonwealth, and submit to the obligations and duties of civil society in return for security. For Hooker, while in Book I he argues that in framing a civil order we must presume man to be "inwardly obstinate, rebellious, and averse from all obedience unto the sacred laws of his nature....a wild beast",[37] men in the state of nature are also said to be "inclined" to civil society. While both Hooker and Hobbes seek to qualify Aristotle's view of the naturally sociable nature of man, Hobbes' qualification to this view is far greater. For while Hooker regards men as "rebellious", he also regards them as amenable to reason whereas for Hobbes, men are convinced by reason only when it is underlined by a passion towards the same end - in this case the fear of violent death and the corresponding passion for self-preservation.

There are two differences involved here, whose importance may be overrated, and the first of which does not lead to the second. Firstly, for Hooker, men are on the whole naturally inclined to society, while for Hobbes they are forced into it through their mutual fear, society being a compromise of loss of some liberty in exchange for security. And secondly, for Hooker the parts of civil society are animated and held together by law, whereas for Hobbes civil society is in the final analysis or crucially held together by sovereignty, the indivisible absolute authority and power vested in the sovereign. For Hobbes law is secondary, and the same as the sovereign's will. Thus law is the instrument of the sovereign, through which his will and the obligations and duties of the citizens are conducted, their rights for the most part being only negatively within the scope of the law. However these two lines of argument have the same outcome, for Hooker goes on to identify the sovereign as the proper and only authority for positive law. Thus the rule of law is conducted through the sovereignty of the Prince. While Hooker and Hobbes therefore argue, in comparison, reversely (Hooker from law to sovereignty and Hobbes from sovereignty to law), in practice, in its effect on political society, it comes to the same result, namely that the sovereign alone has authority to make positive law, which expresses the law of nature which is the same as the dictates of right reason; that public activity is conducted through law, and that there is no effective right of resistance on the part of the citizens. Furthermore, in both writers the character and role of the social contract, as a legal mechanism, is of crucial importance, and while the burden of Hobbes' argument is from sovereignty to law, it is worth noting that the instrument through which the commonwealth is formed and a sovereign instituted - covenant - is a legal instrument and is valid because it is legal.

The situation, which follows from Hobbes' conception of sovereignty, of the lack of an effective right of resistance on the part of citizens, and the corresponding position of the sovereign as above the law, has occupied many writers on Hobbes. What twentieth century commentators find vexing is the seemingly facile assumption, found in both Hobbes and Hooker, that the right of resistance is only of theoretical interest, that it is unlikely to become a question of practical concern in the commonwealth or polity they envisage. Hobbes and Hooker both argue that the only situation in which the question of a right of resistance could even arise, is that in which the sovereign not only ceases to act through the legal framework (of positive law, expressing the laws of nature in positive form) he has established for public conduct, but also flagrantly contravenes that which the laws of nature enjoin in general terms, that the object of the commonwealth (and so of the sovereign) is the welfare of its citizens. Entailed in the second part of this double proviso is the notion that the sovereign may act, if necessary, through edicts which express his will more immediately, which impose particular obligations on citizens not found substantively in the general rules of positive law. What worries many twentieth century commentators is that if the sovereign were to disregard the framework of positive law or to take measures not sanctioned within the general terms of its rules, he does not seem to incur any effective penalty and could not, seemingly be resisted. In other words, in the extreme case it would seem that Hobbes' careful distribution of legal rights and obligations which ensure the welfare of citizens as well as the order and stability of the commonwealth as a whole, degenerates rapidly into a situation in which law becomes meaningless and the sovereign may rule through absolute power according, if he wishes, to his own whims. Many commentators find this apparent implication particularly puzzling in Hobbes, not only because much of his argument is spent in attempting to establish that the sovereign's power derives from the authority vested in him by the consent of the citizens, but also because the background which Hobbes had in mind when writing *Leviathan* seems to be precisely a situation which illustrates the failure of a system like Hobbes' to account for the extreme case. That is, the events of the 1640s in England seem to have arisen precisely from a situation in which the dissatisfaction of a large number of citizens with the character of their sovereign's method of ruling led to civil war and the breakdown of authority altogether.

However, Hooker's and Hobbes' statements on this subject become more intelligible as answers to this question (how is it that there is no real right of resistance against a sovereign who abuses his power?) if three considerations are taken into account. Firstly, the problematic character of the question revolves, in part, around the kind of social contract that is understood to have established the commonwealth or polity. The character of the social contract as outlined by Hobbes and Hooker must be distinguished from those which later became current in the works of political thinkers. The theory of the social contract, as it was developed in the late seventeenth and eighteenth centuries, was closely associated with the idea of the right of resistance and the doctrine of popular sovereignty. Hooker and Hobbes both differ radically from this conception of the social contract; in both the social contract serves primarily to account for the transformation of a multitude of individuals into a commonwealth of citizens. That is, for Hobbes and for Hooker the social contract is understood first as a philosophical rather than an ideological metaphor for the emergence of a commonwealth or polity based on the twin notions of sovereignty and authority. The kind of contract Hooker has in mind is not a formal contract of government of the kind that figures in the writings of some of his more radical contemporaries, but rather the ancient laws and customs of the realm, which it is the duty of the sovereign to observe. These laws and customs derive their validity partly from immemorial usage, partly from positive law, and ultimately from their source in divine law. For Hobbes the character of the contract (actual or notional) derives from the laws of nature recognised and acted upon by each man through his natural reason and on the basis of his passion and fear.

Thus for Hobbes and for Hooker the idea of contract is primarily a means of explaining how society and government came into existence. And they both argue that political authority, though derived from those who take part in the contract, cannot be withdrawn by them at will. This leads to the second consideration, that Hooker and Hobbes do not place *no* restriction on the sovereign's use of his absolute power and his indivisible authority - in both the sovereign is answerable to God. While twentieth century readers do not in general find this a convincing restriction, for Hooker and Hobbes it was a line of argument sufficient to assure that the sovereign would rule to ensure the welfare of the commonwealth of citizens. Thus their statements make sense when Hooker and Hobbes are considered as writers for whom divine judgment on the sovereign is to be taken seriously. And thirdly, for Hobbes the events of the 1640s illustrate not only the consequences of the breakdown of a weak political authority and the need for a sovereign whose authority is unassailable by those who consented to it, but also illustrates the power of religious fanaticism. In our eagerness to embrace Hobbes

as a writer who shares our secular understanding of the connection
between sovereignty and authority, we overlook the distinction
between a civil war fought for secular political ends, and a civil war
to be taken seriously as a religious war fought for religious ends but
whose resolution must be political because the stage on which it is
fought is a human, earthly one. For Hobbes the power of religious
fanaticism lies not only in its political consequences but also in its
appeal to the most potent dimension of a man's life, his religious
beliefs, that which links him to a world infinitely greater in every
way than the life on earth. But earthbound as he is during his
lifetime, the solution to man's wars must be political, he says.
Perhaps the reason for the sense of anticlimax and tameness that
greets the reader at the beginning of the third Part of *Leviathan* (after
the spectacular progression of the first and second Parts he is denied
even a definition of Christian commonwealth) lies precisely in
Hobbes' recognition that because the potency of the religious dimension of man's life exceeds that of any earthly dimension, it must
be severely harnessed to those lesser capacities that make life on
earth possible, peaceable and tolerable - that is, to natural reason and
the laws of nature that follow from recognising the constructive as
well as the destructive sides of man's passions, the artifice of
covenant by which the commonwealth is established, and the given
relation between sovereignty and authority on which it is based. If
a harmonious life on earth is to exist, religion must serve politics.[38]

Thus, if Hobbes' and Hooker's statements on this subject are to
make sense, the question to which they are answers must be understood as not 'how is it that there is no real right of resistance
against a sovereign who abuses his power?', but 'how is it that a
commonwealth can be constructed through the artifice of man?' It is
interesting to note at this point that the question of a 'lack' of an
'adequate' provision for a right of resistance exercises commentators
on Hooker much less than it does those on Hobbes. Three reasons
may be advanced to account for this. Firstly, God through his
creation of the hierarchy of laws, plays a larger part in Hooker's
argument than in Hobbes', so that the force of divine sanction and
judgment of the sovereign's conduct is more accessible to twentieth
century readers. Secondly, in Hooker, God is said to be subject to his
own First Eternal law, and therefore it is easier, by analogy, to regard
the sovereign as subject to law too, and thus less likely to succeed in

the exercise of a completely arbitrary power. And thirdly, the background against which Hooker wrote is considered to be more stable than for Hobbes; therefore Hooker has less reason to be concerned with a right of resistance, and is thus less culpable of 'neglecting' a 'proper' discussion of it. In other words, we are prepared to consider that Hooker's context is sufficiently different from ours, to allow that the issue at stake may have been a different one. However, it may be argued that the issue at stake for Hobbes was also different from ours. For Hobbes, Hooker's argument could not be convincing, because in his own context it had already, in practical terms, failed. Its failure could be located in that it leaves the appeal to divine revelation apart from that established in the ecclesiastical polity, as a weapon in an earthly conflict, too accessible and therefore too much of a threat to a political solution. It therefore serves to confuse in men's minds the (undoubted) significance of the religious dimension of man's life, with the business of his life on earth. For Hobbes, the solution involves a strict separation of these areas. And it is because of this that Hobbes is then, ironically, taken in the twentieth century as a writer for whom there is no significance attached to man's life. The argument that has been developed above gains its crucial support from noting that while we are prepared to accept that for Hooker sovereignty lies ultimately in Heaven and nowhere unambiguously on earth,[39] the absence in Hobbes of a right of resistance can only be satisfactorily accounted for if we accept that for him too, while it is the citizens who invest the sovereign with authority, the corresponding link is not with them but with God.

Turning once more to Hooker's and Hobbes' statement of procedure, it may be observed that both statements are metaphors. In one sense, this is an unexceptional point, since such brief statements are bound to operate as shorthand guides whose multiple significance requires some unravelling in the light of the course of the argument. In another sense, however, the point is worth some consideration, since the character of the metaphors Hooker and Hobbes have chosen, indicate the manner in which the two writers approached their inquiries. Hooker's metaphor is one which stresses the value of progression or development. It suggests two broad kinds of imagery. Firstly it suggests both the course of a man's life, that each experience in a man's life may give strength unto all that follows; and the movement of water from spring to river to sea, accumulating the

water from tributaries along the way, gaining in breadth and strength
as it moves. This is an image of continuity and change, of movement
from one identification to another without perceptible break, remaining of the same character throughout;[40] it is an organic metaphor. Secondly it suggests the imagery of building, of the construction
of an artifice or structure such that each part becomes incorporated
into the whole. Here it is a mechanical metaphor, and again "every
former part" has a double focus, being both characterised as a
particular and as contributing to the character (the "strength") of "all
that follows" and finally to the whole. As a mechanical metaphor it
suggests design, forethought, an artificer; and as an organic metaphor it suggests the undesigned but perfect course of nature, or
rather the natural course of all things, according to the design of the
Divine Maker but unknown to themselves. Thus the metaphor as a
whole suggests that the design of the artificer, in the work of artifice,
is also itself a "part" which "gives strength" to another artifice
according to the design of another artificer.

Hobbes' metaphor has the tone of a classical tag, and is curious
for also having a biblical association (although so does 'Leviathan')
when some of the other indications in his work suggest that religious
considerations are not of primary importance in his thinking. It also
expresses, however, in shorthand form, his epistemological position
that the only way to knowledge is through one's own experience,
and presents the image of experience as an intelligible account
which can be read. According to Hobbes' distinction in chapter 5
between the only two forms of knowledge, the results of prudence
may be uncertain while the results of science are "infallible";[41] in
chapter 7 he says that science or the knowledge of consequences "is
not absolute but conditional".[42] Both forms of knowledge are,
however, known as part of experience.[43] Thus knowledge cannot be
gained through external means such as the authority of books, but
only through the fruits of (in prudence) and right ordering of names
(in science) in experience.

It is also interesting to note that Hobbes' metaphor stresses the
profoundly private nature of experience and so of knowledge (though
the possibility of a shared or public knowledge is offered through
agreement on the definitions of words), whereas Hooker's metaphor
in respect of knowledge stresses its development and the strength
which emerges from it and is gained through its acquisition. In

rhetorical terms, then, Hobbes stresses that conviction arises from agreement (based on personal experience - which, because it can, and must, be "read" is a kind of book from which his general condemnation is excepted) on the first elements and their subsequent constructions, whereas Hooker emphasises that conviction is the outcome of a gradual process of recognition of the strength of an argument. In both writers the notion of an unbroken thread characterises the argument which carries conviction, but the emphasis in Hobbes is on the validity of its initial components, and in Hooker on the continuity of its development. Furthermore, the same considerations can be seen to operate in the overall structure of the two works. The pace of the argument of the *Laws* is gradual and its general tone optimistic, whereas in *Leviathan* the overall development of the argument towards the emergence of the figure of *Leviathan* is made up of a severely analytical attention to a long series of discrete particulars which may be rendered in a set of (static) definitions. Hooker seeks to account for a part - law - and argues towards a general acceptance of his view, which extends in the course of the work to encompass the whole polity. Hobbes seeks to account for the whole - civil society - and argues by way of a 'proof' of each discrete part along the way.

These reflections on the understanding of the two metaphors would be incomplete with respect to the *Laws* without some consideration of the importance, for Hooker, of custom and tradition. For as an organic metaphor, Hooker's statement of procedure also suggests the imagery appropriate to the growth and effect of custom and tradition in human affairs. One of the most notable expressions of the importance of custom and tradition in Hooker's thinking in the *Laws* is found in his argument that while "matters of perpetual necessity to all men's salvation" are "both fully and plainly taught in holy Scripture", it is "not necessary" for the structure of the Church "to be in such sort there prescribed". The former are "not capable of any diminuition or augmentation at all by men, the other apt to admit both".[44] That is, in "things indifferent" (those not crucial to salvation), and whether the Church in England should take the form of an episcopally-based hierarchy or not is one such, the Scripture does not prescribe and leaves to the "convenience" of man. As Hooker argues, "the necessity of polity and regiment in all Churches may be held without holding any one certain form to be necessary in them all",[45] and:[46]

> to mention what the Scripture of God leaveth unto the Church's discretion in some things, is not in any thing to impair the honour which the Church of God yieldeth to the sacred Scripture's perfection. Wherein seeing that no more is by us maintained, than only that Scripture must needs teach the Church whatsoever is in such sort necessary as hath been set down; and that it is no more disgrace for Scripture to have left a number of other things free to be ordered at the discretion of the Church, than for nature to have left it unto the wit of man to devise his own attire.

Hooker's argument for hierarchical organisation of ecclesiastical polity as the most fitting form for the Church in England, having reduced the argument of his opponents to a matter of 'unnecessity', concentrates on the tradition of episcopacy in the Church that extends back to the Apostles, and on the force of the analogy between hierarchy in the universe, in the structure of law and the structure of human societies. His argument rests on the notion that custom and tradition represent the choices of men throughout the past of what is most convenient for them, on the basis of their exercise of their natural reason. Although Hooker is now often seen as the father of Anglicanism, he wrote precisely because he wanted to reassert what he saw as a traditional view, a view which took full account of tradition and custom. For him, the Elizabethan settlement and episcopacy in the Church of England are good not only because they are God-given, but also because they represent the extension of a tradition, which is suited to the English people as shown in the continuity of the custom they reaffirm. The only new element, as far as Hooker is concerned, is that Elizabeth rather than the Pope is now the head of the Church of England, and this for Hooker does not represent a new departure but a modification which strengthens the tradition. Indeed in one sense Hooker is not preaching a particular religion but discussing the kind and degree of liberty proper to national churches within the universal visible Church, according to their different traditions.

Hooker's argument for the intelligibility of custom and tradition in terms of natural reason is, in part, directed against the Puritans' dislike and suspicion of natural reason. He identifies the source of their distrust in the strict separation they make between flesh and spirit in man, a dualism which in the end destroys the validity of the

gifts given to man by God in nature, including his natural reason and
arts and sciences. But that which is known to man of Divine Law in
Scripture may also be known through reason, Hooker argues:[47]

> ....the general principles thereof are such, as it is not easy to find men
> ignorant of them. Law rational therefore, which men commonly use
> to call the Law of Nature, meaning thereby the Law which human
> Nature knoweth itself in reason universally bound unto, which also
> for that cause may be termed most fitly the Law of Reason; this Law,
> I say, comprehendeth all those   things which men by the light of
> their natural understanding evidently know, or at least-wise may
> know, to be beseeming or unbeseeming, virtuous or vicious, good or
> evil for them to do.

The importance of reason for Hooker as opposed to the Puritans
is, then, twofold. He not only describes how the externals of Church
government have been determined by time, place, custom and
circumstance in the history of the Church, but also argues that such
things can demonstrably be left to men's judgment, discretion and
reason to determine in a manner that God would approve, as shown
by the silence of Scripture on the particular forms in "things indifferent". Hooker's preparedness to accept an account of the changes
in the structure and ceremonies of the Church in terms of time, place
and circumstance modifying a tradition, point to the historical
character of Hooker's understanding, which is not found in the
Puritans (nor, incidentally, in Hobbes). Almost everything of importance for the Puritans takes place for them outside time, and the
only certainty for them on earth is the coming Day of Judgment.
Because they view the past, present and future all in terms of this
messianic event, their attention is focussed not on the human historical
level but on the divine historical level, in which all events have and
only have a divine significance. In contrast, Hooker argues that the
significance of the human historical level lies in the recognition of
the value of customs, traditions, human continuity and change. The
authority of positive law and the authority of Divine laws in Scripture
do not conflict but complement each other, for the natural and
human worlds are not only fixed in the hierarchy ascending to God,
but are also imbued with God, whose laws are written in nature and
in men's hearts. "Where understanding therefore needeth", says
Hooker, "in those things Reason is the director of man's will by
discovering in action what is good. For the Laws of well-doing are

the dictates of right Reason".[48] As Munz observes, "To Hooker, the appeal to historical precedent and to history in general is always an appeal to human reason".[49] Thus there is in Hooker a direct connection between natural reason, custom, natural law and divine law. His understanding of natural reason comprehends the significance of custom and tradition, a dimension not found in Hobbes. For Hooker, natural reason is demonstrated in the way men in the past have organised their public arrangements, whereas for Hobbes natural reason is valued for its essentially private character, and for the Puritans it has little value at all.

It has already been argued so far that Hooker's work deserves to be called political philosophy in the same sense that we understand Hobbes' work as being, if a label is required, on the grounds that the scope of Hooker's interest in law involves him in a comprehensive discussion of the major categories of political philosophy, in terms of the relation of law to sovereignty, obligation, rights and duties and the social contract. Hooker's status as a political philosopher may also be examined from another set of considerations, those which identify his arguments about religion as political in character - where religious argument is political argument.

Hooker's arguments about religion serve two main and related purposes, firstly to provide a thoroughly-argued justification for the Elizabethan settlement, which in effect establish the tenets and scope of what later became known as the Church of England, and secondly to refute the claims of the Puritans for a quite different conception of Church polity. Indeed, the conception of the Puritans, based on the principles found in Scripture alone, acknowledging only revelation and faith as the basis of knowledge about and action in the Church, rejecting knowledge gained through natural reason, and rejecting the palpable evidence of the effects of political and historical considerations in the organisation of an activity within the Church, all contribute to the conclusion that the Puritans envisage a Church which is not a polity at all.

Both of Hooker's purposes are served by the progressive narrowing of focus that characterises Hooker's discussion of Church polity in the course of the *Laws*. In Book III Hooker begins the discussion of the laws governing ecclesiastical polity, following the discussion of law in general in Book I and of the scope of divine law in scripture in the human world in Book II. And, having considered some aspects of "Church polity" in general, that is, those which affect the Christian church as a whole, he again narrows his focus, and continues the discussion of the character of church polity as it concerns the polity of the Church in England. Thus Book III the polity of Church of England is seen as the most important category of ecclesiastical polity under discussion. And, as Hooker develops his argument in Books III and IV, it becomes clear that for him the polity of the Church of England cannot be separated from the polity of England as such.

It is important to distinguish between Hooker's and Hobbes' references to 'Puritans'. During Hooker's lifetime the Puritans were dissenters within the broad all-embracing scope of the Church in England, and the only serious contender for the faith of Christians in England was the "Romish" Church. By the time *Leviathan* was written, however, the Church had a narrower focus and Puritans and other dissenters operated largely from outside the established religion. The change from the Church in England to the Church of England, was from a Calvinistic Anglicanism to an Armenian Church of England. Puritans were now more like their popular image, and politically dangerous in a way not found in Hooker's time, that is, once their views were being expressed in Parliament in a platform against the Royal prerogative. The change is from Puritans inside the Church to dissenters expelled from it and forming their own churches and parties. It is a development from 'Puritan' as a general label to describe reformers, to the fragmentation of dissenters into groups of Presbyterians, Independents and the manifold smaller sects. Thus in Hooker's time the Church in England encompassed a whole spectrum of anti-Papal thought, although some dissenters had already broken away. By the time Hobbes was writing *Leviathan* the Church of England had become more circumscribed, and attempted to pursue a middle course between Catholics on one side and the Puritan and independent sects on the other. Furthermore, while Hooker's Church was identified with Elizabeth I, in Hobbes' time the discredited (in some eyes) or at least embattled (in others) Charles I could try to claim to represent that unity but could not unambiguously be said to hold it. And, after James I had antagonised so many by his claim to rule by divine right in the temporal field of civil society, the unity achieved (even though precariously) by Elizabeth as herself the head and symbol of both Church and Nation,

was indeed difficult to justify in the present. With the beheading of
Charles I and the reign of Cromwell, the idea of a stable unity of
Church and Nation took on a new meaning, and the effect of this on
the idea of the Church of England was significant. The character of
the Church of England necessarily changed along with the changes
in the character of its opponents and allies.

The political character of theological controversy in the late
sixteenth and early seventeenth centuries is a point which is, in one
sense, not in dispute. The character of political activity and thought
was, throughout this period, so deeply imbued with the inheritance
of religious considerations, that theological controversy in its turn
could not be seen as other than polically significant. Since, however,
Hooker's work tends to be regarded, in twentieth century currency,
as largely within the preserve of theology and the history of law,
detached from its political groundwork, it is worth restating the
connection. Theological controversy during this period is not simply debate about various ways of interpreting the corpus of texts (the
Bible, the works of the early Church Fathers and the profusion of
commentaries, and the thought of Calvin and his follows), but must
be seen in its setting, which concerns the relation between religious
and political authority in England.

The sixteenth century theological controversies in England are
a good example of the religious institutions exploring their relation
to the newly-emerging political unit. For what is theologically
significant to stress in a framework of Papal supremacy over Christendom, is different from that in a framework of the Elizabethan
settlement affecting a population divided in its religious allegiance.
To a large extent the controversies arose from the consequences of
developments in religious observation inspired by political changes
implemented by Henry VIII and Elizabeth, and from the political
consequences of Calvin's thinking. But here as well, the political
character of the controversies that arose cannot be divorced from
their theological character. Indeed, since the terms in which political
debate takes place are for the most part those of another activity
(nowadays the vocabulary and terms of debate being largely those
of economics and technology); that is, since the terms of politics itself
(authority, democracy etc.) are abstractions whose meaning depends
upon the concrete situation involving other activities to which they
refer, the identification of the theological character of political

debate in the period under discussion, involves no fundamental problem. And the point around which the theological/political controversies revolved was the redefinition of theological significances within the altered political structure ushered in by Henry VIII and Elizabeth. Religious debates, movements and heresies appear, from their labels ('latitudinarianism', 'Armenianism', the 'Vestarian' debate) formidably unintelligible to the lay reader, and seem to predicate a wide knowledge of theology before they can be understood. However, on examination, the issue at stake in each case can be seen to make sense in terms of its political rather than its solely theological consequences.

In Book II of the *Laws*, Hooker is concerned with the refutation of various quotations from Scripture held by the Puritans to be crucial in the argument for their claim that in Scripture and only in Scripture is the law laid down, that divine law for man in Scripture equals all law for man, and that this law applies to every action of a man's life. Hooker argues for different interpretations of these quotations, along the lines that while divine law is certainly laid down in Scripture, it is also found out by other means, and that it does not apply to all of a man's actions. Only the things that Scripture directly prescribes as lawful or unlawful are divine laws; those choices in which it does not prescribe a certain way are "things indifferent". Hooker is here arguing that the limits of divine law in Scripture are narrower than the Puritans would suppose, and that this does not lead to a less lawful man, since in "things indifferent" man will use his "discretion" or judgment according to reason, to do what is right in the particular case, even if it not be directly laid down in Scripture. Thus while the limits of explicit divine law are narrower, the conditions in which good actions and right choices are made is not. As Hooker sums it up,[50]

> There is no necessity, that if I confess I ought not to do that which the Scripture forbiddeth me, I should thereby acknowledge myself bound to do nothing which the Scripture commandeth me not.

In "things indifferent", Hooker maintains, "there is a choice, they are not always equally expedient".[51]

What Hooker is doing in Book II is attempting to refute the arguments of the Puritans in their own terms, on their own ground of Scripture. But the burden of the *Laws* as a whole is to oppose the type of Church government of autonomous groups of elders advocated by the Puritans, and defend the episcopally-based hierarchy in Church government of the Elizabethan settlement, on the grounds not so much of theology but of political necessity and feasibility. In this, Hooker's approach is very similar to that of Hobbes. Both writers reject the Puritan system on the grounds that it divides the authority that men consent to, between Church and Nation; and that moreover, the presence of a *number* of autonomous groups of elders would lead to an even greater fragmentation of authority which would, in turn, result in civil disturbance and conflict. Furthermore, both writers argue the theological case that because God is omnipotent, absolute, eternal etc., His ways and purposes cannot be fathomed by man, are not open to man's scrutiny, whereas the Puritans claim such knowledge.

Hooker and Hobbes both see very clearly that civil and Church authority must be unified in one person, for the sake of civil peace, and although Hooker's argument is framed largely in theological terms while Hobbes' appeals to an essentially private natural reason, both arguments are concerned to establish a point about the conditions and character of politics. For Hooker it follows from the episcopal structure of Church polity that its highest office is joined with the highest office in the hierarchical order which oversees temporal affairs, held by the (civil) sovereign. Hooker and Hobbes both recognise that the first criterion for peaceable association in a commonwealth of polity is that Church and civil authority be unified in one person, and the force of both their arguments is to accuse their adversaries of political naivety.

The threat of political fragmentation was very real in the views propounded by religious fanatics in the sixteenth and seventeenth centuries. The evidence discussed in the works of Cohn and Yates[52] indicates that the strength of such fanaticism has been often underestimated in twentieth century accounts of the history of ideas in this period. Cohn and Yates establish the importance of currents of thinking and movements in the Medieval and Renaissance period that in our time would not be considered as significant aspects of the history of ideas. Whatever the excesses of these two books, they are important contributions to our understanding of the background against which the writings of men like Spenser, Sidney, Hooker and Hobbes are to be read, for they point to the recurrence and fervour that highly radical and unorthodox interpretations and uses of

Scripture and religious life attracted throughout the period from the twelfth to the seventeenth century.

Several interesting consequences for understanding Hooker and Hobbes follow from the evidence described by Cohn and Yates. Firstly it is possible to distinguish more clearly between the orthodox mainstream of the Reformation (including the emergence of the Church of England) from the manifold radical sects that arose in its wake. Once Luther looked to Scripture rather than the Papacy for religious authority, others began to authorise their own individual interpretations in the same way. Thus the ostensible Royalist/ Roundhead division in the middle of the seventeenth century can now be seen as the orthodox tip of the political iceberg. Hobbes' advocacy of either King or Cromwell becomes intelligible in the light of the threat posed by the wealth of competing fanaticisms whose leaders offered no prospect of political stability. And the "fanatics" against whom Hooker and Hobbes are writing can be recognised more clearly, and as a potent threat that helps to account for their writing of their works.

Secondly one can recognise the extent to which any elements of millenarian and apocalyptic thinking are absent from Hooker's and Hobbes' works, and understand why. In view of the association between such thinking and politically dangerous religious fanaticism throughout the period, it can be seen that the absence of millenarianism is not a sign of modernity in their works but a rejection of the fanaticism occurring in their contemporary contexts. Furthermore, the height of revolutionary millenarian thinking in England occurred with the Ranters in 1649-50 - that is, at the time Hobbes was writing *Leviathan*. Thus there is here a direct link, not just a background one, between the climate of fanaticism and the writing of Hobbes' work. And it is interesting to note the proximity of the accusations of atheism against Hobbes following the publication of *Leviathan*, to the accusations of atheism against the Ranters in a Parliamentary debate which resulted in a law against them in 1650. Charges of atheism in this period carried a powerful political load, quite apart from their strictly theological significance.

And thirdly the works of Cohn and Yates demonstrate, as do other sources of evidence, how the history of ideas in this period is necessarily religious in character. In terms of politics and thought today, the power of sixteenth and seventeenth century religious fanaticism is almost not credible. But in the context of the dominance of religious thought in all thought at that time, it becomes more intelligible. The force which fanaticism had illustrates the extent to which thinking was dominated by the preoccupation with the relation between life on earth and the divine world, the religious character of the understanding and meaning of the universe as a whole, and salvation and life after death.

Intellectual histories of this period that concentrate upon the orthodox mainstream of thinking are, therefore, providing a somewhat distorted picture. For they neglect the whole movement of thinking and action that helps to account for works in the acknowledged mainstream such as *Leviathan*. Although these popular movements are neglected on the grounds that they have no coherent intellectual basis, it is worth noting that many of those who contributed articulately to them were former monks and other educated men, who used their education and knowledge of works recognised as scholarly in order to pursue the logic of whatever brand of fanaticism they favoured. In sum, the intellectual history of the period need not be restricted to the scholastics and their detractors and the different controversies that arose between them, on a strictly philosophical basis.

Thus it may be seen that another point of significant similarity between the works of Hooker and Hobbes, which relates to their concern with a unified authority, is found in the urgency which both writers felt, to write, against the context of their political backgrounds. The popular image is of Hooker's work as the product of a serene golden age, in contrast with Hobbes' work which is seen as the product of an intensely turbulent political conflict. However, the tenuous quality of the stability in Hooker's time is well drawn by him in the final two pages of Book IV, which indicate how miraculous the re-establishment of the Church in England under Elizabeth had seemed ("raised as it were by miracle, from the dead...."), after its establishment by Henry VIII but overthrow by Mary. With historical perspective, we tend to regard Henry's actions as the decisive ones and see Mary's reign as an interlude which could not succeed in stemming the tide of change. But to Hooker and to both his patrons and adversaries, it seemed by no means sure that Elizabeth's re-establishment of the Church of England was secure and would endure. It had been overthrown by Mary, and was again under attack, from a different quarter. Thus it was crucial to Hooker to argue as convincingly as possible, so that the Church's integrity would be preserved. Hooker's "via media", then, means in theological terms the Elizabethan Anglican notion of the cooperation of grace (through faith) and reason, and in political terms the middle way between the fanaticisms of Puritans and Catholics.

One of the reasons for the currency of the popular image of Hooker's work lies in the mellifluous "golden" quality of his prose, in contrast with the sharp and taut quality of Hobbes'. There are two points to be made here. Firstly, even if these ascriptions were accurate, they would not in themselves be decisive in indicating the character of political stability or ferment in the two periods. And secondly, when the prose of the two writers is examined, a rather different picture emerges. Within the undoubted fluidity of Hooker's prose,[53] there is a tightness and economy of argument which neither Hobbes nor other writers of the period surpass. And in Leviathan, the impression that each word has been wrenched out of a severe and arduously logical train of systematic thought, is accompanied by another, quite different impression, that of a writer who keeps his predominantly 'poetic' instinct under restraint but cannot prevent a wealth of imagery flowering into a full-blown allegory which provides one level of continuity in the work. In Hooker's work the elements of the rhetorical structure all work to the same end or effect, whereas in Hobbes they work toward different effects, and it is this conjunction that causes *Leviathan* to strike the reader as both fascinating and ambiguous.

Finally, the rhetorical structures of the *Laws* and *Leviathan* can be compared in terms of the two writers' use of metaphor, imagery and references to other works. Perhaps contrary to expectation, Hooker does not use many metaphors in the substance of his argument. Many analogies are made to elucidate his points, and he makes frequent reference to the overall conception of hierarchical order instinct with correspondence. In Book III in particular, the imagery of light and sight is prevalent ('by the light of God', 'by the light of reason', 'shineth forth', 'out of darkness most clearly shined', starlight etc.). And Hooker's work is characteristically free of the imagery, often used in conjunction with that of light and sight in other writers on religious matters, associated with hell, the sinful nature of man, the wrath of God and the terrors of Judgment Day for sinners.

Organic images such as in "For as civil law, being the act of the whole body politic, doth therefore over-rule each several part of the same body",[54] abound throughout the work to express the connections understood by Hooker between the levels of the hierarchical order, and serve also to reinforce the links between his arguments.

Hobbes on the other hand, uses an abundance of metaphor in the substance of his argument as well as an overall allegory which is at the same time organic and mechanical, and which explicitly provides a fund of imagery in addition to the incidental metaphors, through which the argument is developed. But Hobbes' explicit allegory is similar in function to Hooker's more implicit references to the hierarchical order, on which the coherence of the development of his argument depends; the implicit character of Hooker's references may be accounted for by the common currency of the conception of overall hierarchical order among his contemporary readers.

Some of Hobbes' images recur over several chapters, reinforcing the continuity and potency of a theme and heralding by a kind of shorthand the reappearance of a theme. For instance, in chapter 3 Hobbes introduces the image of unguided mental discourse as a "wild ranging of the mind",[55] and later on, after speaking of regulated mental discourse, he comes to speak of remembrance, and says,[56]

> Sometimes a man knows a place determinate, within the compass whereof he is to seek; and then his thoughts run over all the parts thereof, in the same manner, as one would sweep a room, to find a jewel; or as a spaniel ranges the field, till he find a scent; or a man should run over the Alphabet, to start a rhyme.

It is interesting to note that this passage, containing four different images to express his meaning, along with a sentence stating the Latin derivation of the word, constitutes Hobbes' whole treatment of remembrance; his reliance on forms of argument other than demonstration, and particularly upon the variety of language to express meaning, indicates the limits of describing Hobbes' prose in terms of a severely logical analysis. The ranging image occurs again in chapter 8 when Hobbes describes indifference. A man of no great passion, an indifferent man, may be a good man and give no offense to anyone and yet, says Hobbes,[57]

> he cannot possibly have either a great fancy, or much judgment. For the thoughts are to the desires, as scouts, and spies, to range abroad,

and find the way to the things desired: all steadiness of the mind's motion, and all quickness of the same, proceeding from thence: for as to have no desires, is to be dead.

It becomes clear through the 'ranging' image that for Hobbes, thinking is not a merely passive activity but a dynamic movement of thoughts, and that thinking is firmly encompassed within the overall conception of motion.

But among the abundance of Hobbes' imagery and use of metaphor, those which have received most attention are those associated with arithmetic, money, geometry and science. Mental reckoning as addition and subtraction, words as counters, reasoning as the conceiving of a sum total or as a remainder, language as counters at the sovereign's disposal, and the value or worth of man as his price, are some of the most explicit examples. Hobbes' use of this language has led some commentators to conclude that it reveals a fundamentally "mechanistic-materialist" view of man and civil society in Hobbes' thinking, and as a sign that Hobbes belonged to or helped to inaugurate the new scientific age.[58] However, the flourishing of curiosity about the natural world, and the intellectual excitement surrounding geographical discoveries and advances in astronomy and other sciences in the Elizabethan period, alongside the continuing interest in such things as alchemy and witchcraft, resulted in a wealth of additional imagery attesting to the correspondences in the hierarchical order, rather than in a different habit of mind. Furthermore, arithmetic, geometry and astronomy had been three of the seven subjects in the curriculum since early Medieval times; the use of the imagery and metaphors provided by these subjects in Hobbes is by no means novel. Among other sixteenth century writers Hooker, for example, uses a geometric metaphor to great effect to describe the character of the polity:[59]

....therefore as in a figure triangular the base doth differ from the sides thereof, and yet one and the selfsame line is both a base and also a side; a side simply, a base if it chance to be the bottom and underlie the rest: so, albeit properties and actions of one kind do cause the name of a commonwealth, qualities and functions of another sort the name of a Church to be given unto a multitude, yet one and the selfsame multitude may in such sort be both, and is so with us, that no person appertaining to the one can be denied to be also of the other.

But it is precisely in Hobbes' appeal to and use, in the very substance of his argument, of imagery and metaphor and allegory (whatever the character) that links him with the earlier tradition of thought. The particular vocabulary may sometimes be novel but the habit of mind that uses them in this way is a Medieval and Renaissance one. What is important is not that Hobbes uses some images which are taken from contemporary scientific thought, but that he used images in a thoroughgoing way at all.

Hooker often quotes the Bible, the Church Father and classical Greek and Latin writers, in particular Tertullian, in support of his argument, and many of his arguments are directed against or begin by refuting, quotations from the contemporary Puritan writer Thomas Cartwright. And it is interesting to note incidentally the prominence of imagery to do with poisons, disease, infection and purging, in the work of Cartwright quoted by Hooker, particularly evident in Book IV. Hobbes by contrast, makes almost no quotations of nor footnotes to authorities in his argument or in support of it. In Parts three and four of *Leviathan*, Hobbes quotes copiously from the Bible, and much of chapter 42 (the longest is the work) is devoted to refuting the views of Cardinal Bellarmine, but in the context of religious discussion throughout the period, this practice was considered not as a normal form of quotation, but as a necessary dimension of any argument one wished to propound. The absence in general of quotations from authorities in *Leviathan* is another example of Hobbes demonstrating in his rhetoric what he is at pains to establish in his arguments, in this case that only right reasoning and the reading of oneself leads to knowledge, and conversely that,[60]

> they that trusting only to the authority of books, follow the blind blindly, are like him that, trusting to the false rules of a master of fence, ventures presumptuously upon an adversary, that either kills or disgraces him.

This chapter has been concerned with five themes that have emerged in studying Hobbes and Hooker with a view to presenting a comparative treatment of the *Laws* and *Leviathan*; three of these themes are about Hobbes and Hooker, and two are about writing about Hobbes and Hooker, or indeed about any other political thinker. The word 'theme' here has been deliberately chosen for, in addition, the argument of this chapter has been concerned to indicate the way in which these five threads of discussion interact. The first theme has been the nuts and bolts one of identifying what seemed to be the most significant aspects of the two writers' works, within the limits of a comparative discussion; and since the discussion of Hobbes at this level is the subject of other chapters, more attention has been given to Hooker and to the points of significant comparison between the two works. The first theme, then, has involved the examination of Hooker's major preoccupation, law (and the way in which divine law, the natural law of reason and positive law all inform both Church and temporal matters in the single polity), and of his conceptions of custom and tradition and the hierarchical structure of Church government; and has attempted to demonstrate that the character of his work brings it within the scope of political philosophy. It has also involved the discussion of the ambiguous character of Hobbes' treatment of the relation between religion and civil matters in a "commonwealth ecclesiastical and civil", a discussion which, by its nature, can arrive at no conclusive resolution. But whatever the ambiguity in Hobbes' position, the common ground between Hobbes and Hooker here is clear. Both writers are opposed to "fanatics" of all colours, not religion itself; two consequences follow from this. Firstly, Hobbes and Hooker both address themselves to the problem of civil order, understood as a problem which can only be resolved by placing religion in the context of politics, of civil association seen as a whole. Both are concerned with the effects of religious organisation on civil order, and with the consideration of civil association as having written into it religious considerations. Both see ecclesiastical hierarchy as expressing religious unity, and the system of doctrine, administration and practices advocated by Puritans and Catholics alike as expressing (for different reasons) religious disunity. And both are led therefore, although from different directions, to advocate a state Church, such that religious and civil authority are vested in one Sovereign whose authority is indivisible. And secondly, both writers must be studied in the context of politics preoccupied by its relation to ecclesiastical, theological and religious considerations and activity - a context acknowledged for the study of Hooker but less often for the study of Hobbes. This first theme has also involved the comparative discussion of Hobbes' and Hooker's understandings of natural reason, the contract which generates a commonwealth or polity, the connection between authority and sovereignty, and the way in which the absence of a right of resistance in both their works may be understood in consequence. In particular, the study of Hobbes' view on the right of resistance leads to the conclusion that the first two Parts of *Leviathan* do not stand on their own as completely describing the political or temporal dimension of civil society, and require the third Part.

The second theme has been concerned with some of the elements in the rhetorical structures of the two works, as another aspect of their comparison. The discussion focussed upon their titles, statements of procedure, the use of argument in terms of religious considerations as argument about the conditions of politics in a commonwealth or polity, and the use of metaphor and imagery. The manner in which discussion of these matters becomes, at a touch, a discussion of matters of substantive meaning, is the subject of the third theme. One of the purposes of this chapter has been to illustrate that rhetorical considerations provide a means of entering those preoccupations, assumptions and conditions which are most significant in the work of any particular writer. Thus the third theme has been concerned with the way in which, in the case of Hobbes and of Hooker, rhetoric leads to or introduces meaning; or rather with how rhetoric itself is a level of meaning, how the consideration of the particular rhetoric of a work is also, at the same time, a consideration of its meaning and significance.

The fourth theme has also been concerned to make a general point about writing about political thinkers, with Hobbes and Hooker seen as particular examples. For one of the objects of this chapter has been the comparison not simply of what might be called Hobbes' and Hooker's techniques of government (what the two writers said about categories such as authority, sovereignty, obligation, rights, law and the constitution of government), but of that which touches upon a broader and more fundamental comparison of their political philosophies - a discussion which attempts to account for why the two writers considered these categories as significant and in what manner. Thus the emphasis changes from a discussion in terms of a number of categories whose importance and relative importance is preconceived, to one in terms of the character of Hobbes' thought and the character of Hooker's thought, as it is expressed in *Leviathan* and the *Laws*. The advantage of this approach is that, although the resulting discussion may be much less neat and tidy, it might allow the scope of whatever may emerge as significant

a greater possibility of indeed emerging. For the points of significance and the continuities and dissimilarities of and between the
two works are expressed in their political philosophies understood
as coherent wholes, and only then become intelligible in terms of the
categories of the techniques of government. And while the character
of a particular political philosophy can only be approached through
what the writer has actually said, this chapter has attempted to show
that 'what the writer has actually said' is expressed not only in
arguments in which terms like 'authority', 'sovereignty' etc. occur
and reoccur, but also in the elements of rhetoric and rhetorical
structuring the writer has chosen for their expression and development. The study of a political thinker which begins and ends only
with a discussion of the categories of the techniques of government,
might be felt to lack an account of why and how they are connected.
The reason why a thinker should consider say, 'authority' significant,
is not found simply in his discussion of it alone; the question of why
'authority' is significant in the work of a particular political thinker
is a question about his political philosophy seen as a connected
whole.

The fifth theme has attempted to demonstrate that in the light
of the significant continuities between Hooker's and Hobbes' political
philosophies, the claim by some twentieth century commentators
that Hobbes' *Leviathan* represents a 'radical new departure" in the
history of political thought, require some revision. Such claims rest
on two sources of evidence, its contemporary reception and an
examination of the text itself. In view of the connections which can
be drawn between Hobbes' thinking and that of earlier writers such
as Hooker, Sidney and Spenser, the examination of the text of
Leviathan discloses the transitional character of Hobbes' thinking.
And if it is understood as coherent within its own terms, it cannot be
claimed as either the pale imitation of an earlier political philosophy
nor as the precursor of a later one. In consequence, the significance
of the contemporary reception of *Leviathan* may be found in the
political context at the time of its publication, rather than in the
acceptance of a too literal interpretation of the charges of atheism
levelled against Hobbes. These charges may be accounted for by
considering the context of the inflamed and polarised political
conditions in which they were made, rather than by considering
them only at their face value.[61] *Leviathan* is a work of political phi-

losophy and as such cannot be read simply as an apology for either side in the Civil War. The attacks made against *Leviathan* are those on a work which is at the same time profoundly political and singularly lacking in practical solutions to what were seen to be the substantive issues at stake. In terms of its propaganda value and effect, and practical prescriptions (the level of attention which its combination of emphases primarily attracted) then, it was fair game for attack on all sides.

NOTES

1. Among the best contributions to the debate on these problems are those of J. Dunn, "The Identity of the History of Ideas", in *Philosophy*, Vol. XLIII, 1968, Q. Skinner, "Meaning and Understanding in the History of Ideas", in *History & Theory*, Vol.8, 1969, and "The Limits of Historical Explanations", in *Philosophy*, Vol. XLI, 1966, J.G.A. Pocock, "The History of Political Thought: A Methodological Enquiry", in Laslett & Runciman ed., *Philosophy, Politics and Society*, Oxford, 1962, C. Condren, "Three Aspects of Political Theory", in R. Lucy ed., *The Pieces of Politics*, Macmillan, 1975, and M. Oakeshott, "The Activity of Being a Historian", in *Rationalism in Politics*, OUP, 1962.
2. One of the stock examples of the consequences of this view being K. Popper's *The Open Society and its Enemies*, 2 vols., Routledge & Kegan Paul, London, 1945.
3. The question of connections in thinking was discussed in chapter 2.
4. Included in Walton's edition of Hooker's *Works*, OUP, 1845.
5. The aim in this chapter is to compare the thinking of the two writers, rather than to show a line of derivation from one to the other. This point, together with Hobbes' characteristic reluctance to advertise the extent of his reading of other authors, renders the absence of evidence that Hobbes had read Hooker arguable, and does not in any case invalidate the comparison undertaken here.
6. *Laws*, p146. All page references to the *Laws* are to the Walton edition, OUP, 1845.
7. *ibid* p148.
8. "no art is at the first finding out so perfect as industry may after make it", *Laws* p167, and "Man in perfection of nature being made according to the likeness of his Maker resembleth him also in the manner of working; so that whatsoever we work as men, the same we do wittingly work and freely", *Laws* p169. The value Hobbes accords to artifice ("Nature, the art whereby God...", *Leviathan* p5) represents an appeal to the same tradition of thought.
9. *Laws* p287-288.
10. *ibid* p427.
11. *ibid* p43.1
12. Lewis, *English Literature in the Sixteenth Century*, OUP, 1973, p457
13. *Laws*, ed. Walton Vol. II, p485.
14. *ibid* p493.
15. Lewis, *op.cit.* p455.
16. *ibid* p457.
17. It is at this point that Munz's book, *The Place of Hooker in the History of Thought*, Routledge & Kegan Paul, London, 1952, fails in its self-appointed task. The three alternative relationships between "Church" and "state" which he sets out as the only theoretical possibilities, and from which he argues the case for the failure of Hooker's 'via media' as a form of the second alternative, do not allow for the dimension crucial to an understanding of Hooker's thought that Lewis properly stresses.
18. *Laws* p228.

19. Titles formed by the word "or" (expressed or understood) dividing a metaphor or latin phrase from a series of words which elucidate it, were common throughout the sixteenth and seventeenth centuries. The usage points to the habit of mind throughout the period which placed far more significance on metaphorical language than later became acceptable. During this period the force of metaphor was understood as a reminder to the reader of any subject to an overall divinely-created order. Examples include Thomas Scot's *Philo-mythie or Philomythologie wherein Outlandish Birds, Beasts, and Fishes are taught to speake true English plainely* (1616), Francis Bacon's *Sylva Sylvarum or a Natural History in ten Centuries* (1629), Luke Fawn's *A Beacon Set on Fire: or the Humble Information of certain Stationers, Citizens of London, to the Parliament and Commonwealth of England* (1652), and Alexander Ross' *Arcana Microcosmi: or the hid Secrets of Man's Body discovered: in an Anatomical Duel between Aristotle and Galen concerning the Parts thereof: in an Anatomical Duel between Aristotle and Galen concerning the Parts thereof: With a Refutation of Doctor Brown's Vulgar Errors, The Lord Bacon's Natural History and Doctor Harvy's Book De Generatione, Comenius, and Others...* (1658).

20. Very long titles, and titles with very long subtitles were also common throughout this period, as some of those in the previous note illustrate. Hobbes' title can be seen to be really quite pithy compared with some of those of his contemporaries. The composition of Hobbes' title contains a well-distributed balance of and tension between the words, whereas in some, these qualities are lost in the accumulation of secondary clauses. In these cases the importance of an initial metaphor is crucial in maintaining some focus for the title.

21. The title of Hobbes' *The Elements of Law, Natural and Politic*, on the other hand, contains a comma, which avoids this kind of ambiguity, making the title clearly understood as "the elements of law, both natural law and politic law".

22. For example, William Warner's *Pan his Syrinx or Pipe* (1584), the anonymous *Willoby his Avisa* (1594), Thomas Pierce's *The Self-Avenger Exemplified* and *Self-Condemnation Exem-plified* (1658), Matthew Wren's *Monarchy Asserted* (1659), the anonymous *Insolence and Impudence Triumphant* (1669), Thomas Tenison's *The Creed of Mr Hobbes Examined* (1670), William Lucy's *An Answer to Mr Hobbs His Leviathan* (1673), Matthew Hale's *Reflections by the Lord Chiefe Justice Hale on Mr Hobbs his Dialogue on the Lawe*, Charles Blount's *Miracles, No Violations of the Laws of Nature* (1683), Robert Boyle's *An Examen of Mr T. Hobbes his Physians Natura Aeris* (1662), John Bramhall's *Castigations of Mr Hobbes His Last Animadversions, in the Case concerning Liberty and Universal Necessity* (1658), Thomas Cooper's *The Mystery of Witchcraft: discovering the truth thereof* (1617), and Alexander Ross' *Leviathan drawn out with a Hook, or Animadversions Upon Mr Hobbs His Leviathan* (1653).

23. *Leviathan* p5.

24. *ibid* p305. And so, through the simple rhetorical device of defining in terms of a derivation from Latin, Hobbes has effectively dismissed the issue so important in Hooker, of whether the organisation of the Church ought to be hierarchical or not.

25. As with the word "thinking", discussed in chapter 4.

26. *Leviathan* p232.

27. *ibid* p77.

28. *ibid* p76-7.

29. *ibid* p242.

30. *Laws*, Vol.II, p582.

31. *Leviathan*, p6.

32. *Laws*, p147.

33. *ibid* p361.

34. In the course of Book III.

35. Lewis, *op.cit.*, p459.

36. *Laws*, p184, emphasis added.

37. *ibid* p184-5.

38. Hobbes makes this point very clear in *Behemoth*, ed. Molesworth Vol. VI, p221, p227. It is interesting how closely connected for Hobbes are the questions of the right of resistance and the role of religion in the commonwealth.

39. Lewis, *op.cit.* p458.

40. This image is also used in the work of Michael Oakeshott very effectively, to describe the course of history as the historian's subject.

41. *Leviathan* p30.

42. *ibid* p40.

43. Even reasoning, acquired by industry, can only be knowable as experienced.

44. *Laws* p340.

45. *ibid* p288.

46. *ibid* p293.
47. *ibid* p178-9.
48. *ibid* p167-8.
49. Munz, *op.cit.* p70.
50. *Laws* p249.
51. *ibid* p239.
52. Norman Cohn, *The Pursuit of the Millenium*, Granada (Palladin), London, 1970 (1957), and Frances Yates, *The Occult Philosophy in the Elizabethan Age*, Routledge & Kegan Paul, London, 1979
53. George Edelen, "Hooker's Style", in W. Speed Hill, ed., *Studies in Richard Hooker*, Cleveland, Case Western Reserve Univ. Press, 1972, p276, locates this effect in the "generally low density of his prose", which he says "results from a deliberate emphasis on the whole rather than the part. Like Spenser, Hooker seeks his effects by the page, not the line".
54. *Laws* p196
55. *Leviathan* p14
56. *ibid* p15
57. *ibid* p46
58. For example, S. Mintz, *The Hunting of Leviathan*, CUP, 1962; R. Peters, *Hobbes*, Penguin, 1956; J. W. N. Watkins, *Hobbes' System of Ideas*, Hutchinson Univ. Library, London, 1965
59. *Laws*, Vol. II, p485-6
60. *Leviathan* p30
61. It is interesting to note that in D. Christie-Murray's *A History of Heresy*, New English Library, London, 1976, Hobbes' views on religion are considered as heterodox rather than heretical, and that their heterodoxy is seen to lie in his rejection of the Mosaic authorship of the Pentateuch and his Erastinianism, and not in any way in any atheistic tendencies.

CHAPTER 7
Allegory and Philosophy in *Leviathan*

Following the discussion in previous chapters of some aspects of Hobbes' language in *Leviathan*, the discussion of the engraved title-page and the comparison of the ways in which the use of language expresses meaning in Hooker's *Laws* and Hobbes' *Leviathan*, this chapter is concerned with the verbal imagery which forms the allegory of the Leviathan. In the examination of the allegory of the Leviathan, the issues raised in the earlier chapters converge. The argument has three levels of purpose. It is concerned firstly to describe the allegory of the Leviathan as one of the aspects of Hobbes' rhetoric. The discussion involves the examination of the features of the allegory – the mechanical and organic sources of imagery, the importance of movement, and the conception of artifice. The allegory is introduced by Hobbes in the figure of the Leviathan in the Introduction, and developed in the course of the work in the language Hobbes uses to discuss the character of the "civil and ecclesiastical commonwealth".

The second concern of the argument of this chapter is to indicate the philosophical character of the allegory. This involves seeing how the allegory holds together the whole philosophical view Hobbes presents in *Leviathan* – the way in which the allegory may be understood as the central feature of the rhetoric of *Leviathan* seen as a philosophical identity.

The third level of the argument takes these concerns a step futher, in proposing that what is said about the function of the allegory in *Leviathan* holds not only for this particular text but implicitly for other texts as well. The function of the allegory in *Leviathan* may be seen as an example which suggests a more general point – that any philosophical work which seeks to present a view as a whole, a coherent unity, contains in its use of language metaphors whose significance are particular to that specific work. The texture of meaning that hangs on such metaphors operates like the allegory of the Leviathan, and the philosophical character of the whole text requires the understanding of that texture. This aspect of the concerns of the thesis takes up the argument begun in the first two chapters on rhetoric and the role of figurative language and analogical reasoning in philosophical understanding.

What would *Leviathan* lack, without the allegory? What does it provide that is not provided in other ways? This is the question to which the discussion in this chapter addresses itself.

The features of the allegory are initially sketched by Hobbes in the Introduction to *Leviathan*. These are sources of imagery with which the figure of the Leviathan is associated, the kind of movement which enlivens the figure, the specific analogies between man, machine and commonwealth that are drawn, and the conception of artifice that Hobbes articulates which provides the key to the relationships drawn between the 'levels' of the allegory. These are the features of what, during the course of the work, becomes recognised as an allegory. In describing these features, some of the ground covered in previous chapters needs to be recalled, to indicate its particular reference to Hobbes' language and meaning. In particular there is an overlap with the content of chapter 5 – due to the relation between the verbal and pictorial expressions of the allegory. In the following few pages, some of the same points arise as did in chapter 5, but it is necessary to repeat them, since in chapter 5 they arose from the engraving, and here they arise independently from the language Hobbes uses in the Introduction and later on.

What is immediately clear in the Introduction, and what is crucial, is firstly the multiple character of the figure of the Leviathan, the multiple levels to which attention is directed, and secondly that Hobbes' allegory is not fantastical, supernatural or exorbitant. There is nothing about the figure of Leviathan or about the way the allegory operates in the course of the work, that is un-natural. It is intelligible in terms of artifice (that by which man imitates the natural world created by God, including man) alone, and thus comes within the province of Hobbes' own stricture, in the Answer to Davenant's Preface to *Gondibert* that poets and other writers ought not to go beyond the "conceived possibility of nature". Thus, and this is important to Hobbes, his own allegory of the figure of Leviathan can be understood in terms of this accepted area, since there is nothing singly about it which goes against or beyond nature, for while Leviathan expresses many things, he never ceases to be a natural man; the conception of a natural man is never lost.

Mechanical and organic imagery

The kinds of imagery introduced by Hobbes in the Introduction fall into two groups, mechanical and organic, and the important point to bear in mind is that the figure of the Leviathan is portrayed as both a mechanism and an organism at the same time. In the course of the work the mechanical imagery is continued through the metaphors associated with arithmetic, geometry, money and science – those subtle products of man's industry which express best to Hobbes the rules and laws of mechanical operation – and the organic imagery is continued through the working out of the correspondences implicit in the term 'body politic'.

In the Introduction, however, the mechanical imagery is more general, and derives from Hobbes' use of the metaphor of the engine to describe the movement which animates man's physical body. The specific analogies drawn are between the heart, nerves and joints of man's body, and the automata made by man's artifice – springs, strings, wheels, and the composite artifact of the watch. The significance of this mechanical imagery to describe man lies in the conceptions of artifice and movement which Hobbes thereby introduces.

Hobbes then introduces organic imagery, as a palimpsest upon the mechanical, to describe the commonwealth as an artificial man. Thus sovereignty, magistrates, reward and punishment, wealth and riches, the people's safety, counsellors, equity and laws, concord, sedition, civil war, and pacts and covenants – the major features of the commonwealth – correspond to the soul, joints, nerves, strength, memory, reason and will, health, sickness, death and original creation of man.

Hobbes furthermore emphasises that both these sets of imagery describe the parts of a body which is a whole, an integrated composition. The mechanical imagery is seen in terms of "giving motion to the whole body", and the organic imagery describes a commonwealth which is an integrated composition. In particular, the pacts and covenants, says Hobbes, are the means "by which the parts of this body politic were at first made, set together, and united", and they correspond to the generation of man by God in the creation. And it is interesting to note that the generation of man by God is said by Hobbes to have taken place by an act of speech, a pronouncement of will, in the statement "let us make man". This is important in terms of Hobbes' concerns, for two reasons. Firstly, an act of speech is a natural and not a supernatural or magical occurrence (such as generation, for instance, by a bolt of lightning, would be). And secondly, it confirms the connection between God and man in the significance of speech; this is one of the many correspondences between the natural, human and divine levels of the universe that Hobbes draws upon.

As the work develops, the organic imagery associated with the 'body politic' becomes more prominent than the mechanical, in Hobbes' account of the commonwealth. The language of the 'body politic' runs right through *Leviathan*, and its presence is by no means arbitrary to his meaning. For example, the description of sovereignty as the soul of the commonwealth in the Introduction[1] is repeated in chapter 21 and extended: "The sovereignty is the soul of the commonwealth; which once departed from the body, the members do no more receive their motion from it".[2] And in chapter 28 Hobbes points again to two levels of the sovereign's 'body' or "person" when he says "the sovereign, considered in his natural person, and not in the person of the commonwealth".[3]

It is important to note how deliberately Hobbes uses this body imagery for it indicates how he approaches the understanding of civil society. Another example is found in Hobbes' discussion of public ministers in chapter 23. He continues the imagery used with great force in chapter 22 which refers back to that used in the Introduction and says, "in the last chapter I have spoken of the similar parts of a commonwealth: in this I shall speak of the parts organical, which are public ministers".[4] Of ministers of general administration Hobbes says, "this kind of public ministers resembleth the nerves, and tendons that move the several limbs of a body natural".[5] And again "These public persons, with authority from the sovereign power, either to instruct, or judge the people, are such members of the commonwealth, as may fitly be compared to the organs of voice in a body natural".[6] Furthermore, those public ministers with authority from the sovereign to procure the execution of judgment given – "every act they do by such authority, is the act of the commonwealth: and their service, answerable to that of the hands, in a body natural".[7] For Hobbes it is extremely important to specify the way in which the sovereign may delegate authority and power without himself losing it, and without it dissolving its indivisible and absolute character; to speak of ministers as nerves and tendons and as the voice and hands, indicates exactly the relationship he wishes to specify.

Hobbes' description of public ministers abroad illustrates again how he uses the correspondences between the body natural and the body politic, in the imagery, to discuss the features of his commonwealth – this time the way in which ministers as public persons "represent" the sovereign. A public minister abroad, he says, is "yet a minister of the commonwealth; and may be compared to an eye in the body natural. And those that are appointed to receive the petitions or other informations of the people, and are as it were the public ear, are public ministers, and represent their sovereign in that office".[8] For Hobbes, those who "represent" the sovereign remain entirely dependent upon him, as the working of an eye or an ear is dependent on the well-being of the body as a whole, In this way, Hobbes precludes the introduction of any connotation of autonomy or independence in the notion of representation.

The same kind of argument underlies Hobbes' discussion of law, justice and force in chapter 26. The "two arms of a commonwealth", he says, "are force and justice; the first whereof is in the king; the other deposited in the hands of the parliament. As if a commonwealth could consist, where the force were in any hand, which justice had not the authority to command and govern".[9] "Therefore", Hobbes continues, using the correspondence to stress the identification of the sovereign with "the person of the commonwealth", "it is not that juris prudentia, or wisdom of subordinate judges: but the reason of this our artificial man the commonwealth, and his command, that maketh law: and the commonwealth being in their representative but one person, there cannot easily arise any contradiction in the laws....In all courts of justice, the sovereign, which is the person of the commonwealth, is he that judgeth".[10] Hobbes' use of language in this passage also provides an example of how he puns on the word "person", to signify both a natural person and someone who holds public office and stands for, represents or 'personates' the sovereign. This pun, like that on the word "member" to signify both a natural person who is a member of a corporate body and a limb or organ of a natural body, which has already appeared in some of the passages quoted, is found throughout the text: it is a point to which the discussion will return.

One of the notable ways that Hobbes develops and extends the body imagery is through metaphors associated with sickness and health to describe the condition of the commonwealth.[11] Thus on the one hand he says, for instance, "For it is with the mysteries of our religion, as with wholesome pills for the sick: which swallowed whole, have the virtue to cure; but chewed, are for the most part cast up again without effect";[12] and he speaks of "the infirmities" of a commonwealth as "the diseases of a natural body",[13] "the diseases of a commonwealth, that proceed from the poison of seditious doctrines" and the disease that results from the use of private judgment,[14] of "democratical writers" as mad dogs that have "bitten" monarchy "to the quick" and whose "venom" is a "continual torment" to the well-being of the commonwealth,[15] and of the "epilepsy" that results from the darkness of School distinctions.[16] These are just a few of the many examples in *Leviathan* of this imagery.

On the other hand Hobbes develops the imagery of health and nourishment to describe a well ordered commonwealth. He calls the power of levying money "the nutritive faculty", and talks of such "nourishment, as is necessary to life, and motion",[17] and speaks of "the antidote of solid reason".[18] This imagery is perhaps most explicit in chapter 24, which is entitled "Of the Nutrition, and Procreation of a Commonwealth". Hobbes talks in terms of "diet", "appetite", "hurt",[19] "sustentation" and "nourishment".[20] One of the most interesting examples is money as the blood of a commonwealth. Hobbes describes the circulation of money in the economy of a commonwealth as "the sanguification of the commonwealth: for natural blood is in like manner made of the fruits of the earth; and circulating, nourisheth by the way every member of the body of man".[21] One of the effects of the use of money is "to make commonwealths more, and stretch out their arms, when need is, into foreign countries"; however money is "unable to endure change of air" and its effect is at home only.[22] Hobbes goes on to discuss the "conduits" or channels or arteries through which the blood of money is conducted; "And in this also, the artificial man maintains his resemblance with the natural; whose veins receiving the blood from the several parts of the body, carry it to the heart; where being made vital, the heart by the arteries sends it out again, to enliven, and enable for motion all the members of the same".[23] This passage describes both the body natural and body politic or artificial at the same time; it also refers to the offices of public ministers and to subjects, both immediately insofar as they have natural bodies and mediately in that they help to make up the body politic. The language of this description is, furthermore, particularly apt for Hobbes' understanding of the commonwealth, for the circulation of the blood of money is movement around, and through the parts of, an organism.

At this point in the text it is the vocabulary of law which is combined with the imagery of the natural and politic body, through the vocabulary of the anatomy of human bodies. And, as if in case any reader had missed the significance of the imagery, Hobbes drums home the connection between the commonwealth, the sovereign and the natural and politic "person", when he says "For seeing the sovereign, that is to say, the commonwealth, whose person he representeth...."[24]

The two sides of this imagery are contrasted by Hobbes when, at the end of chapter 22, he says [25]

And this is all I shall say concerning systems, and assemblies of people, which may be compared, as I said, to the similar parts of men's body; such as be lawful, to the muscles; such as are unlawful, to wens, biles, and apostems, engendered by the unnatural conflux of evil humours.

Hobbes' description of what occurs when a commonwealth is dissolved provides a good example of how he speaks about the character of civil society through the language of the natural body:[26]

For the sovereign is the public soul, giving life and motion to the commonwealth; which expiring, the members are governed by it no more, than the carcase of a man, by his departed, though immortal, soul. For though the right of a sovereign monarch cannot be extinguished by the act of another; yet the obligation of the members may. For he that wants protection, may seek it anywhere; and when he hath it, is obliged, without fraudulent pretence of having submitted himself out of fear, to protect his protection as long as he is able. But when the power of an assembly is once suppressed, the right of the same perisheth utterly; because the assembly itself is extinct; and consequently, there is no possibility for the sovereignty to re-enter.

As with the other images already discussed, those associated with the death of a natural body do much more than merely embellish or dramatise Hobbes' argument. The language he uses indicates exactly the kind of relationships between the parts of the commonwealth he wishes to make. In the passage just quoted,

Hobbes' account of the way in which subjects ("members" in two senses at once) may seek protection elsewhere once a commonwealth is dissolved, whereas an assembly does not have this right, is lucidly conveyed through the metaphor of the death of a natural body.

Hobbes uses the body imagery sometimes to specify the parts of the commonwealth and their relation to the whole, and sometimes to stress the identity of the whole with both the sovereign and the commonwealth of subjects. The continuity of the imagery enables Hobbes to explain the connections between the parts, the character of the parts and to arrive at a conception of the commonwealth as a coherent whole. It also enables him to move from one level of attention in his discussion to another (the whole, the parts, the particularity of the parts, concrete example) without the development of the discussion seeming forced or discontinuous, and to focus upon any one level as a level related to others. Furthermore, the understanding that is expressed through the imagery provides Hobbes with the means of speaking about the commonwealth which is neither wholly abstract (in the sense that 'rights', 'obligation' etc. are abstract) nor wholly in specifics (in the sense that the actions of particular men or parliaments are specific).

Hobbes' description of the commonwealth along the lines of a body politic, and he frequently uses this term in the text, recalls the body politic imagery which was not only prevalent, but was the predominant means of accounting for the commonwealth in discussions about civil society throughout the Medieval and Renaissance period. During this period, the body politic metaphor was understood to supply the means of explaining the relation between man, King, commonwealth and God; the way in which the King was the mortal representative of God, represented also the body politic as well as having himself a natural body, was crucial. And secondly, civil society was understood in terms of the human, organic body directly – a whole made up of parts which worked together as an organism. Discussions in which the King is described as the head etc., were very common.

The use of the body politic imagery was understood as one of the most powerful examples of the correspondence between the levels of the created world; the body politic imagery was such a potent 'argument' for the character of the commonwealth because of the correspondences between the natural world, man, society and God on which it drew. To speak of a commonwealth in terms of a body politic was to place it within an acknowledged and ordered framework of understanding and meaning and significance, and to speak about God and man in one breath.

Hobbes' use of this imagery is comprehensive. Not only are the relations between the natural body, man, the commonwealth and the sovereign found in his language; the correspondence with God is also present. He calls the sovereign "that mortal god",[27] and argues in chapter 30 that the obedience due to the sovereign in law is of the same kind as that owed to God in the commandments.[28] In his discussion of images in chapter 45, Hobbes draws a connection between three levels – God, sovereign and magistrates: "So an earthly sovereign may be called the image of God: and an inferior magistrate, the image of an earthly sovereign";[29] and at the end of chapter 28 the correspondence between the mortal and immortal Kings is repeated:[30]

> Hitherto I have set forth the nature of man, whose pride and other passions have compelled him to submit himself to government: together with the great power of his governor, whom I compared to Leviathan, taking that comparison out of the two last verses of the one-and-fortieth of Job; where God having set forth the great power of Leviathan, calleth him King of the Proud. 'There is nothing", saith he, 'on earth, to be compared with him. He is made so as not to be afraid. He seeth every high thing below him; and is king of all the children of pride'. But because he is mortal, and subject to decay, as all other earthly creatures are; and because there is that in heaven, though not on earth, that he should stand in fear of, and whose laws he ought to obey; I shall in the next following chapters speak of his diseases, and the causes of his mortality; and of what laws of nature he is bound to obey.

While Hobbes' own attitude to the spiritual scope of religion in civil society may be ambiguous, he exploits the full force of the correspondences between the levels of the created world in his use of the body imagery. And although Hobbes is often careful to say "resembleth" or "is like" or "compared", though this is by no means always the case, the connections being made by Hobbes are closer than comparisons between separate things. The way in which Hobbes uses and develops the body imagery throughout the work gives it an irreducible presence in the expression of his thinking. In particular, Hobbes' use of this imagery provides the answer which is convincing to questions like 'why is the authority of the sovereign indivisible and absolute?' and' why are subjects obliged?'

The imagery of the body politic is additionally appropriate for Hobbes because of his insistence that he is describing a subject which is composed only of matter, corporeal matter. Like the body politic of Medieval and Renaissance discussions it is neither invisible nor incorporeal, but clearly visible in the person of the sovereign, the natural body of the King and the natural bodies of subjects.[31] In consequence, the way in which the sovereign carries the authority of the persons in the corporate body, is also neither mystical nor incorporeal, but through the notion of an actual or implicit covenant having taken place. Thus the generation of the commonwealth rests not on an act of faith, but on the fundamental natural powers of men, for it is an expression of aspiration and passion and wish, as well as an intellectual expression of reasoning, all expressed in embodied form. The combination of passion and reasoning acting in concert through the movement of bodies coming together in the covenant, provides the means which, Hobbes argues in *Leviathan*, is the only sure grounding for knowledge in general and the perpetuation and security of the commonwealth in particular.

Hobbes' organic imagery, as well as exploring the implications of the body politic, also draws upon two other and related sources of metaphorical explanation which exercised an enormous force throughout the Medieval and Renaissance period – that of the relation between father and children, and that between God and man directly. The family relationship and kinship, in which the father is the head and protector, was used to account for all social and political relations, and is also evident in the paternal appellation of the Roman clergy. The image of Leviathan is, among other things, that of a father who protects and embraces and guides his children (the children of Pride) so that they may then lead their lives and pursue their own felicity. And the relation between God, the epitome of the father, and man was expressed again in the divine qualities attributed to kings. The figure of the Leviathan, then, as well as being a mechanism made by the artifice of man, a natural man, a king, and the sovereign expression of the corporate commonwealth, is also an intensely personal paternatlistic figure and a mortal God.

Movement

The kind of movement which animates the figure of the Leviathan, is both that of automata, "engines that move themselves by springs and wheels as doth a watch", and that of organic development such that the very life of an organism is registered in and known by its motion – "for seeing life is but a motion of limbs".[32]

The metaphor of movement for life itself, is crucial for Hobbes, for on it depends the analogy he wishes to draw between the study of physical bodies in the sciences, the study of artificial bodies in the arts, and the study of man and the commonwealth in philosophy. For Hobbes the universe is an integrated composition, any aspect of which can be examined according to a common set of presuppositions of inquiry. The examination of physical bodies is a study of their motion and their matter. The same applies to artificial bodies in the arts and philosophy, and while some commentators on Hobbes have taken this to be evidence of Hobbes' 'scientific' approach to the study of man and society; it also witnesses the perhaps more fundamental point that for Hobbes, the natural and artificial world are not separated along the lines drawn by modern science but are profoundly related. They are necessarily fused in the study of man and civil society because the study of men in commonwealths is a study of an entity which is both natural and artificial.

Furthermore, for Hobbes the man-made quality of a mechanism remains one of its most important features, and in *Leviathan* the creation of the commonwealth by men never ceases to be important. Thus while the springs and wheels of Hobbes' mechanistic imagery are driven from outside themselves to create motion, and the organic images are driven by motion internal to hearts, nerves, tendons and blood, the two converge again because the motion of organic entities can also be seen in terms of mechanism and vice versa. In both kinds of image, then, the motion is both involuntary and generated by a voluntary act of creation – by man's artifice, or God's.

The metaphor of movement for life itself, in respect of the life of an organism being registered in and known by its motion, is also important to Hobbes in describing the relation *between* voluntary and involuntary motions in man. In the first chapters of *Leviathan* Hobbes examines the voluntary motions of man such as speaking, which are artificial, and the involuntary motions – the passions – which are natural. Man's voluntary motions are propelled by a passion or desire towards or away from an object, whether in the physical world or in the mind. One of the conclusions Hobbes draws from this line of argument is that since the natural motions of man are the passions, and since trains of reasoning and speech are driven by the passions, it is imperative that the commonwealth be safeguarded from the subversion resulting from destructive passions aroused by rebellious preachers. For destructive passions are no less natural to man than creative ones. In this way, then, Hobbes arrives at one of his most specific programmatic points from the consideration of the kinds of motion in man.

The combination of mechanical and organic movement which gives life to the figure of the Leviathan becomes, as the allegory develops in the course of the book, an analytical movement. The allegory is animated not by chronological movement, but by analytical procedure. That is, we begin with the whole image of the Leviathan, a natural and artificial being, a living mechanism, and in the rest of the book the analytical implications, ramifications, consequences, characteristics and significances are followed. It is a journey, a quest, and a search not across land and in time, but in the mind. There is constant movement from one level to another, from body to man to commonwealth to sovereign to God and back again and, as in all allegory, it is through the journey that a familiar but also unfamiliar entity becomes "less conditionally understood", in Oakeshott's terms. In *Leviathan* it is a man, the image and concept of a man which is familiar, and the commonwealth of Leviathan which emerges as the understood.

One implication of the significance of movement or motion, for Hobbes, is made clear in chapter 11 where he identifies the nature of man with the unceasing seeking of felicity. This in turn is seen as "a perpetual and restless desire of power after power, that ceaseth only in death", which Hobbes sees as "a general inclination of all mankind".[33] As well as showing how a passion can have both creative and destructive potential, this movement is readily intelligible in terms of both the organic and mechanical imagery already used to discuss man – a natural inclination of men and the movement of a machine which, once wound up, is in perpetual motion.

On the level of the kinds of reasoning used in *Leviathan*, Hobbes uses two methods to advance his argument in addition to the metaphorical, although it is important to add that these are all strands of a single overall argument and so separable only for analytical purposes. These two methods are commonsense introspection and the much advertised resolutive-compositive method, and in *Leviathan* they act in concert, the first largely on the level of the examination of human nature and the second largely on the level of the exploration of civil society.

An interesting feature of the second method, so far as the movement within the text is concerned, is that the resolution and composition take place concurrently. The way in which the notion of "civil and ecclesiastical commonwealth" is resolved into its component parts by Hobbes, and at the same time the task of composition or reconstruction is taking place, can be seen as two threads of movement in the work, in opposite directions. The result, however, is not confusing, for both threads of movement start from the initial image of the figure of Leviathan; the resolutive-compositive method emphasises the importance of wholes. The resolutive movement focuses upon that aspect of the image by which it is an integrated figure made up of parts which can be analysed, whereas the compositive movement begins with that aspect of the image according to which it is the natural and acquired powers of man that characterise him. The mutual dependence of the two kinds of movement is expressed by Hobbes in the figure of the Leviathan, wherein the sovereign depends on the subjects who compose him and subjects depend on the sovereign they form. The same notion of simultaneous resolution and composition is captured throughout the work, in passages such as, "For the good of the sovereign and people, cannot be separated. It is a weak sovereign, that has weak subjects; and a weak people, whose sovereign wanteth power to rule them at his will".[34] In this way Hobbes argues very effectively against any form of limited or divided authority.

The two kinds of movement are further related to the figure of Leviathan, for it is through the reconstruction of Leviathan the natural man that the reconstruction of Leviathan the image of civil association takes place. The first Part of *Leviathan* is not only an analysis of parts and a process of gradual composition but is also a discussion of man as a metaphor for civil society. Because the image of the constituted civil society is presented in the Introduction, the reader attends to the argument of the first Part on two levels, man and the commonwealth. The discussion is explicitly about the character of man but the correspondence with commonwealth is present as a figure.

Perhaps this prefiguring of the discussion of the second and third Parts in that of the first accounts for the lack of surprise the reader feels about the way Hobbes develops his argument in the later Parts of the work. One example of this is found in chapter 14, which is still in the First Part. In the discussion of primarily legal matters in chapter 14, Hobbes refers, but only in passing, to the "common power set over" men which can ensure that a covenant is not invalid.[35] But although this "common power" is not described or defined here, he nevertheless exercises an enormous presence in the argument; the presence of the sovereign – which derives from the Introduction – provides the context in which this discussion makes sense. The legal matters discussed in chapter 14 already presuppose a "common power" whose character is that of a sovereign who is none other than the Leviathan. The import of the discussion is for the generation of civil society, in the institution of the Leviathan sovereign – which are not explicitly considered until the second Part. The features of Hobbes' commonwealth - the kind of absolute power a sovereign must have, that he is not a party to the covenant, that he governs by his will (passions more fundamental than reasoning), that his authority requires citizens' obligations and his prerogative to use force, his monopoly of power, his representing the rights of all citizens in his person - are all already presupposed in outline in chapter 14.

At three crucial points in his argument, Hobbes uses the notion of the mechanism of 'transference' to indicate the kind of movement that has occurred. In chapter 4 he speaks of the "transfer" of mental discourse into verbal;[36] in chapter 14 he says that obligation is created by the "transferring" of rights;[37] and in chapter 21 he discusses the manner by which sovereignty is "transferred" on the death of a sovereign or by conquest or acquisition.[38] By the use of the metaphor of transference,[39] the force of the argument of chapter 4 is felt later in the work, and the arguments of the later chapters are reinforced by the repetition; the movement is again in two directions. Thus in chapter 14 the argument is strengthened, for just as when mental discourse is "'transferred" into spoken discourse, nothing changes in quality, so, Hobbes is arguing, when men covenant to form a commonwealth, their nature is not changed at all but they have "transferred" some of their rights. Thus there is a continuity in the argument in the movement of transference.

The movement that characterises the allegory of the Leviathan is complex, but its complexity is held together by the dominating presence of the figure of the Leviathan. The initial presentation of Leviathan is of a whole whose parts need to be explored, and by the end of the work Leviathan is understood as a composition of parts and as a reconstituted whole. In this way the image of the figure of Leviathan may be seen to both precede and be the conclusion of Hobbes' inquiry; a process which corresponds to his resolutive-compositive method.

Artifice

The different levels of Hobbes' allegory are linked together by the notion of artifice. He refers to this notion in those sections of the work that are concerned with the correspondence between man and commonwealth in the body of the sovereign, summed up in the term 'Leviathan, a mortal god'. Hobbes speaks of that "artificial man"[40] and "artificial body",[41] and extends the metaphor by talking of an "artificial animal", "artificial life", "artificial soul", "artificial joints", "artificial reason and will", [42] "artificial bonds", "artificial chains",[43] and an "artificial eternity".[44] But he is also using the notion of artifice at other points. When Hobbes speaks of the sovereign, "considered in his natural person, and not in the person of the commonwealth",[45] or says that "the persons counselling are members of the person counselled",[46] the pun on the word "person" is trading on the double meaning Hobbes gives it – the natural person and the artificial person. The same identification of natural and private person with public and artificial person is being made when Hobbes says, "the law of nations, and the law of nature, is the same thing. And every sovereign hath the same right, in procuring the safety of his people, that any particular man can have, in procuring the safety of his own body",[47] and when he says "if by 'all together'" is understood "the collective body as one person", "which person the sovereign bears, then the power of all together, is the same with the sovereign's power".[48]

The notion of artifice presented by Hobbes in the Introduction, "Nature, the art whereby God hath made and governs the world, is by the art of man, as in many other things, so in this also imitated, that it can make an artificial animal",[49] draws upon a long history. For instance Spenser in the *Faerie Queene* says, "For all that nature by her mother wit / Could frame in earth, and forme of substance base, / Was there, and all that nature did omit, / Art playing second natures part, supplied it".[50] In the *Anatomy of Melancholy*, Burton says "Man, the most excellent and noble creature of the world, the principal and mighty work of God".[51] Nicholas of Cusa argues in a similar vein:[52]

> For as God is creator of real entities and natural forms, so man is creator of rational entities and artificial forms, which are nothing except similitudes of his intellect, as creatures are similitudes of the divine Intellect.

The way in which the conception of artifice was understood to enable man to express truth, and in a way that overcomes our problem of the discrepancy between form and content, has been discussed in a previous chapter.

Hooker subscribed to the same tradition of thought when he says, "no art is at the first finding out so perfect as industry may after make it",[53] and "Man in perfection of nature being made according to the likeness of his Maker resembleth him also in the manner of working; so that whatsoever we work as men, the same we do wittingly work and freely".[54] And Sidney argues this same relationship between nature and artifice:[55]

> There is no art delivered unto mankind that hath not the works of nature for his principal object, without which they could not consist, and on which they so depend....Only the poet, disdaining to be tied to any such subjection, lifted up with the vigor of his invention, doth grow in effect into another nature, in making things either better than nature bringeth forth, or, quite anew, forms such as never were in nature....Nature never set forth the earth in so rich tapestry as divers poets have done.

The conception of artifice which these, and other, writers share is very different from the neo-classical and scientific conception of artifice as second-rate, synthetic and unnatural. In the Medieval and Renaissance understanding, the way in which poets and other users of language imitate not the visible world naturalistically but the world of experience and perception, is the same as the way the designers of engraved title-pages produce works that are knowingly artificial, describing in pictorial terms what is, representationally an illusion. There was understood to be, in this way, a metaphorical relationship between visual picture and verbal expression. In *Leviathan* it is through this conception of artifice that both the allegory and the allegorical title-page express the themes of the author and express the coherence of the whole.

The artificial character of Leviathan, and the importance of the metaphor of the natural body, then, are both characteristic of fifteenth and sixteenth century writing. Artifice by man upon the natural world given by God (the natural world itself being the product of His artifice), is the traditional means of accounting for the generation of things, and of man's role in the generation of things, where man is intermediate between the natural world and God the Supreme Atrificer. In the same way, seventeenth century political theorists were concerned with explaining the generation of the commonwealth, since its character in the present was seen to depend upon the way in which it came about. Hobbes' account of the generation of the commonwealth is particularly striking, for in *Leviathan* the complex relationship between nature and artifice is used to great effect; people *make* the Leviathan, civil association, through covenant with each other to set it up, and compose the Leviathan, the commonwealth. They make a mechanism, an artificial mechanical entity, and *compose* it out of their natural bodies to form an organic corporate body.

Man becomes both analogous to God, exercising the same kind of energy in the human world as God exercises in the whold natural world including man in the form of artifice, and imitates God. The metaphor of the natural body which expresses this conception, litters sixteenth century discussions on almost every subject. Again, the force of the metaphor lies in the natural body being itself already understood as a microcosm of the world, which would otherwise be incomprehensible. The natural body is a figure of the created world – with, that is, the hierarchy of correspondences, the integrity of the whole governed by God and with specific parts – even before being used by writers to describe particular relationships. Man is the most skilful creation of God, and in making man, God's most excellent skill was used, and the physical complexity of the body – which in sixteenth-century understanding includes the soul and the heart, that is the spiritual dimension and the affections and passions, as opposed to our modern restriction of the physical body to the biological entity – is imitated by man in the complexity of his artifice.

Another aspect of what is meant by the creation of civil society in the Leviathan *by the artifice of man* is that it is by a self-conscious act that men form a commonwealth. They are not impelled into it without deliberation. And consequently, it also expresses the recognition of the authority of the sovereign's laws and his right to make them.

The question of artifice can also be seen in terms of artifice versus empirical knowledge of the phenomenal world, and here it helps to clarify the way in which Hobbes is a system builder. Hobbes saw his works on natural philosophy, human nature and civil philosophy as an integrated system which accounts for the whole created universe. This adds weight to the very idea of overall system in the allegory of the Leviathan. *Leviathan* is not just a set of principles, but an argument sustained by an overall governing conception, found in the figure and allegory of the Leviathan. 'Body' and 'motion' are the principal characteristics of the subject of *Leviathan*, as well as in others of his works; in this work they point not to an empirical but to a philosophical reality. Philosophy, for Hobbes, deals not with facts and events but with hypothetical causes and consequences; in this sense the empiricist's outlook is foreign to his works on natural philosophy as well. But in *Leviathan* the way in which artifice is the key to this understanding is explicitly stated. The conceptions of 'body' and 'motion' are stated in the title, in the phrase "matter, forme and power", and are expressed in the work where men are described as both "the matter"('body') and "the makers" (making is 'motion') of the commonwealth.[56] Hobbes' most abstract philosophical point (body and motion are the features of any subject of inquiry) is expressed, in the language of the allegory in *Leviathan*, in the image of men forming and making the commonwealth, with their natural bodies and by their artifice.

The figure of the Leviathan works as a metaphor and an allegory rather than as an analogy, because what Hobbes is describing is the character of men itself, not just on a model of or analogy with physical bodies. Hobbes' 'artificial man' assumes a view of reality which is different from ours. In our 'empirical' world, reality is commonly thought of as an independent, external place quite apart from the different perceptions of it in the experience of different individuals. This view of a stable, fixed reality 'out there' is fostered by the sciences. In the sixteenth and seventeenth centuries however, what is 'out there' and what is perceived, were thought to be much more closely related. Hobbes' 'artificial man', if written by a twentieth century author, would perhaps at best be seen as an analogy. In the sixteenth and seventeenth centuries, however, such conceptions were taken seriously, and were seen as shadowing forth a reality much more significant than mere empirical reality. The notion of allegory expresses this view of the complexity of reality, and it is the conception of artifice which shows how man helps to make what is real.

The way in which Hobbes' mechanical and organic imagery work together in the figure of the Leviathan is, then, a direct result of his conception of artifice. The mechanical and organic imagery of the work describe the same figure, Leviathan, and they are connected through artifice, for mechanism is both natural in itself (for it is not supernatural or magical) and an imitation of the operation of organisms. Hobbes' view of artifice means, perhaps most importantly, that the Leviathan is something *made* by man, an organic mechanism which operates and works according to the same principles on which man himself works. Thus the Leviathan is both a man and a corporate body of men, a natural man and a man writ large by the artifice of man.

Leviathan as a philosophical allegory

The philosophical character of Hobbes' allegory can be described in terms of the use he makes of the correspondences between parts and whole and public and private 'persons'.

At the beginning of chapter 5, Hobbes uses the notion of parts and whole to talk about reasoning, both expressly and through the metaphor of addition and subtraction of parts, to form or from a whole:[57]

> When a man reasoneth, he does nothing else but conceive a sum total, from addition of parcels; or conceive a remainder, from subtraction of one sum from another; which, if it be done by words, is conceiving of the consequence of the names of all the parts, to the name of the whole; or from the names of the whole and one part, to the name of the other part....In sum , in what matter soever there is place for addition and subtraction, there also is place for reason; and where these

have no place, there reason has nothing at all to do.

The same notion is present wherever Hobbes wishes to specify the relationship between individual men and the sovereign. This occurs whenever the imagery of the body politic is used and also when Hobbes says, for example, that both the power and the honour of the sovereign "ought to be greater, than that of any, or all the subjects".[58] The correspondence between parts and whole also operates between the levels of abstraction and specificity in the work, as when Hobbes says, after describing the "laws of sovereignty" in general terms, "to descend to particulars", and then proceeds to set out what the people should be taught.[59]

Hobbes proposed to create a system, a philosophical system of explanation which accounts for everything. And a system, as well as being a complex thing (as implications are explored, parts explicated, connections made and significances drawn) must also be a simple thing, capable of being grasped by the mind in its entirety, as a single whole. As Oakeshott points out in his Introduction to *Leviathan*, the system in Hobbes is not that of a piece of architecture, "with civil philosophy as the top storey", but that of a "single 'passionate thought' that pervades its parts....not the plan or key of the labyrinth", but "rather, a guiding clue"[60] implicit in the parts and in the development, that through which the parts and their development make sense, are understood as coherent. Thus, Oakeshott concludes, "the civil philosophy belongs to a philosophical system, not because it is materialistic but because it is philosophical".[61]

This is where the image of Leviathan comes in. For as well as proposing a system of all philosophy, Hobbes proposed in *Leviathan* a system of all civil philosophy. His conception of what a commonwealth is, is the central point of this system, and its image, expressing the coherence of the whole, is the image of the figure of Leviathan. In other words a system, as well as being a corpus of thought or ideas is also a design. It will have an individual rhetoric, and to identify the particularity of that rhetoric is to point at that design. In *Leviathan* the design of the system is summed up in the figure of Leviathan.

Furthermore, because the image that expresses the whole as a single simple thing (and only an image *can* do this), must be explicated through and derivable from the necessarily linear development of the parts in a written work, in *Leviathan* this crucial connection is made through the device of the allegory of the Leviathan. The allegory is the level of attention in the reading of the work to which the reader refers whenever he wants to see how this or that part relates and connects to the whole. To read the parts, the linear development of the thinking in the arguments advanced in the work, as though they were separate, would be to miss the most important aspect of it. The need, in philosophy, to attend to the parts, in their own right and *as* parts of a whole, is inescapable. The constant glances towards the construction of the whole, leads to the understanding of the whole that is, and must be, the most profound. The whole in *Leviathan*, summed up in the figure of the Leviathan and explicated in the parts of the work through the allegory of the Leviathan – for the linear development is above all else a story – is an image grasped in all its simplicity as well as its complexity.

In chapter 22, "Of systems subject, political, and private", Hobbes is concerned with the kinds of systems of association which arise once the commonwealth is established. In the first sentence he uses the notion of whole and parts to distinguish between the commonwealth and any other form of association:[62]

> Having spoken of the generation, form, and power of a commonwealth, I am in order to speak next of the parts thereof. And first of systems, which resemble the similar parts, or muscles of a body natural. By systems, I understand any numbers of men joined in one interest, or one business.

Hobbes then goes on to outline the difference between the systems in a commonwealth in terms of those which are public or political, and those which are private:[63]

> some are political, and some private. Political, otherwise called bodies politic, and persons in law, are those, which are made by authority from the sovereign power of the commonwealth. Private, are those, which are constituted by subjects amongst themselves....no authority derived from foreign power, within the dominion of another, is public there, but private.

In this and later chapters Hobbes is careful to state when the sovereign's acts are those of every subject, and when they are simply his own; the correspondence between public and private person provides Hobbes with the means of explicating the multiple character of the Leviathan. For instance he says,[64]

> In a body politic, if the representative be one man, whatsoever he does

in the person of the body, which is not warranted in his letters, not by the laws, is his own act, and not the act of the body, nor of any other member thereof besides himself: because further than his letters, or the laws limit, he representeth no man's person, but his own. But what he does according to these, is the act of every one: for of the act of the sovereign every one is author, because he is their representative unlimited; and the act of him that recedes not from the letters of the sovereign, is the act of the sovereign, and therefore every member of the body is author of it.

In chapter 22 Hobbes is concerned with this correspondence mainly as it enables him to reflect upon the many sided phenomenon of civil unrest. But it also occurs in many other places throughout the work. He speaks often of "private men",[65] "private persons",[66] and of "public and private ministers",[67] "public and private reason"[68] and "private authority".[69] He also refers to "the king of any country" as "the public person, or representative of all his own subjects",[70] and to public and private worship: "public, is the worship that a commonwealth performeth, as one person. Private, is that which a private person exhibiteth".[71] On the same theme, Hobbes says a little later that "seeing a commonwealth is but one person, it ought also to exhibit to God but one worship; which then it doth, when it commandeth it to be exhibited by private men, publicly. And this is public worship; the property whereof, is to be uniform".[72] This is an extremely dense piece of argument – insofar as the commonwealth is a unity formed from the multitude of subjects (that is, when they wear the hats of subjects rather than of private persons simply), there is an implication for religious observance. This is explicated in terms of private and public persons, and thus Hobbes arrives at public worship. The argument is rounded off with the idea that the single unity of the commonwealth leads to uniformity in the character of public worship. Hobbes reasons not that the Church of England is the best church, but that its constitution (national) and its relation to the civil commonwealth require it to be preferred to any other church; this line of reasoning is also directly against puritans and other religious dissenters and independents of all kinds.

Hobbes also uses the correspondence between public and private in the first Part of Leviathan. In chapter 15 he distinguishes between public and private, between those laws of nature "which only concern the doctrine of civil society", and those "things tending to the destruction of particular men". He says that those such as drunkenness and other kinds of intemperance "are not necessary to be mentioned, nor are pertinent enough to this place", because they have primarily a private application.[73] And in the following chapter Hobbes argues that when a man's actions "are considered as representing the words and actions of another, then is he a feigned or artificial person",[74] and that when a multitude of men "are made one person....it is the unity of the representer, not the unity of the represented, that maketh the person one".[75]

The correspondence between public and private 'persons' is very closely related to that between political and private, or political and natural, or artificial and natural. And its presence in the first chapters of the second Part of *Leviathan* forms one of the continuities with the argument of the first Part. In chapter 17 Hobbes speaks of "that great Leviathan" whose authority "given him by every particular man in the commonwealth", and in whom "consisteth the essence of the commonwealth", is "one person, of whose acts a great multitude, by mutual covenants, one with another, have made themselves every one the author". It is "he that carrieth this person, is called sovereign, and said to have sovereign power; and every one besides, his subject".[76] And in chapter 19 Hobbes takes up the point again, when he discusses how the "politic person" of the sovereign and his "natural person" differ, as a difference between that which is public and that which is private.[77] Another example is found where Hobbes considers civil law, which, he says, differs from other law in that "it addeth only the name of the person commanding, which is persona civitatis, the person of the commonwealth".[78] The persona civitatis, we are to understand, is that public, political and artificial person embodied in that private and natural person, the sovereign representative of the commonwealth, Leviathan. Hobbes' use of language, in this way, is extremely evocative – he has only to say "persona civitatis" , and the reader supplies the rest of what Hobbes is referring to.

The importance of allegory lies in the way it can tell us about something at more than one level. It isn't one thing 'really' saying something else, but a story – narrative, descriptive, composed of development of some sort – which means something, or has significance, simultaneously on several levels. The most interesting kind of allegory, in the present context, is that in which the significances of the different levels are themselves interacting – when they knit together to say something that isn't captured by any one single level, but is captured in the whole, the whole story.

What would *Leviathan* be without the allegory? Without the language that forms the allegory, the work (no longer to be called *Leviathan*) would consist of a set of doctrines without a cohering philosophy, and its rhetoric would lack its central feature. Although questions like 'what did Hobbes say about obligation, authority etc.' are undeniably important to an understanding of his political thought, they do not by themselves represent an account of his political philosophy. By themselves Hobbes' views on these matters cannot amount to a political philosophy because by themselves they cannot form an overall view of civil society but only locate some of its parts. What sustains them in the overall political philosophy and provides the means of establishing their interconnections, is the figure of the Leviathan and the imagery, sense of movement, conception of artifice, and the correspondences between parts and whole and public and private 'person', which are the principal features of Hobbes' allegory.

Without the allegory the work may still be political thought of some kind, but it would not be political philosophy. In using allegory Hobbes is not employing something otherwise foreign to philosophy. He is utilising the metaphorical character of philosophical understanding explicitly, drawing out through his use of language the metaphorical process present in all philosophical thinking. The allegory is not something extra, but is exploiting with particular richness and imagination what is necessarily present in all philosophy.

One of the features of allegory is that it is as the story develops or unfolds that the significances accumulate; they are not set out only once and for all in an explicit way – it is the gradual emergence of significances that is important. In *Leviathan* it is as Hobbes expounds his views on various specific matters that the image of the figure of the Leviathan is correspondingly invested with more and more significance. The exposition of the theory, the development of the allegory and the elucidation of the character of the image all take place at the same time.

The role of the allegory in the work as a whole revolves around the way in which, having read the text, the image of the Leviathan can be understood to capture and contain the full meaning of the text. That is, a single image is used to grasp the whole significance of Hobbes' thinking; the image Hobbes chose is that of the Leviathan, unravellable into an artificial man, a natural man, a natural body, a mechanical body, a father, a monarch, a God, and a unity or association or whole composed of parts. The unravelling takes place through the course of the work.

A second way of describing what the Leviathan expresses, looks at what the image means in terms of the act of covenant. Natural men covenant with each other and in doing so create and form the commonwealth, represented by the sovereign. Through their action of covenanting, they create something new. Leviathan is thus three things in one – the commonwealth they create, the multitude together that composes it, and the sovereign, the artificial man of the sovereign they make, who is also a natural man. Furthermore, it is through the means of the allegory of the Leviathan that the interests of the sovereign are identified with and identical to those of the commonwealth, and the interests of its subjects (who are natural persons) are identified with and identical to those of the sovereign (the artificial person who 'represents' them). There are three major levels here and, more crucially, the identification between them all. And the identification that is argued in the text is also expressed in the image.

A third way of describing the Leviathan is to point to how the figure is a man, a commonwealth of men, and a Christian commonwealth all at the same time. The understanding of the Leviathan is not linear but like experience itself, significant in several different ways simultaneously, and in ways which are profoundly related and which affect one another. The features of the allegory are thus 'like life' in the same sense as those of Spenser's allegory – not in terms of naturalistic representation or the registering of the outward form, but as a description of experience whose levels can be analytically distinguished as themes. Like Spenser's allegory then, Hobbes' allegory of the Leviathan works at various levels and explores different thematic questions. In *Leviathan* the themes of man, commonwealth and Christian commonwealth correspond to the natural, human and divine levels of God's creation, and to each other. Thus Leviathan is firstly a man, a natural body as well as a public 'person' made of man's artifice. Secondly Leviathan is the constituted commonwealth, which works like a man, a human organism. It is based on the correspondence between man and civil society, but is also more closely connected since men literally compose it. The way in which sovereignty, obligation, law, contract, rights and duties, liberty, public officers, subordinate associations, military might and power all work in the commonwealth, is indicated by the features of the image. And Leviathan is thirdly a Christian commonwealth, a body of men united in, and uniformly worshipping God whose representative, head of the national church, is the sovereign.

These themes correspond to the divisions in the work itself – in the First Part, Leviathan as a man is considered, in the second Part Leviathan as a commonwealth, and in the third Part Leviathan as Christian commonwealth. In the fourth Part Hobbes discusses the enemies of the Leviathan, those people and ideas which threaten it. The figure of the Leviathan thus represents each of the three conceptions and ties them together, since they are profoundly related to each other as well as all stemming from the same central image. For Oakeshott, the "single 'passionate thought'" that pervades Hobbes' system is "the continuous application of a doctrine about the nature of philosophy".[79] In terms of the argument advanced here, Hobbes' "doctrine about the nature of philosophy" rests on the perception of whole systems in terms of their composite parts and movement. It follows that parts and their relations can only be understood fully in terms of the whole. In this study of Hobbes, the "single 'passionate thought'" which runs through *Leviathan*, which captures the whole multiplicity of levels to which attention is directed in a single image, and which expresses the philosophical wholeness of the work, is the figure and the allegory of the Leviathan.

NOTES

1. *Leviathan*, p5.
2. *ibid* p144.
3. *ibid* p208.
4. *ibid* p156.
5. *ibid* p157.
6. *ibid* p159.
7. *ibid* p159.
8. *ibid* p160.
9. *ibid* p176.
10. *ibid* p176.
11. This imagery recalls that used to great effect by Machiavelli.
12. *Leviathan*, p242-3.
13. *ibid* p210.
14. *ibid* p211.
15. *ibid* p214.
16. *ibid* p215.
17. *ibid* p216.
18. *ibid* p214
19. *ibid* p163.
20. *ibid* p164.
21. *ibid* p164 And by "money" Hobbes is referring not to paper money but to coins of precious gold and silver.
22. *ibid* p165.
23. *ibid* p165
24. *ibid* p162.
25. *ibid* p156.
26. *ibid* p218.
27. *ibid* p112.
28. *ibid* p222.
29. *ibid* p426.
30. *ibid* p209.
31. The recognition of the physical embodiment of the subject matter of his inquiry does not require Hobbes, as it did not require earlier thinkers, to take a 'scientific' view of corporeal matter.
32. *ibid* p5.
33. *ibid* p64.
34. *ibid* p227.
35. *ibid* p89.
36. *ibid* p18.
37. *ibid* p86. Hobbes uses the word 24 times in chapter 14.
38. *ibid* p144.
39. Because of the special significance Hobbes attaches to the word at several crucial points in the argument, it takes on a metaphorical character in his work.
40. *ibid* p3, p138, p165, p176, p126.
41. *ibid* p468.
42. *ibid* p3.
43. *ibid* p138.
44. *ibid* p126, p127
45. *ibid* p208
46. *ibid* p229-230.
47. *ibid* p232.
48. *ibid* p119.
49. *ibid* p5.
50. Spenser, *Faerie Queene*, IV, xx, 21 in J. C. Smith and E. De Selincourt ed., *The Poetical Works of Edmund Spenser*, OUP, 1912.
51. D. Bush, *English Literature in the Earlier Seventeenth Century*, OUP, 1962, p297.
52. N. Struever, *The Language of History in the Renaissance*, Princeton U.P., 1970, p45-6.
53. Hooker, *Laws*, ed. Walton, OUP, 1845, p167.
54. *ibid* p169.
55. Sidney, *An Apologie for Poetrie*, London, 1595.
56. *Leviathan*, p210.
57. ibid p25.

58. *ibid* p120.
59. *ibid* p221.
60. In M Oakeshott, *Hobbes on Civil Association*, Blackwell, Oxford, 1975, p16.
61. *ibid* p16.
62. *Leviathan* p146.
63. *ibid* p146.
64. *ibid* p147.
65. *ibid* p178, p199, p200, p201, p202, p203, p213, p225, p226, p240, p252, p383, p395, p446, p448.
66. *ibid* p200, p225, p227, p255, p271.
67. *ibid* p177.
68. *ibid* p291.
69. *ibid* p329.
70. *ibid* p270.
71. *ibid* p236.
72. *ibid* p240.
73. *ibid* p103.
74. *ibid* p105.
75. *ibid* p107.
76. *ibid* p112.
77. *ibid* p122-3
78. *ibid* p172.
79. Oakeshott, *op.cit.* p16.

CHAPTER 8
Conclusion

The previous chapters have examined different aspects of the thesis that in studying Hobbes' *Leviathan* and attempting to make sense of the work as a whole, the study of Hobbes' rhetoric and the study of his philosophy coincide. Rather than restate the arguments advanced in each of the chapters, this conclusion summarises the themes that have been developed in the course of the argument in support of the thesis.

The first theme has involved considering *Leviathan* in the historical setting of philosophy and culture to which it belongs. It has become almost a commonplace among commentators on Hobbes to pay tribute to the effect of the new scientific cosmology on Hobbes' thinking. However, the set of ideas about man, nature, the divine world, hierarchy, art, artifice, intellectual inquiry and the use of language that characterise the preceding age are perhaps more fundamental in understanding Hobbes' philosophy. It has been argued that the change from an outlook which saw a divine inspiration and presence as the basis from which human inquiry proceeded, to one which saw science as the key to understanding the world, can be studied in the change that took place in literary criticism in the seventeenth century and that Hobbes' outlook is closer to the earlier rather than the later view. It has also been argued that in Hobbes' account of the character of man in *Leviathan*, the fundamental human powers to be reckoned with and on which his deliverance might rest are not his capacity for reasoning but his passions. Reasoning and passions may well work hand in hand, but for Hobbes reasoning merely "suggests" the means while the passions dictate the ends. Furthermore, the need to establish civil society arises, according to Hobbes, from the natural physical equality of men to injure each other, which can only lead to war in the state of nature. What Hobbes proposes in *Leviathan* is that the natural condition of mankind is remedied by the artifice of man in the figure of the Leviathan – an argument that imaginatively uses the traditional understanding.

A second theme has been about unity, analysis and composition in a piece of philosophical writing. It has been argued that a piece of thinking is made up of connections between perceptions and that this process is a metaphor-making one. A piece of writing is an expression of the author's thinking and involves a use of language which is also metaphorical. The structure of a piece of philosophical writing, where the role of metaphor is at its most highly developed, can be examined in terms of how it is both and simultaneously a gradual composition which results in a unity or whole, and an analysis of the parts of the author's thinking. In *Leviathan* this is dramatically explicit in Hobbes' resolutive compositive method.

The third theme has been concerned with the significance of rhetoric in understanding a text, in the language a writer uses to express his thinking. Specifically it has considered the manner in which the language Hobbes uses is connected to the political philosophy he expounds; it has been about the significance of language for philosophy in *Leviathan*. Hobbes' *Leviathan* has been examined, the, by looking at the rhetoric of the work; that is, through the way in which the language Hobbes uses not merely reflects (like a static mirror reflection) his thinking but expresses and organises his thinking. Hobbes' use of language, including his imagery and metaphorical use of words, and the way in which he argues, have been discussed more broadly than in the allegory alone. But the allegory and figure of the Leviathan remain the central point of the discussion, and this thus leads to the fourth of the themes of the thesis.

The fourth and central theme has been about the relationship between rhetoric and philosophy in Hobbes' *Leviathan*. It has sought to show how the figure and allegory of the Leviathan – the primary features of the work's rhetoric – express the unity of the work and provide a way of understanding how the work hangs together as a piece of philosophy. The thesis has aimed to disclose how, in the attempt to make sense of the work as a whole, the study of Hobbes' rhetoric and the study of his philosophy coincide. Understanding *Leviathan* involves understanding his thinking as, at the same time, philosophy and rhetoric. It is a piece of thinking which examines the conditions upon which civil society must be established and elucidates the character of the civil society that results; and it is a piece of thinking which can be studied by attending to the manner in which it is expressed, in the use of language employed by Hobbes. In particular this has involved recognising the significance of the figure of the Leviathan and the allegory in the work that develops the implications of this figure. The image of the Leviathan is the central feature of the rhetoric of *Leviathan* seen as a philosophical identity. It holds together the whole philosophical view Hobbes presents in the work; it is the pivot of the thinking and writing as a whole. To see *Leviathan* 'as a whole' in this thesis means, not to reduce or elevate its different aspects to a single level of abstraction at which the different levels of the inquiry disappear, but to consider the overall image through which all the points Hobbes wishes to make in the work about sovereignty, obligation, authority, rights, law, religion and so on, can be seen as parts of an integrated composition. The coherence of the work lies not in this or that theory or doctrine but in the image from which the theories and doctrines hang and help to compose the character of the image.

The fifth theme of the thesis follows from the fourth and is concerned with the more general point that can be seen in it. What has been said about the relationship between rhetoric and philosophy in *Leviathan* also has a wider application. It can be argued that not only *Leviathan*, but any philosophical text contains and revolves around a focus upon which its unity as a philosophical identity rests, and that this focus can be examined as the central feature of the work's rhetoric.

Illustrations
Examples of Seventeenth-Century
Engraved Title-Pages

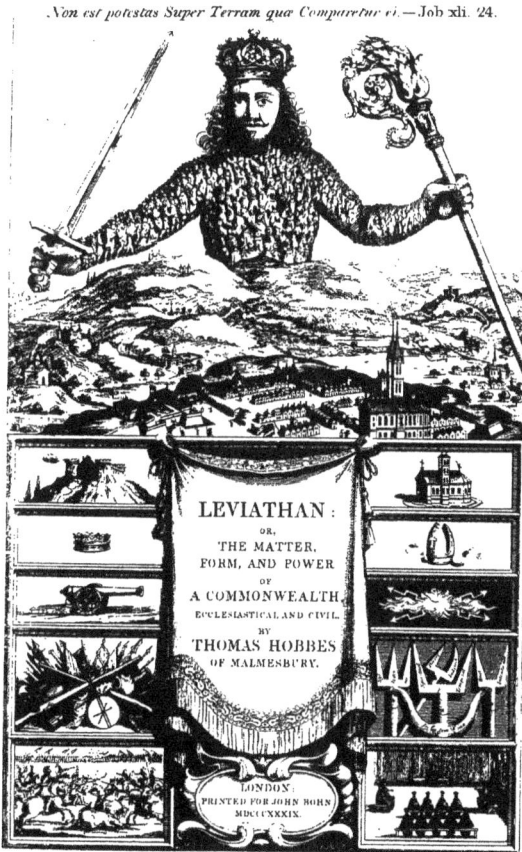

Thomas Hobbes *Leviathan*, 1651
Engraved title-page by Abraham Bosse (?)

Thomas Hobbes, *De Cive*, Paris, 1642
Engraved title-page by "Math. F."

Thomas Hobbes, *De Cive*,
Amsterdam, 1647

Title-page by anonymous engraver

Thomas Hobbes, *De Cive*, Amsterdam, 1647
Engraved title-page by anonymous engraver
Reproduced by permission of
The Librarian, Glasgow University

Thomas Hobbes, *Philosophicall Elements of*
Government and Civill Society, 1651
Engraved title-page by Robert Vaughan
Reproduced by permission of The Librarian, Bodleian Library

Thomas Hobbes, *Philosophical Rudiments concerning Goverment and Civil Society*, 1651
Engraved title-page by Robert Vaughan
Reproduced by permission of The Librarian, Aberdeen University

THE
WORKES
of.
Homer
Engl: by T. Hobbes

London Printed for W: Crooke at the green Dragon. without Temple Barre. 1677.

Thomas Hobbes, translation of *The Workes of Homer*, 1677

Title-page by anonymous engraver

Thomas Hobbes, translation of Thucydides'
History of the Peloponnesian War, 1629
Engraved title-page by Thomas Cecil

Richard Hooker, *Of the Lawes of Ecclesiastical Politie*, 1662
Engraved title-page by William Hole

Michael Drayton, *Poly-Olbion*, 1612
Engraved title-page by William Hole

John Bulwer, *Anthropometamorphosis*, 1653
Engraved title-page by Thomas Cross

Bibliography

PRIMARY SOURCES

Aristotle, *Rhetoric and Poetics*, Modern Library edition, Random House, N.Y., 1954.

John Bunyan, *The Pilgrim's Progress*, Dent, London, 1967.

Robert Burton, *The Anatomy of Melancholy*, ed. Floyd Dell and Paul Jordan-Smith, Tudor Publishing Co., N.Y., 1927.

Catalogue of Engraved Title-Pages, Prints and Drawings Room, British Museum, London, undated but pre-1905.

Sir Sidney Colvin, *Early Engravings and Engravers (1545-1695)*, Longmans, for British Museum, London, 1905.

Margery Corbett and Michael Norton, *Engraving in England in the Sixteenth and Seventeenth Centuries. A Descriptive Catalogue with Introductions. Part III The Reign of Chalres I*, Cambridge University Press, 1964.

Oliver Lawson Dick, ed. *Aubrey's Brief Lives*, Penguin, 1949.

John Dryden, *Essays*, ed. W. P. Ker, Vol.II, Clarendon, Oxford, 1926.

Emblems and Entrances: An Exhibition of Woodcut, Engraved and Etched Title Pages of English Books 1500-1700, held in the Hunterian Library, University of Glasgow, April 1970.

Arthur M. Hind, *Engraving in England in the Sixteenth and Seventeenth Centuries. A Descriptive Catalogue with Introductions*

Part I The Tudor Period, Cambridge University Press, 1952.

Part II The Reign of James I, Cambridge University Press, 1955.

Thomas Hobbes, *Leviathan or the Matter, Forme and Power of a Commonwealth Ecclesiasticall and Civil*, ed. Michael Oakeshott, Blackwell, Oxford, 1946.

Richard Hooker, *The Laws of Ecclesiastical Polity*, ed. Isaac Walton, 2 vols., Oxford University Press, 1845.

Alfred Forbes Johnson, compiled *A Catalogue of Engraved and Etched English Title-Pages. Down to the death of William Faithorne, 1691*, Bibliographical Society, Oxford University Press, 1934.

G. W. Kitchen, ed. *Spenser, Faerie Queene, Book I*, Clarendon, Oxford, 1905.

Hugh Macdonald and Mary Hargreaves, *Thomas Hobbes. A Bibliography*, Bibliographical Society, London, 1952.

Sir William Molesworth, The *English Works of Thomas Hobbes of Malmesbury*, 11 vols., John Bohn, London, 1839-45.

Sir William Molesworth, *The Latin Works of Thomas Hobbes*, 5 vols., John Bohn, London, 1839-45.

Henry R. Plomer, *A Dictionary of the Booksellers and Printers who were at work in England, Scotland and Ireland from 1641 to 1667*, Bibliographical Society, London, 1907.

Sir Philip Sidney, *An Apologie for Poetrie*, printed by James Roberts for Henry Olney, London, 1595.

G. Gregory Smith, ed. *Elizabethan Critical Essays*, 2 vols., Oxford University Press, London, 1904.

J. C. Smith and E. De Selincourt, ed. *The Poetical Works of Edmund Spenser*, Oxford University Press, 1912.

Edmund Spenser, *The Faerie Queene*, ed. A. C. Hamilton, Longman, London, 1977.

J. E. Spingarn, ed. *Critical Essays of the Seventeenth Century*, 3 vols., Oxford, 1908.

Ferdinand Tönnies, *The Elements of Law, Natural and Politic by Thomas Hobbes*, Frank Cass, 1969.

C. F. Tucker Brooke, ed. *The Works of Christopher Marlowe*, Clarendon, Oxford, 1964.

Howard Warrender, ed. *Thomas Hobbes. De Cive. The English Version*, Oxford University Press, 1983.

Howard Warrender, ed. *Thomas Hobbes. De Cive. The Latin Version*, Oxford University.

SECONDARY SOURCES

Paul J. Alpers, ed. *Edmund Spenser. A Critical Anthology*, Penguin, 1969.

Maurice Ashley, *England in the Seventeenth Century*, Penguin, 1952.

Herschel Baker, *The Wars of Truth: Studies in the Decay of Christian Humanism in the Earlier Seventeenth Century*, Harvard University Press, 1952.

Owen Barfield, *History in English Words*, Faber, London, 1954.

Owen Barfield, *Saving the Appearances. A Study in Idolatry*, Faber, London, 1957.

Peter Bayley, ed. *Spenser, The Faerie Queene. A Casebook*, Macmillan, London, 1977.

Deborah Baumgold, *Hobbes's Political Theory*, Cambridge University Press, 1988.

D. R. Bell, "What Hobbes does with words", *The Philosophical Quarterly*, XIX (1969), pp.155-158.

Anthony Black, *Monarchy and Community. Political Ideas in the Later Conciliar Controversy 1430-1450*, Cambridge University Press, 1970.

Max Black, *Models and Metaphors. Studies in Language and Philosophy*, Cornell University Press, N.Y., 1962.

J. E. Bowle, *Hobbes and his Critics. A Study in Seventeenth Century Constitutionalism*, Jonathan Cape, London, 1951.

C. W. Brown, "Thucydides, Hobbes and the Linear Causal Perspective", *History of Political Thought*, X (2), 1989, pp215-256.

K. C. Brown, ed. *Hobbes Studies*, Blackwell, Oxford, 1965.

K. C. Brown, "The Artist of the *Leviathan* Title-Page", *British Library Journal*, 4 (1978), pp24-36.

Stephen J. Brown, *The World of Imagery. Metaphor and Kindred Imagery*, Kegan Paul, Trench, Trubner, London, 1927.

Vincent Buckley, *Poetry and Morality. Studies on the Criticism of Matthew Arnold, T. S. Eliot and F. R. Leavis*, Chatto & Windus, London, 1961.

Kenneth Burke, *A Grammar of Motives*, Prentice-Hall, N.Y., 1945.

Kenneth Burke, *A Rhetoric of Motives*, University of California Press, Berkeley, 1969.

Peter Burke, *The Renaissance Sense of the Past. Documents of Modern History*, Edward Arnold, London, 1969.

Douglas Bush, *The Earlier Seventeenth Century 1600-1660*, Clarendon, Oxford, 1962.

David Christie-Murray, *A History of Heresy*, New English Library, London, 1976.

Joan Cocks, *The Oppositional Imagination*, Routledge, London, 1989.

Norman Cohn, *The Pursuit of the Millenium. Revolutionary Millenarians and Mystical Anarchists of the Middle Ages*, Granada, London, 1970.

R. G. Collingwood, *The Principles of Art*, Oxford University Press, 1958.

Irene Coltman, *Private Men and Public Causes*, Faber, London, 1962.

Conal Condren, "Three Aspects of Political Theory", chapters 5-7 in Richard Lucy, ed. *The Pieces of Politics*, Macmillan (Aust.), 1975.

Conal Condren, *The Status and Appraisal of Classic Texts*, Princeton University Press, N.J., 1985.

Conal Condren, "Radicals, Conservatives and Moderates in Early Modern Political Thought: A Case of Sandwich Islands Syndrome?", *History of Political Thought*, X (3), 1989, pp525-542.

William E. Connolly, *Politics and Ambiguity*, University of Wisconsin Press, 1987.

Elizabeth J. Cook, "Thomas Hobbes and the 'Far-Fetched'", *Journal of the Warburg and Courtauld Institutes*, 44 (1981), pp222-232.

David E. Cooper, *Metaphor*, Aristotelian Society Series, Volume 5, Blackwell, Oxford, 1986.

Margery Corbett and Ronald Lightbown, *The Comely Frontespiece. The Emblematic Title-Page in England 1550-1660*, Routledge & Kegan Paul, London, 1979.

Hardin Craig, *The Literature of the English Renaissance, 1485-1660*, Collier-Macmillan, London, 1966.

Ronald D. Crane, *The Languages of Criticism and the Structure of Poetry*, University of Toronto Press, Toronto, 1953.

Maurice Cranston and Richard Peters, ed. *Hobbes and Rousseau*, Anchor Books, N.Y., 1972.

Frederick C. Crews, *The Pooh Perplex*, Robin Clark, 1979.

Brenda Davies, *Civil Philosophy: Science and Politics in the Thought of Hobbes*, unpublished Ph.D. thesis, University of London, 1966.

Jacques Derrida, "White Mythology: Metaphor in the Text of Philosophy", *New Literary History*, VI, 1 (1974) pp5-74.

Peter Dixon, *Rhetoric*, Methuen, London, 1971.

Cornell March Dowlin, *Sir William Davenant's Gondibert, Its Preface, and Hobbes' Answer*, Philadelphia, 1934.

J. Dunn, "The Identity of the History of Ideas", *Philosophy*, XLIII (1968), pp85-103.

William Empson, *The Structure of Complex Words*, Chatto & Windus, London, 1951.

William Empson, *Seven Types of Ambiguity*, Peregrine, London, 1965.

S. Morris Engel, "Analogy and Equivocation in Hobbes", *Philosophy*, XXXVII (1962), pp326-335.

Roger Fowler, ed. *Essays on Style and Language*, London, 1966.

Rosemary Freeman, *English Emblem Books*, Chatto & Windus, London, 1948.

Theodore M. Gang, "Hobbes and the Metaphysical Conceit - A Reply", *Journal of the History of Ideas*, XVII (1956), pp418-421.

David P. Gauthier, *The Logic of Leviathan. The Moral and Political Theory of Thomas Hobbes*, Clarendon, Oxford, 1969.

M. Gavre, "Hobbes and his Audience: the Dynamics of Theorising", *American Political Science Review*, LXVIII (1974), pp1542-56.

Allan H. Gilbert, *Literary Criticism. Plato to Dryden*, American Book Co., N.Y., 1940.

E. P. Goldschmidt, *The Printed Book of the Renaissance. Three Lectures* on *Type, Illustration, Ornament,* Cambridge University Press, 1950.

M. M. Goldsmith, "Picturing Hobbes's Politics?", *Journal of the Warburg and Courtauld Institutes,* 44 (1981), pp232-237.

Doris A. Graber, *Verbal Behaviour and Politics,* University of Illinois Press, 1976.

Robert Gray, "Hobbes' System and his early Philosophical views", *Journal of the History of Ideas,* XXXIX, 2 (1978), pp199-215.

W. H. Greenleaf, *Order, Empiricism and Politics. Two Traditions of English Political Thought 1500-1700,* Oxford University Press, 1964.

W. H. Greenleaf, "A Note on Hobbes and the Book of Job", in *Hobbes,* ed. Department of Philosophy, University of Granada, Granada, 1974.

Ian Hacking, *Why does Language matter to Philosophy,* Cambridge University Press, 1975.

Jean Hampton, *Hobbes and the Social Contract Tradition,* Cambridge University Press, 1986.

Eric A. Havelock, *Preface to Plato,* Blackwell, Oxford, 1963.

Terence Hawkes, *Metaphor,* Methuen, London, 1972.

David Held, *Political Theory and the Modern State,* Oxford, Polity Press, 1989.

Helen Hervey, *Truth and Knowledge in the Philosophy of Hobbes,* unpublished Ph.D. thesis, University of London, 1952.

Mary B. Hesse, "On Defining Analogy", *Aristotelian Society Proceedings New Series,* LX (1959-60), pp79-100.

J. H. Hexter, "The Burden of Proof", *Times Literary Supplement,* October 24th, 1975, pp1250-2.

Christopher Hibbert, *Charles I,* Corgi, 1972.

Christopher Hill, *Intellectual Origins of the English Revolution,* Clarendon, Oxford, 1965.

Christopher Hill, *The World Turned Upside Down,* Penguin, 1975.

Philip Hofer, *Baroque Book Illustration. A Short Survey,* Harvard University Press, 1951.

Edwin Honig, *The Dark Conceit,* Faber, London, 1951.

F. C. Hood, *The Divine Politics of Thomas Hobbes. An Interpretation of Leviathan,* Clarendon, Oxford, 1964.

Wilbur S. Howell, *Logic and Rhetoric in England 1500-1700,* Russell & Russell, N.Y., 1961.

Wilbur S. Howell, *Poetics, Rhetoric and Logic; Studies in the Basic Disciplines of Criticism,* Ithaca, Cornell University Press, 1975.

Isabel C. Hungerford and George C. Vick, "Hobbes' Theory of Signification", *Journal of the History of Philosophy*, XI (1973), pp459-82.

Samuel Ijsseling, *Rhetoric and Philosophy in Conflict. An Historical Survey*, Martinus Nijhoff, The Hague, 1976.

D. G. James, *The Life of Reason. The English Augustans. Hobbes, Locke, Bolingbroke*, Longmans, London, 1949.

Linda Gardiner Janik, "Lorenzo Valla: The Primacy of Rhetoric and the De-moralisation of History", *History and Theory*, XII (1973), pp389-400.

Terry Jones, *Chaucer's Knight. The Portrait of a Medieval Mercenary*, Weidenfeld & Nicolson, London, 1980.

David Johnston, *The Rhetoric of Leviathan*, Princeton, 1986.

Gregory S. Kavka, *Hobbesian Moral and Political Theory*, Princeton, 1986.

Maurice Keen, *The Pelican History of Medieval Europe*, Penguin, 1969.

Dorothea Krook, *Three Traditions of Moral Thought*, Cambridge University Press, 1959.

Richard Kuhns, "Metaphor as Plausible Inference in Poetry and Philosophy", *Philosophy and Literature*, III, 2 (1979), pp225-238.

W. M. Lamont, *Godly Rule: Politics and Religion 1603-60*, London, 1969.

F. R. Leavis, *English Literature in our Time and the Unviersity*, Chatto & Windus, London, 1969.

Gordon Leff, *The Dissolution of the Medieval Outlook. As Essay on Intellectual and Spiritual Change in the Fourteenth Century*, Harper & Row, N.Y., 1976.

J. R. Levenson, *Confucian China and its Modern Fate*, 3 vols., Routledge & Kegan Paul, London, 1958, 1964, 1965.

C. S. Lewis, *The Allegory of Love. A Study in Medieval Tradition*, Oxford University Press, 1936.

C. S. Lewis, *History of English Literature in the Sixteenth Century, excluding Drama*, Oxford University Press, 1953.

C. S. Lewis, *The Discarded Image. An Introduction to Medieval and Renaissance Literature*, Cambridge University Press, 1964.

C. S. Lewis, *Studies in Words*, Cambridge University Press, 1967.

Jack Lively and Andrew Reeve, eds. *Modern Political Theory from Hobbes to Marx, Key Debates*, Routledge, London, 1988.

A. C. Lloyd, Paper 2 at Symposium "Thinking and Language", *Aristotelian Society Supplementary Volumes*, XXV (1951), pp35-64.

G. E. R. Lloyd, *Polarity and Analogy. Two types of Argumentation in Early*

Greek Political Thought, Cambridge University press, 1966.

Hampus Lyttkens, *The Analogy Between God and the World. An Investigation of its Background and Interpretation of its Use by Thomas Aquino*, Almquist & Wiksells, Uppsala, 1952.

Margaret Macdonald, "The Philosopher's Use of Analogy", and "The Language of Political Theory", chapters 5 & 9 in A. Flew, ed. *Essays on Logic and Language*, Blackwell, Oxford, 1951.

A. M. MacIver, "The Instrumentality of Language", *Aristotelian Society Proceedings, New Series*, LXII (1961-62), pp1-20.

John MacQueen, *Allegory*, Methuen, London, 1970.

Joseph Mali, "The Poetics of Politics. Vico's 'Philosophy of Authority'", *History of Political Thought*, X, 1 (1989), pp41-70.

R. M. Martin, "On the Semantics of Hobbes", in B. H. Baumrin, ed. *Hobbes Leviathan: Interpretation and Criticism*, Wadsworth, California, 1969.

K. R. Minogue, "Parts and Wholes: Twentieth Century Interpretation of Thomas Hobbes", in *Hobbes*, ed. Department of Philosophy, University of Granada, Granada, 1974.

Samuel Mintz, *The Hunting of Leviathan. Seventeenth-Century Reactions to the Materialism and Moral Philosophy of Thomas Hobbes*, Cambridge University Press, 1962. ·

John B. Morrall, *The Medieval Imprint. The Founding of the Western European Tradition*, Penguin, 1970.

Peter Munz, *The Place of Hooker in the History of Thought*, Routledge and Kegan Paul, London, 1952.

Iris Murdoch, Paper 1 at Symposium "Thinking and Language", *Aristotelian Society Supplementary Volumes*, XXV (1951), pp25-34.

Iris Murdoch, *The Sovereignty of Good*, Routledge & Kegan Paul, London, 1970.

Iris Murdoch, *The Fire and the Sun. Why Plato Banished the Artists*, Clarendon, Oxford, 1977.

Michael Murrin, *The Veil of Allegory. Some Notes toward a Theory of Allegorical Rhetoric in the English Renaissance*, University of Chicago Press, Chicago, 1969.

George Nadel, "The Philosophy of History before Historicism", *History and Theory*, III, 3 (1964), pp291-315.

M. Natanson and H. W. Johnstone, eds. *Philosophy, Rhetoric and Argumentation*, Pennsylvania State University Press, Pennsylvania, 1965.

Michael Oakeshott, *Experience and its Modes*, Cambridge University Press, 1933.

Michael Oakeshott, *Introduction* to Hobbes' *Leviathan*, Blackwell, Oxford, 1946.

Michael Oakeshott, *Rationalism in Politics*, Methuen, 1962.

Michael Oakeshott, "Logos and Telos", *Government and Opposition*, IX, 2 (1974), pp237-244.

Michael Oakeshott, *Hobbes on Civil Association*, Blackwell, Oxford, 1975.

Michael Oakeshott, *On Human Conduct*, Oxford University Press, 1975.

C. K. Ogden and I. A. Richards, *The Meaning of Meaning. A Study of the Influence of Language upon Thought and of the Science of Symbolism*, Kegan Paul, London, 1923.

Anthony Pagden, ed. *The Languages of Political Theory in Early-Modern Europe*, Cambridge University Press, 1987.

Ch. Perelman and L. Olbrechts-Tyteca, *The New Rhetoric. A Treatise on Argumentation*, University of Notre Dame Press, London, 1969.

J. G. A. Pocock, *The Ancient Constitution and the Feudal Law. A Study of English Historical Thought in the Seventeenth Century*, Cambridge University Press, 1957.

J. G. A. Pocock, "Time, History and Eschatology in the Thought of Thomas Hobbes", chapter 5 of *Politics, Language and Time*, Methuen, London, 1972.

K. R. Popper, *The Open Society and its Enemies*, 2 vols., Routledge & Kegan Paul, London, 1945.

Mario Praz, *Studies in Seventeenth-Century Imagery*, Edizioni di Storia e Letteratura, Roma, 1964.

Anthony Quinton, *The Politics of Imperfection*, Faber and Faber, London, 1978.

Andrzej Rapaczynski, *Nature and Politics: Liberalism in the Philosophies of Hobbes, Locke and Rousseau*, Ithaca, Cornell University Press, 1987.

Gary Remer, "Rhetoric and the Erasmian Defence of Religious Toleration", *History of Political Thought*, X, 3 (1989), pp377-404.

I. A. Richards, *The Philosophy of Rhetoric*, Oxford University Press, 1967.

Melvin Richter, "Conceptual History (Begriffsgeschichte) and Political Theory", *Political Theory*, 14 (1986), pp604-637.

Melvin Richter, "Montesquieu, The Politics of Language and the Language of Politics", *History of Political Thought*, X, 1 (1989), pp71-88.

Melvin Richter, "Reconstructing the History of Political Languages: Pocock, Skinner and the 'Geschichtliche Grandbegriffe'", *History and Theory*, XXIX, 1 (1990), pp38-70.

Arnold A. Rogow, *Thomas Hobbes. Radical in the Service of Reaction*, W. W. Norton & Co., N.Y., London, 1986.

Richard Rorty, *Philosophy and the Mirror of Nature*, Princeton University Press, 1979.

Richard Rorty, J. B. Schneewind and Quentin Skinner, eds. *Philosophy in History*, Cambridge University Press, 1984.

Henry M. Rosenthal, *The Consolations of Philosophy: Hobbes's Secret; Spinoza's Way*, Temple University Press, Philadelphia, 1989.

Ralph Ross et al, ed. *Thomas Hobbes in his Time*, University of Minnesota Press, Minneapolis, 1974.

K. K. Ruthven, *The Conceit*, Methuen, London, 1969.

Gilbert Ryle, Paper 3 at Symposium "Thinking and Language", *Aristotelian Society Supplementary Volumes*, XXV (1951).

George Schulman, "Metaphor and Modernization in the Political Thought of Thomas Hobbes", *Political Theory*, 17, 3 (1989), pp392-416.

Quentin Skinner, "Hobbes' Leviathan", *The Historical Journal*, VII, 2 (1964), pp321-333.

Quentin Skinner, "History and Ideology in the English Revolution", *The Historical Journal*, VIII, 2 (1965), pp151-178.

Quentin Skinner, "The Ideological Context of Hobbes' Political Thought", *The Historical Journal*, IX, 3 (1966), pp286-317.

Quentin Skinner, "The Limits of Historical Explanations", *Philosophy*, XLI (1966), pp199-215.

Quentin Skinner, "Meaning and Understanding in the History of Ideas", *History and Theory*, VIII, 1 (1969), pp3-53.

Quentin Skinner, *The Foundations of Modern Political Thought*, Cambridge University Press, 1978.

Tom Sorell, *Hobbes*, Routledge, London, 1986.

W. Speed Hill, *Studies in Richard Hooker*, Case Western Reserve University Press, Cleveland, 1972.

J. E. Spingarn, *A History of Literary Criticism in the Renaissance*, Columbia University Press, N.Y., 1908.

Thomas A. Spragens, *The Politics of Motion. The World of Thomas Hobbes*, Croom Helm, London, 1973.

J. P. Stern, "Nietzsche and the Idea of Metaphor", *Encounter*, February 1977.

Donald Stewart, *The Concept of Metaphor*, unpublished Ph.D. thesis, University of London, 1972.

Leo Strauss, *The Political Philosophy of Hobbes: Its Basis and its Genesis*, University of Chicago Press, Chicago, 1952.

Nancy Struever, *The Language of History in the Renaissance. Rhetoric and Historical Consciousness in Florentine Humanism*, Princeton University Press, 1970.

C. D. Tarlton, "Levitating Leviathan: Glosses on a Theme in Hobbes", *Ethics*, LXXXVIII (1977), pp1-19.

C. D. Tarlton, "Creation and Maintenance of Government: a Neglected Dimension of Hobbes' Leviathan", *Political Studies*, XXVI (1978), pp307-27.

Clarence Dewitt Thorpe, *The Aesthetic Theory of Thomas Hobbes*, Ann Arbor, 1940.

Robert Thouless, *Straight and Crooked Thinking*, English University Press, London, 1964.

E. M. W. Tillyard, *The Elizabethan World Picture*, Chatto & Windus, London, 1960.

Richard Tuck, *Hobbes*, Oxford University Press, 1989.

James Tully, ed. *Meaning and Context: Quentin Skinner and his Critics*, Polity Press, Cambridge, 1988.

Rosamund Tuve, *Elizabethan and Metaphysical Imagery*, Chicago University Press, Chicago, 1947.

Rosamund Tuve, *Allegorical Imagery. Some Medieval Books and their Posterity*, Princeton University Press, N.J., 1966.

Howard Warrender, *The Political Philosophy of Hobbes*, Clarendon, Oxford, 1957.

J. W. N. Watkins, *Hobbes' System of Ideas. A Study in the Political Significance of Philosophical Theories*, Hutchinson University Library, London, 1965.

George Watson, "Hobbes and the Metaphysical Conceit", *Journal of the History of Ideas*, XVI (1955), pp558-562.

J. Weinberger, "Hobbes' Doctrine of Method", *American Political Science Review*, LXIX (1975), pp1336-53.

Frederick G. Whelan, "Language and Its Abuses in Hobbes' Political

Philosophy", *American Political Science Review*, 75 (1981), p59-75.

Basil Willey, *The English Moralists*, Chatto & Windus, London, 1964.

William K. Winsatt and Cleanth Brooks, *Literary Criticism. A Short History*, Vintage Books, N.Y., 1957.

Peter Winch, *The Idea of a Social Science and its Relation to Philosophy*, Routledge & Kegan Paul, London, 1958.

Sheldon Wolin, *Politics and Vision*, Little, Brown & Co., Boston, 1960.

Sheldon Wolin, *Hobbes and the Epic Tradition of Political Theory*, William Andrews Clark Memorial Library, University of California, 1970.

Frances Yates, *The Occult Philosophy in the Elizabethan Age*, Routledge & Kegan Paul, London, 1979.

Perez Zagorin, *A History of Political Thought in the English Revolution*, Routledge & Kegan Paul, London, 1954.

Perez Zagorin, *The Court and the Country*, Routledge & Kegan Paul, London, 1969.

For Product Safety Concerns and Information please contact our EU
representative GPSR@taylorandfrancis.com
Taylor & Francis Verlag GmbH, Kaufingerstraße 24, 80331 München, Germany

www.ingramcontent.com/pod-product-compliance
Lightning Source LLC
Chambersburg PA
CBHW070355270326
41926CB00014B/2562